ונus Salk · **Tristan Jones,** 71, a British author and adventurer, in Phuket, Thailand, Wednesday of a stroke. He held many records for solo long-distance sailing.

Group Capt

Heart of Oak

BY THE SAME AUTHOR

AUTOBIOGRAPHY

A Steady Trade
Ice!
Saga of a Wayward Sailor
The Incredible Voyage
Adrift

FICTION

Dutch Treat
a novel of World War II

Tristan Jones

Heart of Oak

St. Martin's Press
New York

AUTHOR'S NOTE

To save embarrassment to relatives, the names of some of the characters in this book, as well as the names of the ships on which the author served, have been altered.

"Lili Marlene"
(German Lyric by Hans Leip, English Lyric by Tommie Connor, Music by Norbert Schultze)
© 1940 by Apollo-Verlag Paul Lincke, Berlin.
Copyright renewed.
English lyric © 1944 by Peter Maurice Music Co. Ltd.
Published by permission of the Music Publishing House: Apollo-Verlag Paul Lincke, Berlin.
Sole distributor for the U.S.A. and Mexico: EDWARD B. MARKS MUSIC COMPANY.
Used by permission.   All rights reserved.

Library of Congress Cataloging in Publication Data

Jones, Tristan, 1924-
    Heart of oak.

    Sequel to: A steady trade.
    1. Jones, Tristan, 1924-   . 2. Voyages and travels—1951-   . 3. Seamen—Wales—Biography. I. Title.
G465.J657   1984   910.4'5'0924 [B]   84-1306
ISBN 0-312-36598-5

First published in Great Britain by The Bodley Head Ltd.

First U.S. Edition

10 9 8 7 6 5 4 3 2 1

Dedicated to the men and women of the Royal Navy, the oldest organised fighting force in the world.

ACKNOWLEDGEMENTS

Laurence Everleigh, ex-matelot, R.N.
Gordon Rollason, ex-matelot, R.N.
Eric R. Thomas, ex-matelot, and Boy Seaman, R.N.
David McLeod, ex-matelot, and Boy Seaman, R.N.
Anne Hammond, Eurosports Village (ex H.M.S. *Ganges*)
Lt. Col. P. R. Thomas, R.N. (Rt'd), Royal Naval Sailing Assoc.
John Douglas, ex-matelot, author, H.M.S. *Ganges*
Raymond (Moss) Rawlett, of Key West, for his help in a period of great difficulties.

Quentin Crisp, author, for his statement, in 1981, that the only British men who treated him as a human being were matelots.
Kaleeny Cannon, St Martin's Press, for her quiet, sane efficiency in a mad, shifting world of sound and fury.
                    Key West, San Diego and aboard
                    S/Y 'Outward Leg', 1983

'A ddioddefodd a orfu'
'Who has endured has overcome'
Old Welsh proverb

CONTENTS

FOREWORD

When I first started to write this account of my years in the
Royal Navy, I envisaged it as spanning the years 1940 to
1952. But the whole story is not only about war—or only
incidentally about war. It really is about the forging of a
simple young lad from coastal Wales and the trading barges
of the North Sea, into something—someone else. The later,
'peacetime' naval years of 1945 until 1952 must await their
telling in another volume, *Sons of the Sea*. Events passed
then, between 1945 and 1952, so crowded, so varied; the
post-war story is very different to this one.

In this book I am attempting to describe people and events
as I witnessed them, as they really were. To do this honestly I
must report speech as it was spoken—as everyone else who
witnessed it *knows* it was spoken. Sailors—and especially
Royal Navy matelots—have always had a colourful vocabulary. They used—and still use—many words and phrases
which are not found in everyday English. For that reason I
have included at the end of the story a glossary of Royal Navy
lower deck words and phrases mentioned in the book which
were in everyday use during and after World War II.

Other words and phrases were used by the lower deck
which were also not used then ashore in 'polite' company, at
least in public. These words and phrases I have also included
in the text. To do otherwise would be to misrepresent the
speech of the matelots, as it has been by most other writers
who so far have written about them. Enough is enough. As our
words make our worlds so our words must report our worlds.

The men of the Royal Navy lower deck were not fighting a

9

'polite' war. They generally did not come from 'polite' backgrounds. Mostly their use of 'foul' language was a symptom of poor education and upbringing, which deprived them of a fluent use of the language.

My purpose in reporting speech as I heard it—as we all heard it—on the mess decks and gun stations in His Majesty's ships, is not to pander to anyone's need for gratuitous verbal pornography. My only purpose is to tell how it all was, to me. *Honi soit qui mal y pense.*

The verbally squeamish might avoid reading this book, or they can wait until some bright spark bowdlerizes it; but I make no apologies for the language reported herein. It was the language of heroes—and that, for me, is reason enough to report it as truthfully and as accurately as my memory and my acumen allows.

I have in the past few years met a number of matelots —including veterans of the Falklands War. In many of the ways in which the Andrew in the past was good for young men, it seems not to have changed much. In a few of the ways in which it was bad it obviously has changed a great deal for the better; particularly in the relations between the officers and the lower deck, and in ships' living conditions. I am proud to have belonged to one of the generations of matelots who dreamed of the day when these changes would come about.

Some names of people and of ships have been changed, to avoid embarrassment to anyone who might still live, or to their relatives.

PART ONE

The Forge

'Come, cheer up, my lads! 'tis to glory we steer,
To add something more to this wonderful year;
To honour we call you, not press you like slaves,
For who are so free as the sons of the waves?
   Heart of oak are our ships,
   Heart of oak are our men,
   We always are ready;
   Steady, boys, steady;
   We'll fight and we'll conquer again and again!'

We ne'er see our foes but we wish 'em to stay,
They never see us but they wish us away;
If they run, why, we follow, and run 'em ashore,
For if they won't fight us, we cannot do more.
   Heart of oak . . .

'Heart of Oak',
marching tune of the Royal Navy
'lower deck' (enlisted men).

1. Off to War

Chorus: This is my story,
 This is my song;
 Been in the Andrew
 Too fucking long!
 So roll on the *Rodney*,
 The *Nelson*, *Renown*,
 This three funnelled bastard
 Is getting me down.

During and after 1941 the latter two lines changed to:

 They can't sink the *Hood*
 'Cos the bastard's gone down!

Chorus: Hold your own,
 What d'ye say?
 From China to Chatham's a fucking long way!

'This is my story' Pre-World War II, and probably World War I. 'Roll on' is an expression of anticipation; for example a common saying on convoy escorts was 'Roll on death—let's fuck the angels'. Another example was 'Roll on my twelve' (the enlistment time in peace time was twelve years). The 'three funnelled bastard' in the earlier version indicates one of the County class cruisers. *Rodney*, *Nelson* and *Renown* were battleships, which spent much less time at sea than the cruisers. Sung to the tune of the hymn 'This is my story'. Many Royal Navy ditties were set to Salvation Army tunes.

The war with Nazi Germany had been declared by Britain nine months before, but there seemed to be few signs of it when I made my way to the railway station at Harwich, even though the town was supposed to be one of our major naval ports on the east coast of England. Perhaps it was the early May weather, which was fine, sunny and warm for a change. War just didn't seem to fit in with sunshine and spring in England, at least to me at sixteen years of age, although I suppose I hardly thought about it, but there *was* a war to be fought.

Army police patrols, red covers on their peaked caps, were on the station platform. Sailors in small knots of blue here and there, lounged about, sitting on their kit-bags. There were a few soldiers, some new recruits by the look of them; some older hands too, all with their .303 Mark II Lee-Enfield rifles beside them. Their faces and gestures, as they laughed and joked among themselves, or silently watched the young women who passed, seemed to belie what everyone knew —that only a hundred and fifty miles or so to the south of us, what we knew as Western European civilization was being hammered to the wall by the Panzer tanks and Luftwaffe planes of Hitler's war machine.

I must have looked something of a sunburned shrimp as I rolled along the platform. I'd been deckboy on board the coastal sailing barge *Second Apprentice* for two years since my fourteenth birthday, and, although I hardly realized it at the time, it had been pretty hard going for a young lad, what with hauling anchors and halyards, and hand-loading cargoes, from hand-skinning housebricks to great heavy boulders of coal. By sixteen I was about five feet six, very thin but wiry, and like practically all the sailor-lads from the Coastal Trade I must have had a certain air about me. Looking back it seems to me we mostly all had it—an indefinable cockiness. Not an arrogance, but more as if, in our attitude to others we could say, 'Right, we know what the bloody sea can do; now, what can you do?' Looking back, I realize that this attitude, combined with the air of innocence which all kids of sixteen exude, must have made me appear to much older people as either an incipient rebel or an indomitable little sod, a cross between Tom Brown and the Artful Dodger.

I was dressed in a too-big sea-jersey knitted by my mother back home in Wales, a too-small grey jacket which had certainly seen better days, a striped Welsh linen shirt, a cheese-cutter cap and shiny black moleskin trousers with black boots. I wore all my best clothes—my only shore-going rig. Over my shoulder was a salt-stained blue sea-bag, which contained my working rig; a pile of knitted woollens and linen shirts, holed socks and tatty underwear, all washed during the previous week on board in a bucket with salt-water soap, and my sea-boots, now a size too small. These I would send home, to be passed on to some smaller local lad in Llangareth. I was on my way to the Royal Naval Barracks in Chatham, Kent. There I knew I would be issued with, evidently, the value of a king's ransom in new uniform clothes.

The ticket collector when I passed him on the platform, while a steam engine hissed nearby, grinned down at me. He was a large florid man, who wore only a waistcoat over his shirt in this, for England, warm weather. I returned his grin.

'Off to join the army then, son?' he hailed me.

'No sir, navy.' I shoved my pigeon chest out another mite into the air of England.

A porter passed by on my other side, wheeling a barrow-load of officers' trunks and cases by the looks of them. The big ticket collector greeted him. 'Eh, Fred! How's this one then? Off to join the navy, he is!'

The porter, a little thin man with a huge moustache, stared at me for a moment, then turned his gaze from me and replied, 'Is he, by gum! Now we'll be all right, eh Bill? They won't get past that bugger!'

My grin dropped. There was an awkward silence for a second or two, then the ticket collector said, 'Portsmouth or Chatham, mate?'

It was 'mate' now.

'Chatham,' I replied as I glanced my own glare at the porter. Both men looked a bit embarrassed in the silence.

'Well . . . train leaves in about fifteen minutes,' observed the collector meekly. 'Good luck, Taffy!'

'Give 'em one for me, mate!' exhorted the porter as he trundled off with his barrow.

Not if I can help it, I thought. I felt a bit disappointed somehow. Despite my having been working out of England for two years, and having, as I had imagined, got rid of the more wild parts of my Welshness in gesture and speech, the collector had called me 'Taffy'—an English attempt at the Welsh pronunciation of 'David' ('Daffyd'). I was still marked, to East Anglian eyes and ears at least, as some sort of foreigner; even though I knew I was more British, by far, than any of the English. I came from the heartland of the old, old Brithonic tribes, Merioneth. No one, I knew, had ever subdued *us*. As my Dad had always said, that would have been 'flogging a dead horse'.

In mid-1940 British Railways were still in the hands of private companies. The carriages of the train which left Harwich were still painted in the brown and gold livery of the London and North Eastern Railway Company. The brasswork on the puffing steam engine was still proudly polished and glinted in the sunshine. The train was by no means crowded, and I managed to find a compartment with only one other person in it. He was a tall spare man, from his clothes and demeanour obviously working class, 'one of the lads'. From the way he was busy cutting through one of the real

leather straps with which the carriage windows were hoisted
and lowered, he was either a thief or one of the still-
unemployed. The leather in railway carriages then was
apparently of finest Argentine importation—the British
owned practically all the railways in Argentina in 1940. The
man was about forty-five at a wild guess, clean shaven, with
light ginger hair and pale blue eyes. He was dressed in a
workman's cap, a collarless shirt and grey trousers which had
seen better days. Around his neck he wore a red bandana—a
neckerchief as we used to call it. He winked at me as I
dumped my sea-bag on the overhead netting. Below the
luggage rack were three deep sepia-coloured pictures of
English East Coast sea-side scenes: the pier at Yarmouth, the
harbour at Whitby, that kind of thing. The ladies and
gentlemen in the pictures were all dressed in the garb of the
turn of the century, the gentlemen mostly in black suits and
straw boaters, the ladies in long black voluminous skirts
reaching down over their feet, and surprisingly gay and frilly
white blouses puffed up at the sleeves. Some of the ladies
wore boaters, too, atop their piled-up Edwardian hair-dos.
At sixteen it seemed to me that those long, narrow pictures
were from another world altogether; but I little realized,
never dreamed, that I felt closer to that depicted world of
1900 then, in 1940—much closer—than I would feel to the
world that I see around me forty-three years later. Like, I
suppose, most youngsters, I had no idea of the appalling
gulfs, the yawning chasms ahead of me. Neither had I any
idea of the strange beauty that terror spawns. I was very
much an after-product of the late Victorian age, when 'God's
in his heaven, all's right with the world' was just about all the
sense I could ever get from most 'respectable' people leading
their lives of quiet, polite desperation.

'Fag, Cocker?' The man offered me a Woodbine cigarette.
His fingertips were brown with nicotine stains.

'Thanks, mate,' I replied. No 'sirring' in Third Class.

'Where you off to, then?' He spoke in thick, fast Cockney. His teeth were mere stumps. There was no National Health Service in those days. It was normal enough.

'Chatham,' I replied. 'I'm joining up.' I tried to keep my voice low.

He threw his head back and huffed a short cough. 'You volunteering? Bit young, ain't you? What is it, navy?'

'Yeah. Joining as a Regular. Boy Seaman.'

'Oh, you'll be all right. By the way things are going in France, by the time you're through your training it'll be all over. I was in the last lot. Army, Royal Fusiliers. Got gassed on the Somme. Well, at least the buggers can't get me this time.'

The man turned to the window in a fit of deep coughing. Then, recovered, he stared out of the window at the green fields passing steadily by. After a while he turned towards me again and went on in a smaller voice. 'Main thing, matey, is never volunteer for anything once you're in and when you're doing squad drill always try to get in the middle of the mob. That way the other blokes can cover up for you, see? Try to get in a squad with a big instructor if you can. Those bloody little blokes are always the worst when they got a bit of power over you; all bleeding gate and gaiters, they are, see? Still, I don't know about the navy. Perhaps it's different. They seem to be a steadier lot than we was. You know, not so much bleeding discipline and frigging about over things that don't matter a fiddler's fart, see? The blokes seem to be a lot more cheerful. Still, in the last lot you can understand that, I suppose, because the navy wasn't in the fucking trenches, were they? Excuse my French, I mean most of them had a pretty cushy time, at least on the big ships, from what they told me, stuck up in the Fleet Bases—except for the two big battles where the battleships knocked shit out of each other and they was sinking like bloody ninepins . . . Cor, look at that!' His head swiftly turned as the train pulled into a station. There were two young women sliding by as the train slowed down. 'Bit of all right, eh? Well, matey, at least you'll be all right where crumpet's concerned. They go for the navy blokes a lot more than the army, see? Can't go wrong in your little old navy-blue suit, can you? Bring 'em back a parrot and a bloomin' bunch of bananas—they went on the rations yesterday—and you're in . . . bit of the old quick-touch-me-collar-and-gimme-a-kiss! Good old Jolly Jack! Blimey, wish it was me!'

As this last wish was sent up to heaven more passengers entered the compartment. In the English fashion the rest of the journey to London was passed by everyone in absolute silence. I found myself thinking of my erstwhile shipmates on board *Second Apprentice*, which I had left only a few hours earlier that day. Both Tansy, the captain, and Bert, the mate, had spent years in the Royal Navy. Neither one of them had ever suggested to me that I should not volunteer for anything, nor that I ought to hide my defects behind the more proper actions of others; it seemed to me a shoddy suggestion, and somehow landlubberly. The skipper's and mate's advice had been, more or less, to 'take what's coming to you and do your best for your mates and for the ship'. In a sailing barge, with a crew of only four including the captain, it was the most natural thing in the world to give a hand wherever it was needed, and a reluctant skulker would scarcely have lasted for five minutes on board; in any case, on many an occasion lending a hand was a matter of helping to stay afloat and alive. Now I knew what Tansy and Bert meant when they described somebody who worked shoddily or slowly as 'a blinking soldier' or as 'coming the old soldier'. I found myself feeling lucky not to be joining the army. Besides, to Ted, the other deckhand, and me, an irksome, awkward or heavy job had been considered more of a challenge than a chore. We had vied with each other in performing the task quicker or more efficiently, if only to show the other how much better we could do it. We were not prudish young paragons; we were anything but that, and any other youngster who might have suggested that we were would have soon found himself in a stand-up and knock-down fist fight which would have swiftly and bloodily relieved him of his misapprehensions. Ted and I had been generally known all along the British South and East Coasts, among the crews of the other coastal and narrow seas sailing barges as 'those two cocky bastards off *Second Apprentice*'. So if there was a touch of swagger in my walk, and a mite of pride in my demeanour Tansy and Bert, at least, would have understood it, because they, too, had shared some of the same experiences.

My memories of the trip across London, from Liverpool Street station to Victoria, are vague. This is probably because in later years I was to make the trip so many, many times, that they all seem to melt into one (except for the journeys across the City during the Blitz). There was a naval party of police on Liverpool Street station, especially to meet travelling recruits, and we were soon gathered into a motley crowd of male civilians of all ages from sixteen to mid-thirties, and were each handed a pork pie and a cup of tea by a joking old (that meant over thirty) Able Seaman: 'Here you are then, Wings, cup of the old Rosy Lee, and get this here oggie under your blooming belt, my son.' He handed me a pie.

The Able Seaman was a chubby fellow. His uniform was immaculate, with three gold chevrons on the left sleeve of his blue jumper, and crossed torpedoes on the right. On his chest he wore three rows of medal ribbons. I eyed him with wonder. Here was a sailor who had really been around the globe and back. I didn't know how to address him, so to be safe I called him 'sir' when I thanked him.

Off to War

'Don't you call me "sir", mate,' he frowned at me, but his eyes grinned. 'You only calls officers that. My tally's Nobby, but you can call me "Stripey" if you wants to, Sprog; everyone else does!'

We were piled into a grey-painted double-decker bus and driven across London. There were stacked up sandbags about the doorways to the government buildings around Whitehall, and paper taped over the windows in case of bomb-blasts. Gas masks were carried by almost everyone, besides the police and servicemen. They were slung over civilian clothes in small cardbox boxes. I also remember —who could forget?—the dozens of funny-looking air-raid barrage balloons, looking like so many fat cartoon animals nodding away up in the blue sky on the end of their cables all above the city, and the anti-aircraft guns on the Thames Embankment all manned, all pointing up at an otherwise empty sky. Then there were the eager, motherly ladies of the Women's Voluntary Service in tweed suits and thick stockings on Victoria station, with their tea wagons, and the crowds of soldiers, sailors and airmen through whom we were marched (we were marching by now) by a naval Petty Officer who looked at least sixty, and who wore a whole panorama of medal ribbons which must have been awarded for every British war from the Ashanti onwards. On the main concourse at Victoria station our crew, all still dressed in civilian clothes, all toting suitcases of varying degrees of shabbiness, or parcels, or pillowcases, or sea-bags, were sorted out into three separate squads, and dispatched by train to Chatham or, via Waterloo or Paddington, to Portsmouth or Plymouth respectively. I felt more sheepish than glorious, marching off to war.

Once our Chatham squad was separated from the others, our smaller crowd seemed immediately to take on its own group identity. Then the others didn't seem to matter very much at all. They were strangers now—no longer fellow-strays. The chances were we would never see them again, at least in ships. We were 'the Chatham lads'. We might wind up serving with each other. I recall very well that sense of separateness from all the other servicemen on the station concourse, yet still I remember very little about my fellows in the same draft (we were navy, so it was not a squad now, but a 'draft'). I recall a couple of Scotsmen, one a shepherd from the Highlands, one a hard nut from the mean streets of Glasgow. There were a couple of Geordie coalminers from Newcastle way, and a few East Anglian farmhands, as well as men from the factories of Birmingham and Manchester, and one or two country boys from Oxfordshire and the Cotswolds. And of course some Londoners, freshly turned up to join on to us from the local recruiting office.

Probably the only unusual thing about our little knot of men, young and early middle aged, was me. By tradition a Welsh lad would have been drafted into the Plymouth division of the Royal Navy, but I had volunteered at Harwich so I was counted as an East Anglian, notwithstanding that I hailed from the opposite side of Britain. In any case, as a Boy Entrant I would normally have gone to London first, then to Shotley, where HMS *Ganges* the boys' training ship was located, but more about that anon.

The distance from London to Chatham is about thirty miles or so, but the journey seemed to take hours. At each stop on the line seeming hordes of men in navy-blue and khaki uniforms mounted the train. Every few miles the train was side-tracked on to a siding to allow crammed troop-trains to pass by on their way to the South Coast and the battle now raging in Belgium and France. Nobody seemed to have very much idea of what was going on across the Channel. The British and French armies had entered Belgium to join the forces of that country in fighting the Nazis. Someone, an older recruit, said it looked as if the idea was to set up a static battle-line, as in the First World War, along the banks of the River Meuse—wherever that was. As far as the majority of the men in my carriage were concerned, it might as well have been in China.

It was late afternoon when our train finally pulled in to Chatham station. The platforms were seas of blue. Gimlet-eyed naval police were everywhere. We were soon herded into some semblance of formation by a harassed leading seaman and marched out of the station, down the town High Street and down the long dreary hill road, brick walled in on both sides, to the Royal Naval Barracks. There, at last, we entered through the red-bricked gateway and lugged our way on to the parade ground. It was all strange and overwhelming. Power, male and menacing, was everywhere. All around us squads and battalions of blue-uniformed men drilled and doubled to the loud, harsh shouts and bawls of drill instructors. Above the parade ground, fronting the parade-reviewing platform, set into a rose red brick wall, surrounded by lamp standards decorated with humped dolphins, was the huge legend in gold letters: FEAR GOD—HONOUR THE KING.

After standing in formation but 'at ease', wordlessly watching the fierce action all around us, a Chief Petty Officer and a short Petty Officer showed up carrying a list of our names. One by one, the names were read out: 'Right, when I calls your names out you fall in and double over to the drill-shed wall as fast as Christ will let you and fall in under the name of your respective divisions and God help anyone who gets in the wrong formation! I'll have your guts for garters! Right . . .'

One by one the recruits' names were shouted by Shorty with the Chief silently standing by, and one by one the recruits, looking somewhat clownish in their civilian attire compared to the uniformed men all about us, ran over to the drill-shed wall and stood, stiffer now, under one of the signs: '*Raleigh Div.*', '*Drake Div.*', '*Nelson Div.*', '*Collingwood Div.*' Finally, there was no one left of our original group but me. I stood there, in the now gently falling light drizzle, feeling small, foolish and unwanted. I felt forgotten. I little guessed how soon I would come to welcome that feeling. The Chief Petty Officer, a big man with a face like the Rock of Gibraltar, and a complexion which indicated that he'd sunk enough rum to float the Home Fleet, ambled over to me in his boots and gaiters. He turned round and grimaced at the men now sorted out into their divisional squads by the wall. Then he beamed at me. I smiled back.

The CPO put both hands on his belt and bawled, 'Steady, lad! Get that grin off your mug! Where do you think you are, the bloody Empire Theatre?'

My face straightened rigid.

'What have we here?' yelled the CPO. 'What . . . what would Nelson say? One eye, one hand and one arsehole, eh my son?'

'Er . . . I came down from Harwich, sir,' I managed to mumble.

'Speak up, lad! I had my eardrums busted at Jutland!' His jowls were clean shaven and pink and very close to my face. His eyes were the colour of a pistol. His collar, sparkling white, bit deeply into his thick neck.

I repeated my explanation.

The CPO's voice dropped to an almost tender tone. 'Looks like we got ourselves a little Miss Terry here. We must sort this one out. We don't want to lose the bloody war, do we? We don't want the Jerries dancing for joy because we shuttled you into the wrong place, do we, son? Show me your railway warrant.' He reached out for the green paper which I gave him. It was an Admiralty warrant to allow me to travel from

Harwich to Chatham. It had been handed to me at the Harwich naval recruiting office.

The CPO inspected the warrant cursorily. 'Mmm,' he said in a fatherly tone now. 'Looks like there was a bit of a fuck-up. This time I won't hold it against you. You were supposed to go directly to Shotley, but I'll let you off this time. You get yourself over to the Chief Crusher's Office [Police Office] as fast as you bloody can and they can put you up for the night, then you get the first train up to Harwich in the morning, and they can sort you out again there.'

'Right, Chief.'

The CPO's face darkened. 'You don't call me that on the parade ground, lad. Here I'm "sir".'

'Yes, sir.'

'We don't say "yes" in the Andrew. We say "aye aye".'

'Aye aye, sir.'

'Right. Now, off you go along with this Leading Hand'—a man in his early twenties, wearing a chevron and an anchor on his arm, stared at me. The CPO went on, 'Off you go, like a bleeding bullet, my son, and get yourself a berth and some grub organized.'

'Aye aye, sir.'

'Good. And don't worry about it, but don't do it again. You're lucky it's me. I'm fairly certain the Andrew can manage to bumble along somehow while you get yourself properly organized and you move so fast now, my lad, that your bleeding feet don't touch the deck!'

So I spent my first night in the Andrew in a cell, and entered the stream of the Royal Navy. In it and not. Organized and not. Part of it and not.

The 'crushers' in the Regulating Office were stern but not unfriendly and provided me with a comfortable if hard bed and a thin blanket in one of their overnight cells, whitewashed and stark, and woke me the next morning to a good hefty breakfast, after I had scrubbed out their office, and drove me in one of their vans back to Chatham station.

When I thanked the driver, a Leading Crusher, he replied, 'Bullshit. When you get where you're off to, you'll hate my guts for helping you to get there.'

2. Abandon Hope . . .

Squad: *Ganges* tea is tasty, *Ganges* tea is fine,
It's good for cuts and bruises;
And tastes like iodine . . .

Ganges buns are tasty, *Ganges* buns are fine,
But one fell off the table;
And killed a mate of mine!'

Leading Boy: *'Change step!'*

Chorus: 'Now we're . . . a show'r o' bas-tards,
Bas-tards are we;
We're the *Ganges'* bleeders, the Dockyard Cavalry;
Ta-da-ta-ta-ta-ta-ta-ta . . .
And when we get to Malta—
The C-in-C will say:
'Right up my gut, what a scabby bloody lot,
Are the boys from Shotley way . . . !'
Ta-ta-t-t-t-ta-ta-ta-ta!'

Repeat ad infinitum.

Lower deck marching song (informal). I doubt if anyone who saw it will ever forget the sight and sound of anything up to a hundred *Ganges* Boy Seamen, aged from 15 to 17, shouting this, many still with treble voices, screeching like discordant choirboys, some with angel faces, some with jug-ears, as they marched along, with

Lee-Enfield rifles, in many cases as long as their bearers, at the 'shoulder arms'.

The verses were sung to the tune of 'Onward Christian Soldiers', the chorus to the tune 'The Church's One Foundation', both originally Salvation Army marching tunes.

His Majesty's Ship *Ganges* was a shore establishment—a 'stone frigate'—a group of low buildings and a high ship's mast set on a bleak, windy peninsula on the East Coast of England, between the rivers Stour and Orwell. It was first established in 1865, in Falmouth, on board an eighty-four gun man o' war of 3,600 tons, the original bearer of the name *Ganges*. On board, the otherwise unwanted lads of Britain —the waifs, the strays, the abandoned bastards, the untameable, the Artful Dodgers of Queen Victoria's realm—the so-called scum of British earth, were bullied, beaten, bashed, scourged, half-starved, tormented, pummelled, lashed, keel-hauled, cudgelled, thrashed, swinged, trounced, lambasted, hurt, manhandled, battered, thumped, scared and terrorized into a total submission to the almighty will of My Lords Commissioners of the Admiralty. Then, at seventeen years of age, they were finally sent to sea in Royal Navy ships—some of the finest naval seamen that the world has ever known. 'Once a Ganges boy, always a Ganges boy.'

In 1899 HMS *Ganges* sailed from Falmouth to Harwich. Close by that port she dropped anchor off the Shotley peninsula. To the hell of corporal coercion was added the extra torment of even more bitterly cold winds, more rain, and fogs almost eternal.

In 1906, the rotten old wooden ship was practically sinking at her anchorage, so the training school was shifted ashore on to Shotley peninsula. A mast, 143 feet high, was erected first, a parade ground was laid, then low, spartan buildings were built to 'house' the boys. There was small chance of escape from *Ganges*—only one road led through the foggy marshes and escape in other directions was cut off by two rivers and the North Sea.

For one hundred and eleven years, apart from the latter part of World War II, HMS *Ganges* was utter hell on earth for boys, up to 2,000 at a time, aged fifteen to seventeen.

Ganges finally closed down in 1976 as a naval establishment, and is now a Pan-European sports training complex.

Since I left *Ganges* I have been in many hellish places, including a couple of French Foreign Legion barracks and fifteen prisons in twelve countries. None of them were nearly as menacing as HMS *Ganges* as a brain-twisting, body-racking ground of mental bullying and physical strain.

On the train from London to Ipswich, still in my civvy clothes, I wondered why I seemed to be the only boy bound for *Ganges*. Practically everyone else was several years older than me and already in naval uniform. There were a couple of hundred of them at least, all in blue serge suits with red badges, black boots and with their long overcoats thrown over their kit-bags. The train was so crowded that I had to stand in the train corridor. The sailors didn't speak to me, but laughed and joked among themselves. At Ipswich they all piled on to a line of buses waiting at the station. There I showed my warrant to yet another naval patrolman. He ordered me on to one of the buses. 'Off you go, lad, and quick about it! At the double!'

On the bus, I found myself standing again, pushed up against a tall, skinny man of about twenty-one. 'Getting a lift home, mate?' he asked, grinning.

'No, I'm off to *Ganges*, too.'

Faces around me stared at me. Eyebrows shot up. Skinny

shouted, 'Cor, blimey, you're a bit late, sonny-boy. They stopped taking sprogs months ago. Least that's what we heard, right, lads?'

All around heads nodded in agreement. Someone offered me a cigarette. 'Here, have a tickler.' It was the first time I'd ever heard the word used so.

'They'll send you home,' murmured Skinny.

Someone else said, 'Signed up for twelve, have you, mate?' The bus rattled away along a narrow road. Now we could see the rivers on both sides of the grey peninsula. 'How old're you now, then?'

'Sixteen,' I replied. I tried to keep my voice low.

'Cor, strike a bloody light!' exclaimed the voice. 'And your man's bird don't start 'til you're eighteen! Poor little bastard! That makes fourteen fucking years all told! Fourteen years in this bloody mob!'

There was a general noise of agreement through the bus. I hunkered down on my sea-bag. It made little difference to me. I thought to myself that fourteen years being carried around in naval ships could not be harder on me than fourteen more years in the Trade, loading housebricks and hauling up two-ton anchors every day. What did these recruits know about the sea-life, anyway? I asked myself. From what I'd overheard they had been in the navy no more than six weeks. They were men who had been drafted, or who had volunteered for service for the duration of hostilities. They were 'hostilities only' men—'HOS' in naval slang. They thought they were lucky. They'd be back to civilian life within a few months—back in 'civvy street', and leave all the peacetime cruising around the tropical islands and chasing the girls in Monte Carlo to us professionals in the Regular Navy.

Soon the bus passed by Pin Mill harbour which I knew; I'd sailed there twice. I managed to catch glimpses of several red-sailed barges, just like my recent ship, *Second Apprentice*. They were wending their way up the River Orwell, or were anchored out among the sailing yachts and power boats which still plied the waters, despite the war. I clutched at a seat and leaned over to catch glimpses of the barges. It was like seeing old friends standing on a railway platform as a train rushes through. Soon the barges were gone, and I was back in the limbo between the Trade and the Andrew. Then I—we all, in the bus—caught our first glimpse of the *Ganges* mast. 'They make you climb up that fucker,' said a voice, small, distant and afraid.

'Christ, I can't stand heights,' murmured another voice.

'Hard shit,' said another.

'No, they must have stopped that now,' said someone else. 'They wouldn't risk matelots' lives doing stupid bloody things like that, would they? Not now there's a bloody war on and they need everyone they can get? Wouldn't make sense, would it?'

There was a silence of hopeful agreement, but all the time, as the mast came nearer and nearer, every eye on the bus, it seemed, stared at it and watched it grow and grow, until it towered into the cloudy sky, majestic and threatening, and immense at its base. I wasn't worried about the mast. I was from the Trade. It wasn't much higher than *Second Apprentice*'s mast. I eyed the rigging as we passed, and sniffed the odour of tarred rope; and reckoned I could climb it using my hands only. Two years in the Trade had made me a cocky sod. I'd show these landlubbers. But I said nothing; soon I was too engrossed in staring at hundreds of men all seemingly insanely doubling around the parade ground in squads, this way and that, to the bellowed commands of drill instructors.

We piled out of the buses. All hell was let loose. A huge Petty Officer with a face like a bulldozer bellowed, 'Right, you shower! Fall in three deep! Come on, look lively, you buggers—don't stand there like spare pricks at a wedding! Get your plates moving or I'll have the slew of you on bloody jankers!'

The draft fell into three lines, one behind the other. Bulldozer glowered at us. He struck his cane three times against his gaiter. He grimaced widely then glowered again at us, one by one. He placed both arms behind him and yelled, 'What bloody navy do you think you're in? I said fall in three deep and when I say that I mean three deep, not bleeding three thick! Now . . . fall out!'

Several of us, including me, made the mistake of obeying this order. A few more wily ones, or those perplexed out of their wits stayed put, where they were. Bulldozer's face turned to deep scarlet. 'HALT!' he roared. Everyone froze in his tracks. Bulldozer stamped one boot on the parade ground. 'No one moves unless the order is given commencing . . .' His voice rose to a crescendo, '. . . SQUAD!' His voice fell again. 'Now, let's try again, shall we?' 'SSSSSQQUUUAAD!' he bellowed. Every man's shoulders braced for the blast, 'Fall in three deep, tallest at-the-ends—shortest-in-the-middle!!!' We somehow, half in puzzled panic, half in fear, fell in and in less than the time it takes to tell it there was formed a dazed, resentful order out of a sullen chaos.

There was silence for a full minute after our feet had stopped shuffling around. Shortly, Bulldozer stared at me, still in my civilian sea-jersey, the shortest of us all, right in the middle of the squad. His face cracked a mite. He grinned at me. I kept my face dead straight.

'Hello, hello, *hello* . . .' he said, now in a lower tone. 'What do we have here? Little Lord Fauntleroy, is it? You lost your way, son?' I kept silent, I imagined he must be joking; I didn't know what to do. He glared at me and stepped closer. 'I addressed you. I asked you a question. WELL?'

'I . . . I . . . was sent from Chatham—they made a mistake at Harwich . . .' then I lost my voice. My throat constricted and my mouth was dry.

'Harwich what?' he shouted at me.

'Er . . . er . . . Harwich recruiting office,' I replied.

'Office what?' His face was only inches from mine.

'Office where they recruit for the navy.'

'Navy *what?*'

'I . . . I . . . don't know.'

'Know what, lad?'

'Know . . . I don't know.'

Bulldozer's breath took a sharp intake. Then he yelled, 'What you don't know is your bloody manners!' He now addressed the draft in general. 'Now, you lot, you pin your ears back and listen to this. You all address everyone here with a badge on his left arm or collar, or stripes on his sleeve, anyone, from Leading Hand up to the Admiral of the Fleet, as *SIR!* . . . and God help any one of you who don't!' He turned again towards me. 'That civilian!'

I stiffened my frame.

'Twice around the parade ground at the double! Move it!'

I started to run straight ahead of me.

'Halt!' Bulldozer's voice brought me up all standing. I turned to look at him. I was trying to keep my eyes as dry as my mouth.

'Eyes front! Where do you think you are, bloody Wimbledon?' There was a titter from the squad. 'Shuddup!' from Bulldozer soon stifled it. Again his voice was directed at me. 'Civilian! Left turn!'

I did as I was bid.

'Round the parade ground, three times, at the double . . .

backwards . . . double-quick MARCH!'

I knew I was at *Ganges* all right, even before I officially belonged there, even before I'd doubled around the parade ground once, backwards—even before I'd fallen down and picked myself up thrice.

After the second time around the parade ground—backwards—I was halted by another loud bawl from Bulldozer. I stood in the chilly wind, hot and sweaty under my sea-jersey. The rest of the draft stared ahead expressionlessly. A lieutenant, in shiny black gaiters and boots, was speaking so quietly to Bulldozer that I could not hear him. Then Bulldozer yelled at me. 'Defaulter!' I trotted over to where he stood. The lieutenant turned his head slightly away from me and wrinkled his nose, as if I smelled and the stench was too much for him to bear.

'You!' shouted Bulldozer.

I wanted to cry but I stiffened my shoulders instead. I hated this old bully with all my heart, so much that I could not look him in the eye.

'You!' he repeated. Then in a lower voice, 'Look at me when I give you an order!'

The officer stared into the distance, working his lips back and forth silently.

'What order, sir?' I asked. Then I almost bit my tongue, wishing I hadn't.

Bulldozer seemed about to collapse with apoplexy. His eyes slitted. He breathed hard and exploded. 'First Lieutenant's Report for insolence!'

The lieutenant, who was around twenty-four, without looking at me, murmured something to Bulldozer.

The PO strode back to me. 'Right, get your gear and double over to the Annexe, Boy Seaman,' Bulldozer ordered me in a quiet voice. As he said it he glared at me from under his brows, a look which said, 'And God help you if I ever get you on this parade ground again.'

I doubled over to the pile of cases and kit-bags, picked up my own sea-bag and doubled as fast as I could away from Bulldozer. It was a good five minutes before a crusher pulled me up with a yell, '*Nozzer!*', and asked me where I was going, then sent me in the opposite direction right across the parade ground again, dodging the marching and running squads of trainees, out through the gate and a half mile down a lane to where a large sign said 'HMS *Ganges* Annexe'. It might as well have said, 'Abandon Hope, All Ye Who Enter Here.'

I entered the Annexe gate about two-thirty p.m. By three-thirty p.m. I had been doubled into and out of the Police Office, given a pay-book, been allotted to a class of boys who had already completed two months of training, been shorn of my hair down to within a half inch of my head and doubled by a crusher into the clothing store. There a fat Stores PO, grinning all over his face, slung a cursory glance at my frame, followed it with a heap of blue serge uniforms and heaved a pair of boots at me as black and heavy as coal-boulders. I wondered how I would ever be able to walk in them. It turned out I needn't have worried. No 'nozzer' ever walked in *Ganges*: we ran, and we ran, and we *ran*. If we weren't standing to attention, marching, eating terrible food or exhaustedly sleeping, we *ran*. Everywhere and at all times.

The Stores PO then tossed at me a set of 'sports gear'. This consisted of two pairs of very short trousers or very long shorts—I never did puzzle out which they were. There was also a pair of canvas shoes with leather soles, which were known as 'easy shoes' and which must have surely been the most torturous footwear ever devised. Blisters and sore toes were the order of the day whenever gym shoes were worn.

To this day I remember the scratch of new blue jersey against my otherwise bare skin, and the smell of a new kit of clothes—especially my oilskin overcoat, black and shiny on the outside, bright yellow on the inside, which was so sticky and stiff that it took almost all my strength to pull it apart so I could lay it out. In later years, always, the smell of an oilskin coat took my mind right back to joining-day at *Ganges*. Even now, every time I smell hot steam I recall being doubled down to the showers at *Ganges*, naked and scared.

Everything issued by the Royal Navy was 'Pussers'—a mispronunciation of 'Purser's'. The Purser, in the days of fighting sail, was the ship's accounts and stores officer. Just that—the man who held the purse. Now I was dressed in Pusser's rig. From now on everything I wore, ate, drank, or used for any purpose, while I was in the clutches of the Andrew, would be 'Pusser's'.

From the clothing store, freshly spruced up in a blue uniform about two and a half sizes too big for me, and a round hat which was jammed down on my head by the crusher so hard that it hurt my brow, and my black marching boots, hob-nailed and ponderous, the crusher doubled me back again out of the Annexe gate, along the lane and so into the main *Ganges* barracks. There he doubled me past the red-bricked barracks with their whitewashed sidewalks (walked on only by officers) and into a mess-room crowded with beds made up like fresh sandwiches. At the far end of the mess-room was a large empty space, about half the extent of the room. Its floor—'deck' in *Ganges*—was so highly polished that it looked like glass.

'Right, Nozzer, you've got bed Number Nine,' yelled the crusher. 'Dump your kit there for now and double round to *Benbow* class—they're goin' over the "Devil's Elbow",' said the crusher with a smirk. 'Look lively, lad, you haven't got all day!'

'No, only fourteen years,' I thought.

'You're a lucky nozzer,' said the *Benbow* Division PO when I puffed up to the base of the mast. He was a short man, and sparely set up, although his blue uniform and belt, gaiters and boots made him seem stocky. He must have been around thirty years old—which in the Andrew gave him a mental age of about fifty-five. When I arrived he was pacing up and down before a squad of about twenty boys. The oldest boy in the class could have been no more than seventeen—and only barely that. But as I glanced at them I already felt just a mite more at home. So far in my naval career I had been with older men—eighteen years old and up—and at sixteen a difference in age of two years is like a difference of two decades later on in life. Here I was going to be with my contemporaries—or so I thought.

'Yes,' said the DI, 'you *are* a lucky nozzer *indeed*. We understand as how you've managed already to get yourself posted adrift. Well, you are here to replace Boy Seaman Jenkins. He didn't quite come up to scratch, did he, lads?' the DI bellowed at the boys.

'No, sir,' replied a chorus of voices, some deep, some squeaky.

'What didn't Jenkins do?' yelled the DI.

'Didn't quite come up to scratch, sir!' replied the boys in unison.

The memory brings to my mind visions of Dotheboys Hall.

'Right. Wanted to go home to dear old Mum!' shouted the DI. Then, looking at me with steely blue eyes, stern yet not cruel like Bulldozer's, he went on, 'My name's Petty Officer White. My chums call me Knocker. You call me Sir! Now, my son, let's see if you can do a bit better than the late lamented Jenkins, shall we? Where're you from, my little cherub?'

'Wales, sir.' There was a south-west breeze driving the clouds above.

'Well, well, a little Taff we have, is it, look you,

man . . . !' Knocker shouted out a very poor imitation of a pseudo-Welsh accent. He turned to the class. He was silent for a minute, staring at them. They returned his stare without expression, standing 'easy', which at *Ganges* meant holding themselves slightly less rigid than at 'attention'.

'The last class was all ass, and if I don't get ass . . . *what?*' The DI grinned.

'No one will pass, *sir!*' bellowed the boys.

'Bloody right!' intoned Knocker.

For a moment or two, I was thunderstruck. I'd heard vague rumours about sexual shenanigans in the navy; this was worrying. Then Knocker turned to me with a broad grin on his face. 'Go on,' he said, in a milder tone, 'get fallen in, we've got things to do. We can't stand around all day like pox-doctor's clerks, and anyway you're so doggo I'd rather show the golden rivet to a rattle-snake. And Taff,' he was still grinning widely, 'my mother-in-law is Welsh, so you know what you've got coming if you even as much as *think* of falling by the wayside! You'll get it for her as well as your bloody self! And she's got ten years of nagging and interfering to settle up for! Now, move yourself, Cocker, get fell in . . . !'

As I did as I was bid, shoving myself into the rear rank of the class, Knocker was joined by two other gunnery instructors—'GIs'. They, too, were uniformed the same as Knocker, no belt but instead of holding a short cane, they carried, each one, a length of rope with a monkey's fist knotted into the end. These were known as 'goggers'. For the next half-hour or so both the newcomer GIs attempted to hit as many of the boys as they could with their goggers, as the lads scrambled on to the rigging on their way to the masthead.

At the lower part of the rigging the ratlines—the foothold lines tied between the standing wires—made for fairly easy climbing, although the shrouds swayed like palm fronds in a high breeze as parties of ten boys at a time, with the GIs

wielding their goggers on their legs and rear-ends, tried to
clamber up fast out of the way of the swinging goggers.
Around them the wind blew a good half-gale. Then, towards
the yard-arm, the 'Devil's Elbow' as we called it, the shroud
wires closed up towards each other so that our holds on the
ratlines became smaller and smaller, so much so that we
could grab with only three fingers, and it was almost impossible to get a foothold with our boots. To scramble over the
'Devil's Elbow' meant, momentarily, hanging out over thin
air, with a hundred-foot drop straight below us. We had to go
over the outer ends of the yard-arm—the 'Devil's Elbow'.
No cheating by climbing directly up the mast—that was 'for
sissies and foreigners'. As I slithered over the yard-arm I
could hear all around me the grunts and gasps of nine other
boys as they ascended, driven into near-panic by the goggers.

Knocker had ordered us to 'touch the button'. This was
the mast-head truck, the very topmost piece of the mast,
apart from the lightning conductor which reared above it.
Many boys failed to even touch the top of the button. Those
who did were marked down as 'good lads'. Those who dared
to try to mount the button, to stand upright on the mast-head
truck, were considered heroes. I decided to be a hero despite
the wind. I'd been lucky to get into one of the last boys'
classes to pass through *Ganges* for the rest of the war. I'd
taken the place of someone else (Jenkins). It wouldn't be easy
for the class to accept me straight off the bat; I had to show
them that the ten weeks' training I'd missed wouldn't hold
them back. I aimed for the 'half-moon'—a small platform
just large enough for one man to stand on, which was about
twenty feet below the mast-head. Below me, a hundred odd
feet below, when I made the mistake of looking down, I could
see the tiny figures of the three instructors and the boys
waiting to escape up the mast from the flogging goggers.
Above the half-moon the climb was even more precarious.

There was a Jacob's ladder for the first ten feet, then only the
mast to grab on to and scramble up, with both arms and legs
wrapped as far around it as I could manage. By now my
canvas gym shoes were chafing my feet so badly that I slid
back down to the half-moon and, hanging on to the mast with
one hand, unlaced them and took them off with the other. I
slung the gym shoes over the stay which supported the
half-moon, and bare-footed, made my way again up the mast.
That was the way Ted and I had done it on board *Second
Apprentice*. I'd show those blubberly city lads.

The button, when I finally climbed up to it, turned out to
be a round platform about three feet across. The trick was to
get a good solid handhold on the base of the lightning
conductor and then swing myself bodily up and over the
overhanging edge of the button, so that I was gut down, half
lying on top of it. In *Second Apprentice* Ted and I had done
this a number of times, even when the ship was bouncing
around at sea in the Channel. But there had not been,
on board that sweet ship, the scuffle to avoid whizzing goggers on deck, nor the gasps of fright and fear and effort from
nine other boys scared out of their wits, nor the harsh roars of
command from three bullying petty officers below, nor the
sound of parade-ground commands and the clashing of
bayonets being fixed and the crash of heavy boots from a
thousand feet all around down below, nor the air of utter
menace all around from gently moving White Ensigns, nor
the cold stares of gold-laced officers at their office windows.

I told myself I must show these buggers what a lad from the
Trade could do. With a desperate heave of my whole body as
I locked my hands around the lightning conductor base, I
threw myself outwards, upwards and forwards . . . and
ended, half sobbing with effort and strain, stomach down on
the button. Somehow I clawed up the lightning conductor
rod, with my bare feet seeming to dig into the button, and

remembered to not look down. I stared out over the roofs of
the nearby buildings, right out over the Orwell Estuary. Out
on the estuary a sailing barge, her brown sails rosy in the sun,
was slowly nodding her bow and stern up and down, up and
down, as if she knew that I could do it, and was nodding
approval. From below came the sound of rousing cheers.
Then, above the cheers, I heard Knocker's scream. 'That boy
on the button! GET DOWN HERE!'

As fast as I could I clambered down from the button. This
was even more difficult than getting on to it, as it meant that I
had to get my legs out and over the edge of the button and
then around the mast. But with Knocker's voice bawling
from below, 'Get down on the deck NOW!' I somehow made
it, with my heart in my mouth, slid down the topmast, all the
way to the half-moon, grabbed my gym shoes, scrambled
down the shrouds as fast as I could, jumped down on to the
parade ground and doubled over to where Knocker and the
two other GIs were standing. All three of them glared at me. I
stood, silently heaving, for a minute in front of them, panting
from the effort I had just made. Knocker said, in a low voice,
'*And what are you doing out of the rig of the day?*'

I was dumbfounded. It took me a moment or two to take in
what he had asked. 'I . . . I . . . was getting on to the
mast-head, sir.'

'Out of the rig of the day, not wearing your easy shoes,'
said Knocker. 'Where . . . what did you do in "civvy street",
eh, lad?'

'Deckboy in a sailing barge, sir!'

Knocker stamped his feet and slapped his cane against his
gaiter. 'Oh, oh! So we've got one of *those* with us, have we? A
life on the ocean wave, is it? Think you're on your Daddy's
yacht, do you? Think you can go around dressed like a bloody
Praed Street ponce, eh? In the Andrew you do as you're told,
and if you're ordered to dress in Number Threes with easy

shoes, then that's what you do, see? And you stay rigged like that until you're ordered what else to wear, see? And it don't matter what we're doing, or what's happening—if the bloody ship's sinking and you've got a six-inch shell up your ass—if the rig of the day is easy shoes and Number Threes then that's what you wear until your bloody feet and your ass get blown off! Yours not to reason why, but yours to do and die, GET IT?'

'Yes, sir.'

'Right.' Knocker was silent for a moment. The other two POs scowled at me, fingering their goggers. For a moment I thought I was going to be dismissed again into the anonymity for which I ached. An officer was quietly looking on the scene. Knocker yelled, 'First Lieutenant's report—out of the rig of the day!'

As soon as Knocker said that the officer turned quietly on his heels, a satisfied look on his face, and strode away.

Knocker turned again to me. 'Now up you go again, nozzer, so fast I won't see you . . . and this time come *down* over the Devil's Elbow. Fast.' You didn't argue with the Andrew; I learned that all right. *Fast.*

Later, much later, after a couple more hours of marching, doubling and being shouted at, back in the mess, stamping my name on my kit so that I could later stitch it on my uniforms with red chain-stitch, it seemed that the other lads accepted me. I had become one of them right away, even though I had joined them so late in their course.

'Eh, Taff, you did all right, then!' This from a Birmingham lad who was two sizes too big for his seventeen years, and whose uniform was two sizes too small for him. 'Blimey! Stood on the bloody button *twice and* in the rattle—all on the same day!'

All around me some boys reclined exhausted on their beds,

some polishing their boots ready for next day's muster at five-thirty a.m. Some were out on 'Jankers'—under punishment.

'How long you been in, Cock?' This from a scarred veteran of about sixteen and a half, with a Cockney accent.

'Only joined today—I got shuttled around a bit. Landed in Chatham Barracks by mistake,' I replied. As boys do, I knew that it was vital for me to impress them somehow. Having actually been in a proper naval barracks, no matter for how long, ought to give me some sort of prestige among them. I seemed to be right. There was a respectful silence for a few moments, then a Scots voice piped up, 'Chatham Barracks, on top o' the bloody button *twice*, and Jimmy's . . . all on the same day. Jesus Christ, afore ye know it, you'll be a bloody Admiral, Taff!'

'Or swinging at the bleeding yard-arm,' said another, softly.

3. The Nozzers

Ganges Jaunty's a bastard, a bastard,
The old cunt—he ought to be shot,
And tied to the wall of a piss-house, a piss-house;
And left there to fuckingwell rot!

Singing hi-jig-a-jig, fuck a little pig,
Follow the band,
Follow the band with your prick in your hand—
Singing hi-jig-a-jig, fuck a little pig,
Follow the band,
Follow the band all the way!

Ditty, Royal Navy Lower Deck. It was a favourite in HMS
Ganges, and was sung to the tune of 'Follow the band'.

Life for a boy trainee at HMS *Ganges* was one long harass-
ment from dawn—when the bugler sounded 'Charlie'—
until lights out at nine-fifteen p.m. There was hardly a
minute of the waking day when we boys were not on our feet
and doubling, or sat at attention in a classroom being yelled
at. Even when the 'working' day was over, our time was taken
up hand-sewing our names on to our uniforms (red chain-
stitches, each not longer than the rest). Some of the class were
still busily engaged in this pastime, even though they had
been in *Ganges* for ten weeks. There was always something to

be done, and never enough time to do it. The boy who could find five minutes to sit down and write a letter home was lucky indeed.

Reveille was blared at five-thirty:

> Charlie, Charlie, lash up and stow, me lads;
> Charlie, Charlie, lash up and stow . . .
> Cocoa and biscuits, cocoa and biscuits,
> Cocoa and biscuits, lash up and stow . . .
> Wakey, wakey, lash up and stow, me lads,
> Wakey, wakey, lash up and stow!

Even as the first notes of 'Charlie' blared, the boys were roused by one of the DIs, either banging his cane on the bedrails or grabbing the blanket (no sheets) and pulling the boys bodily out of bed and on to the deck.

> Come along, my lucky lads
> WAKEY WAKEY! you wall-eyed gets!
> Hands off cocks and on to socks
> And Gawd help the last one out
> Of his stinking pit!

Then followed a scramble for the washroom, at the end of the barrack hut. There was always a long line for a cold-water sluice, but we mostly thanked our lucky stars we were too young yet to shave.

The messes were in three sections: first the washroom and drying room, night (indoor) heads and another washroom with a footbath (for scrubbing our feet to avoid chinky toe rot. I don't think anyone avoided it: at night I could hear the bedsprings squeaking for hours where boys were scratching their toes . . . or something). Next there was the mess deck, which took up about a quarter of the remaining space in the hut. This was where we lived. It was crowded with bare furniture; tables and benches. In the middle of the mess deck was a coal stove, highly polished of course. The rest of the mess—about half the total area of the hut—was taken up by the Polished Deck. This was empty. Woe betide anyone who dared to step on to the Polished Deck in boots! The wood planks of the Polished Deck shone like glass. It was kept that way especially for Captain's Rounds. Its main purpose seemed to be to give us something beyond perfection with which to challenge and surpass other messes. There was no other reason for the Polished Deck. It was the ultimate *Ganges* shibboleth. The deck was polished for no other reason than that it was laid down that it had to be polished. The Andrew said so. Ours, in *Benbow* division, shone like ice. God only knows how many young backs had ached, over the years, to bring that cynical sneer of a sheen to those dumb, stupid planks of wood.

Against the walls—we called them 'bulkheads'—of the living section of the mess were arranged the beds, each head to foot, perfectly aligned. Each morning, before breakfast, all the movable furniture was taken out of the mess and the deck was scrubbed by us boys with our bell-bottomed pants rolled up to the knees (and I'd thought the bell-bottoms were to show off jauntily ashore!). While this was going on other boys cleaned out the washrooms, the outside heads and the boats down on the foreshore. This latter was not a bad job on a fine day, but on a cold and foggy morning it was miserable; then the ice clung to the boats' bilges and we chipped it out with marlin spikes and watch out any nozzer who so much as scratched the boats' timbers! On fine sunny mornings the boat party could soon finish their job, then hide behind a clump of grass, safe from the prying eyes of the crushers.

Breakfast was generally cold half-fried, half-poached eggs and a cold greasy rasher of fatty bacon, or 'train smash'

—cold greasy thin sausages in cold greasy tomato mush, or 'herrings in'—cold canned greasy herrings in cold greasy tomato mush, and a 'fanny'—a mess kettle, full of lukewarm tea. Pusser's meals for boys at *Ganges* wouldn't nowadays be fed to swine in any self-respecting pig-farm.

After breakfast we paraded. This was called 'divisions' and lasted about an hour. Then we drilled, all the trainees in formation: 'Squad, from the left . . . dress!' 'Squad . . . by the right, double march . . . left wheel!' On Saturdays divisions was short, so that we could double back to the mess and clean and scrub everything again, and put out kit, otherwise mostly never used, all ship-shape, for the Captain's inspection. While this went on, from the way everyone worried and hurried, and rushed all the time as the posted lookouts reported on the approaching Captain's whereabouts, you would have thought that the King himself was arriving. On Sundays, divisions was two hours long, march and double up and down, up and down. Then we were marched to the barracks church, all except those who declared themselves RC, to half-doze to the droning of the Church of England padre. The Roman Catholics went to an empty mess hut to listen, they said, to the droning of their particular kind of bible bosun.

On Sundays we all wore our Number One uniforms. These were brushed and cleaned and pressed so stiff that we could hardly move in them, even if we had dared to, except when we were marching or doubling. After the Captain had inspected us, and several dozen names had been taken—some for bits of fluff on their suits, some for a collar-tape an eighth of an inch too long or too short, some apparently just for the hell of it—we all marched past the Captain's rostrum.

That was the bit I enjoyed most. That was one of the few occasions at *Ganges* when I felt I was really in the Royal Navy, the oldest organized fighting force in the world, and not some kind of penal institute. Then the Royal Marine band, in their smart dark uniforms and gleaming buttons and sparkling white pith helmets, struck up and played the marching tune of each division as it marched past the Captain on the dais.

Our division's tune was 'Colonel Bogey'. In the centre of our formation there was hardly a boy who was not singing, under his breath, as with rifles or bayonets at the slope, we clomped past the rostrum and the Captain with his four gold rings saluted:

> What did the engine driver say
> When the boiler burst?
> *Bollox!* And the same to you . . .

That was the mornings. The days, except when we had 'Make and Mend'—a 'free' afternoon off, in which to stitch our names on our kit—were full of doubling and marching, or learning by rote the names of a hundred thousand naval things or knots or splices, gunnery terms and fire-fighting. The evenings, after supper, were generally spent getting our boots and uniforms ready for the next day, before 'Lights Out' at nine-fifteen.

For the average, normal, run-of-the-mill boy or HO, Shotley was a bad place to be. For those under punishment it was purgatory. I was very soon in purgatory.

I could see no connection between mindless bullying and efficient seamanship; all the while, it never occurred to me that I was being moulded, shaped, ram-rodded, into the Andrew's idea of what a matelot should be: ideas that had lingered on, pervading everything in the Royal Navy's attitude to the Lower Deck, since long before the days of Vernon and Nelson, ideas and attitudes which went back to even before the days of Raleigh and Drake. First our own personalities, characters; everything that was ours, all that made us who and what we thought we might be, were brutally expunged, until we were little but empty shells. Then the void was crammed with King's Regulations and Admiralty Instructions, Ship's Standing Orders and Orders of the Day—all except one part of our minds and souls, which was defended by the unwritten law of the Lower Deck: *'Thou shalt be one of the lads . . .'* That was the citadel for our sanity.

As *Benbow* Division mustered for divisions the next morning —the day after I arrived at *Ganges*—the DI hailed me over to him. 'In the rattle, you. Stand by to doff your lid,' he said. 'When First Lieutenant's defaulters are called out, you fall out with 'em, see?'

I soon found myself with a half-dozen other defaulters, puffing up the long covered way to the dreaded Quarterdeck on top of the hill. There we lined up tensely and waited for the order to double into the First Lieutenant's presence.

'Jones, T., Boy Seaman, double-quick march, eft, oit, eft, oit . . . Halt!' The Chief Regulating Petty Officer—the 'Jaunty'—who read out the charges seemed to be in his element. Ever since that day forty-four years ago I have been reminded of him and his officious voice every time I've come across a bullying policeman, or a sarcastic office clerk, or a waiter who's bowed and scraped to the rich and powerful for too long, and has caught the complaint of arrogance from his patrons.

The Lieutenant who had been standing by at the base of the mast the day before, and who had strolled away with a satisfied smirk on his face, stood beside the First Lieutenant's table. Now his face was blandly serious.

'Off caps!' *Up, two, three-down.* I whipped off my cap.

As I doubled up before his desk, the First Lieutenant, as befits the Angel of Death, stared at the spot right between my eyes. I crashed to a halt and stood there, breathless, eyes front, at attention.

The Jaunty, a huge fat man, with a brick-red face and what looked like fifty medal ribbons on his left breast, rattled out the charge against me. '. . . DID, on the oomteenth of May, 1940, at oomteen 30 hours . . . in contravention of the King's Regulations and Admiralty Instructions . . . conduct prejudicial to good order and naval discipline . . . remove his deck shoes . . . out of the dress of the day as laid down in ship's standing orders, SIR!'

I felt as if I had been charged with high treason.

The First Lieutenant glared at me. He leaned over very, very slightly and stared down at me. 'Anything to say?' he said. His voice was very, very uppah clahss.

'I . . . I . . . didn't know, sir,' were all the words I could muster.

'Ignorance is no excuse,' said the Jimmy. 'The standing orders are posted in your mess. The rig of the day for your class yesterday was Number Threes with sports shoes. Why did you remove them?'

'To get up to the mast-head, sir.'

'Plenty of other boys have climbed to the mast-head without removing their gear . . . nonsense . . . seven days Number Tens!'

The voice of the Jaunty behind me yelled, 'Seven days Number Tens! On caps! About turn, quick march! Report to the Regulating Office!'

I about turned and marched smartly away, while my mind boggled at the thought of fourteen more years of naval justice.

Royal Navy punishment was doled out by numbers. The lower the number the greater the punishment. Number One, for example, was death by hanging. That was awarded for murder, cowardice in the face of the enemy, treason and burning a ship or a dockyard. Number Two was death by shooting, and so on, with the punishment decreasing as the number increased. Number Ten punishment was the deprivation of all 'privileges' (such as they were). It meant that the sinner had to rise half an hour before 'Charlie' and fall in just as reveille was being sounded, along with other culprits who had transgressed against the King's Regulations and Admiralty Instructions. Then it meant an hour's very strenuous doubling in full working uniform, belt, eighteen-inch bayonet, steel helmet and gaiters, with a heavy Lee-Enfield .303 rifle either at the slope, bruising your shoulder, or held up at full arm's length above your head. In *Ganges*, if the Petty Officer in charge of the 'jankers' detail was feeling a little friendly, it meant doubling up and down Laundry Hill for an hour at full pelt. If the PO had a hangover or 'had a bastard on' (and they usually did) it meant racing up and down Faith, Hope and Charity, the three flights of steps that led to the foreshore down from the signal tower. You had faith when you tackled going up the first flight of steps, hope when you clomped up the second and you needed charity when you staggered up the third. The total distance up the steps was about a hundred yards.

The Petty Officer in charge of the punishment detail on my first morning on jankers was not at all amused at having to rise so early, and seeing me, a new nozzer among the 'old skates' he decided to put me through the hoop. At the bottom of Faith, Hope and Charity, he ordered me to the rear of the single file of boys. Then, half way up the Faith flight he bellowed, 'Rear man to the front!' That meant that I had to double up the steps twice as fast as the others, in order to pass them and take my place at the head of the line. Half way up Hope flight he yelled, 'Front man to the rear!' Then I had to clatter smartly back past the ascending line of skates, so as to take my place at the rear again. Then it was 'Rear man to the front!' and 'Front man to the rear!' twice more till we finally arrived, marking time but still at the double, at the top of the steps. Then the whole performance was repeated in reverse, going down the steps, so that by the time the first return journey had been completed I was panting heavily and half-dizzy with trying to keep my balance as I clattered down the steps.

'About turn—we'll do that again!' smirked the PO. And we did—three times more, with my covering twice the ground. And all the time, even when we doubled up the steps, with the Lee-Enfield rifles at full arm's stretch above the head, I thought of how much easier this was than loading housebricks into a barge by hand, 60,000 at a time, as I'd done onboard *Second Apprentice*. So it went on, double marching in heavy, steel-studded boots, perspiring so much under the coarse blue serge uniform that the sweat stained our white T-shirts blue.

'Right turn! Stand easy!' bawled the PO. Then to me, 'You—the new one! Fall out . . . fall in! Come on! Move! Fall out . . . fall in! Close up front rank! You—the new one!'

Me again.

'Get on the end! Defaulters!' We all stiffened up ramrod straight. 'Hun! Left turn. Rear rank, quick march! Centre rank, quick march! Lead on behind rear rank! Front rank, quick march!'

Now there was a long single file with me in the rear again.

'Defaulters, double-MARCH!'

Off we went at the trot up Laundry Hill. Half way up, the PO bawled, 'Rear man to the front!' He was at it again. So it went on, for yet another half-hour.

It turned out to be that PO's last day on punishment detail duty. The others who followed him were not quite as hard, and the rest of my week's jankers passed a bit more easily. I was the rear man only now and again.

The Nozzers

I knew that I was comparatively lucky. I hadn't been laid into generously with the half-inch thick cane over my thin-canvas-covered rump. Six strokes was usually doled out at any one time and it left bloody weals on many a boy transgressor's rear end. After the fourth time, the caning was twelve strokes, and was carried from the days of fighting sail. That and rum and tobacco—and being boys, we were not entitled to the rum. 'Rum, bum and baccy.' And that was why 'bum' was included—that, and not buggery, as the landsmen thought.

One afternoon a week was put aside as 'Make and Mend'. This meant that the boys had three or four hours in which to 'idle' about unless they still had stitching to do on their nametags. But for us under punishment it meant another hour's doubling up and down the hill or the steps, and when that was over an hour's polishing the corridors of the wardroom—the officers' mess. By the time that was over I was exhausted, but I couldn't lie down on my bed—during daylight hours no one could. That was against the King's Regulations and Admiralty Instructions, and God help the boy found doing it. The only way to rest at all comfortably was to go down to the foreshore and hide behind a hummock. Then if a crusher came along I could pretend to have slipped and fallen down.

Thus passed my first week in the Andrew. The rest of my time in *Ganges* was less strenuous . . . slightly so.

In the months that followed, slowly, so slowly, as each boy ticked off the number of 'Charlies' to go before Christmas leave, the days passed one after the other. We learned by rote, we marched and doubled and scoffed terrible food, and played soccer and rugby and boxed, and I climbed the mast twice more—this time with my easy shoes on. Then, I merely touched the button.

Each week the regular ambulance left *Ganges* taking three or four trainees, HOs or boys, off their heads, to the mental hospital in Chatham. These occasions were spoken of quite casually, in passing, as if the boy or man in question had contracted measles or 'flu and had gone off for a week's rest by the seaside. There was never a thought of commiseration for the loony or his family. It was looked upon as inevitable that some people would go crazy and show it. Others also went crazy—and managed to hide it from Authority—and they, in the long run, were even crazier than those who were carted away. They must have been, to stay in the Andrew when there was the slightest chance of escape.

The funny farm ambulances looked like tumbrils headed for the guillotine.

I had learned a hard lesson. In the Royal Navy there were those who tried to fight it. They came a cropper, or went daft. The only thing to do was surrender to the Andrew all my body and most of my mind. My soul I would keep to myself. The only way to do this was to try to appear and behave in a mediocre, average way; to become one of the herd.

In any group of men or boys thrown together from far parts of the British Isles and Ireland there were bound to be a great variety of backgrounds and characters, although at first encounter this was not so obvious. The standardizing effects of uniform clothes and strict discipline had been at work on *Benbow* division for some weeks. In the classrooms, or out on the parade ground, or pulling the cutters across Shotley Creek, the boys would have seemed, to the casual observer, to have been very much all of a kind. So they had first appeared to me—until I got to know them better in the close confines of the mess.

Of the twenty boys, ten were English, six Scottish, three Irish (one was an Ulsterman, but the other two, from the

Republic, stuck to him like flies to a jam pot); and one Welshman—me. The Scots and Irish, no matter where they hailed from, were considered just that—Scots or Irish; but the English were tallied by the regions from which they hailed, and they tended to stick with their kind in the main—the Londoners with the Londoners, the Geordies with the Geordies, and the Brummies with the Brummies. A particular friend, if he was about the same age, was an 'oppo'. If he was younger, was a 'winger'. If he was from the same city or area, was a 'townie'. The form of address for them, between each other, was 'opps', 'wings' and 'towns'. An English lad could be addressed by any of these tags, but a Scot was invariably called 'Jock', an Irishman 'Mick' or 'Paddy' and a Welshman, 'Taff'. Among the English, anyone from Liverpool area was known as 'Scouse'; from the New-castle area as 'Geordie', and from the Birmingham area as 'Brum'. Anyone not from the British working-class milieu can hardly understand how important to us was placing someone in the right 'slot', but in a country like Britain, so class and region conscious, it was the first rule of social intercourse to know exactly to whom you were talking, and from what level of society he hailed and from which area.

As in practically any group of boys, we had our own general types; there was Slinger Woods, the Cockney class comedian. He could turn even a serious practice at aiming and firing Bren guns into a hilarious affair of stifled laughs and sniffled mirth. There was Gorgeous Geordie, the hand-somest lad in *Ganges*—broad-shouldered, a sculptured face like Adonis, eyes as blue as the sea, golden haired and, as we all had seen when he pranced around the washroom naked, rigged like a donkey. 'A gift for any nice young lady, is our Gorgeous Geordie-boy,' as Slinger put it. It was true, as we all knew to our envy. Gorgeous Geordie's only disadvantage in life was his dialect and vocabulary. His dialect was almost, to us from other regions, impossible to understand, apart from the stock swearwords, which flew from Gorgeous Geordie. Gorgeous couldn't express any one sentence without using 'fookin' or 'coont' at least twice. From what we could understand, Gorgeous Geordie had a friend in Newcastle who was a bank manager. This friend sent him a parcel of food every week, and money, which is why he was always surrounded by some of the other boys, who were not nearly so well endowed, with cigarettes, food, money and whatever it took to have a bank manager friend in Newcastle. Rumour had it that something might be going on, too, between Gorgeous Geordie and one of the crushers who checked the incoming parcels.

Usually any money or anything more than a couple of packets of cigarettes was confiscated by the Regulating Officer, and doled out later, bit by bit, to the boy concerned. This was supposed not to be mindless interference. It was supposed to serve a good purpose. It was supposed to prevent stealing. Stealing only exists where there is envy: 'remove the cause for the envy and the cause for stealing disappears' —that was the theory, and I suppose that it worked in most cases. But in reality any boy who was caught stealing in *Ganges* would have gone through pure hell with his mess mates. Although it never happened in my time in *Benbow* Division, I was told that it had occurred soon after the class was formed. The culprit had been stood in the centre of a ring of all the other lads and pummelled unmercifully until he had dropped. Then the Scots had put in the boot and the lad had been carried away to the sick bay. That was Jenkins, the boy whom I had replaced. He had languished in the sick bay for a week. Upon his return to the class, he had been ostracized —'sent to Coventry'—and in the course of one month had gone barmy. 'Either that or he was working his ticket,' as

Slinger Woods put it. 'Anyway, they carted him off to the funny farm at Chatham.'

By the time I joined *Benbow* most of the boys in the class had become hardened to the steely discipline, but they still grumbled incessantly. They mostly came from working-class homes in the cities, or poor crofters' families in Scotland and Ireland, except for Jock McDonald. He was from the Gorbals, the slum quarter of Glasgow, and he was just about the toughest lad of fifteen I ever knew. No one ever challenged Jock to a stand-up fight by the outside heads, which was the customary way in which disputes between boys were settled. Jock had a vicious right hook and was so fast with his boots that no one could stand up to him for more than a few seconds without being flayed, hammered and kicked into a bloody mess. Jock was always on jankers. He had a running war with the crushers. He dared them to wear him down. They did their best. They doubled him, 'fully booted and spurred' up and down Faith, Hope and Charity until he practically wore a groove in the steps. The crushers tried to run Jock into the deck. They hated Jock and Jock hated them. Finally, while he was on Number Eleven punishment, one of the crushers taunted Jock. Jock fixed his bayonet on to the muzzle of his rifle and charged the crusher. He ran the PO all around the parade ground in full view of the Officer of the Day. Jock was finally subdued by six crushers surrounding him, while another three flung filled sandbags at him until he went down.

Jock was manacled and flung into a cell to simmer down. Then he was stripped naked and left to cool off even more until he was hauled before the Captain's Table. There he was awarded twelve strokes, two years' imprisonment, and to be dismissed from the Service. Then he was returned to his cell.

On the day for Jock's punishment, we boys and all the

HOs, about 2,000 all told, were mustered by divisions on the parade ground, under a grey, threatening sky. We stood there, at ease, for a half hour, while the Royal Marine band played traditional navy marches. Four men-under-punishment under the command of eight crushers, all in Number Ones with gold badges and medals, marched on to the centre of the parade ground. The skates hauled along a vaulting horse from the gym. Behind them, two sick-berth attendants lugged a stretcher. The marine band music stopped and now there was only the slow steady beat of a drum. The vaulting horse was positioned with great purpose and ceremony, until it was just right. Next the Jaunty appeared, bearing two canes. Behind him four more crushers escorted Jock. He was dressed in thin canvas tropical rig, dirty white and somehow very shabby-looking. He was capless, but he held his head high with an air of defiance, as if he were saying, 'Right, you pusser-faced bastards, do your worst—you won't beat me!'

The crushers bent Jock over the vaulting horse and, two to each limb, held him so by his ankles and wrists. Next the Jaunty reported to the Officer of the Day, 'Prisoner present and ready for punishment, sir!'

'Very well, Master at Arms,' replied the Officer of the Day. The Jaunty saluted him and returned to stand by the vaulting horse. To the slow beat of the drum, the OOD reported to the First Lieutenant, who in turn reported to the Captain. 'Very well. Carry out the punishment.' All this was done very steadily and unhurriedly, and all the while we nozzers held ourselves rigidly at attention, heads front, but every eye was on Jock and the Jaunty. I found myself being aware that I wasn't standing at attention for the Jaunty, or the Captain, or the Andrew, but for Jock. By now the rain was coming down thinly and cold water ran down my cheeks as the bass drum beat and the cane came down on Jock's rump, one thwack for every three drum beats. With each thwack I could see and feel the lads around me flinching, and hear soft cries of 'Jesus!' and 'Mary, mother of God!' from the Irish, and 'Fucking bastards!' from Slinger, and all the time the White Ensign drooped over the parade ground, as if in shame.

After the twelfth stroke, Jock was carried off on the stretcher that was waiting, face down, and that was the last any of us ever saw of him. The marine band struck up 'Heart of Oak' and we were marched off back to our messes, to change into working gear.

'Give Jock one thing,' said one voice back in the mess. 'He didn't let out a peep.'

'Fucking hard man—a good Scotsman,' said a Scots voice.

'Bloody good luck to him,' said another.

But there was at least one of us lads who had felt every lash of the cane, and whose memory was seared for ever, and who, while he loved the Andrew and all it defended, would guard from it his own soul—the citadel of himself.

All the time, 'outside' the war situation worsened. In June France fell. Poland, Denmark, Holland and Belgium had already been overrun by the Nazis. On June 4th Churchill had made a speech in the House of Commons and growled that we would fight the Nazis on the beaches and in the fields and in the streets—and we boys and men in *Ganges* made preparations to do just that. We dug trenches on the fore-shore and sharpened our bayonets. Naval trucks were kept ready to take us to other parts of the coastline of East Anglia. One Lieutenant Commander, with a face like a death's head skull, told us in all seriousness that if we, by mischance, lost our rifles and bayonets in battle we could always kick a German to death with our hob-nailed boots. 'Remember, to do your own bit, "on your way out" you only need to take *one*

German with you . . .' Looking back, objectively, I do believe that if the worst had happened we *Ganges* boys would have tried to do exactly that. I recall no defeatism. I often hear nowadays that we didn't know what was going on, or why we were at war, but that was not the case. We knew, all right, what was in store for Britain if the Nazis won. For us boys, and especially a Welsh boy, it was bad enough having to be ordered about in English—but in any other language . . . !

In September the Battle of Britain was in full fling. We were too far north to be under the thick of it, but we saw quite a few dog-fights between our RAF lads and Luftwaffe stragglers or reconnaissance planes, and our own anti-aircraft guns blazed away. Fifty miles or so to the south of us, London was nightly being hammered by the Nazi Blitz and each night we saw the fireglare in the sky.

At sea, the Andrew guarded the tremendous evacuation of Allied soldiery from Dunkirk and, despite heavy losses, had kept the sea-lanes around Britain open under ever-increasing U-boat attacks. In November *Jervis Bay*—a merchantman converted to a convoy escort—went down, all guns blazing, after tackling two Nazi battleships and heading them away from her convoy. A week later our Mediterranean Fleet attacked the Italian Navy at Taranto—at night because their 'Swordfish' planes were too slow for a daytime affair—and crippled three Italian battleships and sunk one. Our Fleet Air Arm lost only two planes, with two damaged. Although we nozzers didn't realize it, this attack turned the sea-war in the Mediterranean and set the stage for Pearl Harbor. It also gained for the aircraft carrier the dominant place in naval strategy which it holds even now. The next week the centre of Coventry was flattened by the Germans.

In December, while the war raged on at sea and in the air all around the kingdom, and as city after city was pummelled in Britain, an event much more significant to us boys, was due to take place. We were going on leave. Jack was 'going up the line'.

4. *Up the Line*

The Jaunty's in the glasshouse with his goolies in his hand,
His ass is making shadows on the wall;
The hairs are growing thick from his belly to his dick,
The rats are playing snooker with his balls.

His sister's name is Lily—she's a whore in Piccadilly,
His mother keeps a knockshop in the Strand;
His father flogs his asshole round the Elephant and Castle,
They're the finest fucking family in the land!

Ditty, Royal Navy Lower Deck, sung to the tune of 'The Road to the Isles'. The glasshouse was any Royal Navy detention centre, or jail. The Elephant and Castle is a famous pub in South London, once much patronized by naval seamen, now unfortunately 'jazzed up'.

As the days passed towards Christmas leave so we boys marked them off, one by one, on our 'Charlie charts'. These were home-made calendars which almost everyone kept, three hundred squares to mark the 300 days of hell which was the training period at *Ganges*. Now that the bitter East Coast weather had turned to winter, with cold North Sea winds and icy sleet lashing the parade ground, the thought of getting away from *Ganges* was all the more delicious. The only people warm now were the officers and staff in their centrally heated wardroom and messes, the boys under punishment polishing their corridors, and the skates pounding up and down Laundry Hill and Faith, Hope and Charity. For a trainee to freeze in his 'spare' time in *Ganges* was the reward for virtue—for toeing the line. It was the mark of what officers called 'a good chap'. I mostly froze.

Slowly, so painfully slowly, the great day approached. Signs of it coming were evident from about mid-November on; already perfectly pressed Number Two uniforms, seven horizontal creases in the trousers, as per King's Regulations and Admiralty Instructions, were even more perfectly pressed. At night the soft snuffles of boys crying to themselves and the creaking of the bedsprings diminished. They were replaced by low excited conversations about who was going to 'get his end away' with whom and where. Gorgeous Geordie said little—with his looks he would be all right anyway. We all knew that his bank manager friend had arranged for Bernards, the naval tailors in Harwich, to send a Number One uniform, with gold badges, to his home in Newcastle, so it would be waiting for him when he arrived. I thought gold badges on Gorgeous Geordie would be gilding the lily.

The day before leave day even the instructors smiled and joked—most of them, too, were going on leave. Discipline was relaxed about one thousandth part of one inch from the letter of naval law. That same day the Irish boys from the Republic left for their leave, in cheap-looking civilian suits provided by the Pusser. The suits were all the same colour and size, and were supposed to stop the Republican fanatics in Eire from attacking or even shooting the lads, while they were on leave. Among the Irish, only the Ulsterman was in uniform. The division of Ireland reached even to HMS *Ganges*. The extra day's leave was granted to the Irish because of the time it would take to cross the Irish Sea. Apart from me, the Paddys were the only ones in the class who had ever been to sea—and that was on the ferries from Belfast and Dublin to Anglesey.

The next morning, when the rest of us were due to go on leave, there would have been no need for the duty crusher to play the 'Charlie' bugle record. We were all up all night, quietly but excitedly packing our duffle-bags and round metal ditty-boxes, making sure that our Number Two uniforms were perfectly clean and pressed, and that the two tapes at the bottom of the jumper 'V' were exactly the right length to pass the OOD's inspection before we were marched to the main gate and piled on to the bus, and making sure that the little bows on the left side of our caps were centred exactly, and that our boots were so highly polished that they looked like obsidian. By the time 'Charlie' blared through the loudspeakers we were all sitting bolt upright in our uniforms, looking like the chorus boys in *HMS Pinafore*.

The OOD's inspection was quite cursory. We didn't know it, of course, but he couldn't stop our leave. If he had found fault with anyone he could only have put him on report for when he returned. He was naturally reluctant to do this, because then the defaulter might take it into his head not to return—to go adrift—and that would mean the expense of sending two crushers to his home town to arrest him and escort him back to *Ganges*.

On the bus to Ipswich station we felt the joy that only boys from *Ganges* could know, at being outside the gates of hell. We sang and shouted obscene ditties about the staff, and 'Maggie May's Drawers', 'The Lobster Song' and 'The Ringer-Ranger-Roo'. It was our way of telling authority, now safely out of earshot, to get stuffed, because we had ten days of unimaginable ease and freedom ahead of us.

They were baggy at the knees, the crutch was full of fleas,
The old Red Flannel drawers that Maggie wore;
When she hung 'em on the line—they started marking
   time,
The old Red Flannel drawers that Maggie wore!

Oh Maggie, Maggie May, they have taken you away;
And I shan't see my Maggie any more,
Just before I went to sea—her lawyer said to me;
Maggie's left you her old Red Flannel drawers!

Now the fellers they came, and the fellers they went—
And the price went down to twenty cents—
From sweet sixteen to ninety-two—
She had to live on—her ringer-ranger-roo! . . .

From the train, as those of us bound through Birmingham
saw, there were many signs of the war—RAF airfields with
Hurricane and Spitfire fighter planes circling overhead and
ranged ready to take off. Every railway station we passed
through had soldiers and airmen on the platforms, and the
women and girls, catching sight of our naval uniforms,
smiled and waved at us as the train rushed through; sailors
were a rarer sight than pongos.

At Birmingham the Scotsmen and Northerners rushed
away to catch their trains, the Brummies took off home, and I
was left alone, the only naval lad, it seemed, on the platform
from whence left the train for Shrewsbury and Wales.

I headed for the station buffet. I felt quite the man now,
with my duffle-bag over my shoulder and my hat-box in my
hand. I had an hour's wait for my train. I ordered a pork pie
and a tea from the counter girl. She was about my age, and
pretty.

'Telford's and a cuppa, love!' I called, bright and breezy.

She smiled at me and screwed up her eyes. They were blue. 'You in the navy?' she asked, as if she would find it incredible if I were.

'No—army,' I replied. 'They ran out of uniforms, see, love?'

An elderly lady appeared from behind the tea-urn. She was chubby and motherly looking. She, too, smiled at my boy's face and the naval uniform I was wearing. 'Don't you take any notice, Rosy. He's having you on,' she told the girl. 'He's a Sea Cadet, that's what he is, aren't you, sonny boy?' This despite the 'HMS' emblazoned in gold thread on my cap ribbon.

A squad of Scottish soldiers, all be-kilted, jammed into the buffet and diverted the lass's attention completely, so that it was too noisy for her to hear my reply: 'Sea Cadet, my ass!'

'Lost your compass, Jack?' yelled a Scots corporal, as he leaned his rifle on the buffet counter. There were too many of them for me to argue with him, and they were a fierce-looking lot, with their tartan tams, hairy knees and fists like legs of ham.

'Britons never shall be slaves!' chimed one of his companions, sarcastically.

'There'll always be an England,' yelled another, 'as long as Scotland stands!' He was part-quoting a popular song of the time.

That got my blood up. I didn't mind the jibes; it was the thought of being mistaken for English that riled me.

'Come to bloody Wales and say that, you fucking sheep-shagger!' I challenged the corporal, as I moved with my pie and cup of tea towards the buffet door. The corporal slammed his kit-bag down on the floor and started toward me just as two red-caps (army policemen) walked in . . . and I thanked my lucky stars.

Up the Line

Once a *Ganges* boy, always a *Ganges* boy! but once a Taff . . .

Later, in the train, I stared through the window as we passed through Shrewsbury, staid and lovely in the wintry sunshine, and then, and then suddenly, quite suddenly, everything changed. The hedgerows somehow looked wilder and more appealing and the roads more ragged and comfortable, and the hills more *knowing*.

Wales.

HMS *Ganges* was then in another world—or some other kind of vague nightmarish plane. The train puffed its way through green valleys, past castles far older than the Andrew, and through little village stations where everyone knew everyone else and greeted one another in Welsh. The *hiraeth* —the longing—left me. I was again in my own world, among my own people, in the land of the shared mystery—the home of the vagrant moon, the beloved of the sea, the spring of the world.

Wales.*

An old countryman mounted the train in Machynlleth. He was ancient. He looked as if he himself had been carved out of the hills. He greeted me in Welsh. 'Going to Barmouth, is it, *morwr* (sailor)?' he asked, showing his toothless gums in a smile. 'Good harbour, there is there . . .'

'Llangareth, *syr*,' I replied.

'Llangareth? Then you must know Sioni ap Rhisiart?'

'Blind Johnny!' I exclaimed. 'Of course I know him! He's dead now—got run over. My Mam told me in a letter.'

The ancient shook his head. 'Gone, is he?' he asked.

* Tristan Jones's childhood in Wales and his early years are fully described in an earlier book, *A Steady Trade* (1982).

'Last September, just after the war started.'

'The poor man. We worked in the quarries together in Blainau long ago. He was a walking miracle; he could make his way along the slippery, sloping ledges, and feel the good slate, and know exactly where to place the charges . . .' The old man thought to himself for a moment then he said, 'Ah, well, perhaps in Heaven they'll give him a new pair of eyes? They'd have to, otherwise he wouldn't know who was who. Be a bit awkward among the angels, that would. Them with their long hair and silk gowns. They'd have him in front of the magistrate if he wasn't careful, eh?' The old man coughed a laugh, just as a woman got into the carriage carrying a goose in a basket. He greeted her—they obviously knew each other—and he told her a funny story about a farmer and his goose. The lady shook with laughter at the end of it, and Dolgellau station hove into view and I was home.

There were a few service uniforms outside Dolgellau station as I waited for the bus. Some of them were worn by slight acquaintances who had joined up. Most of them were in the army, a few in the air force. I seemed to be the only local sailor. Having been affected by the big talk in the mess back at *Ganges*, I half expected some kind of hero's welcome, but no one seemed to notice me. Those who did were more interested in how I had got along with the English, and how were the *Saeson*—the English girls? And how was London? And had I seen any Germans? Was I in the Sea Cadets? When was I going back?

Mam and Angharad were waiting for the bus when it arrived in Llangareth. Mam held my arm and kissed me on my cheek—she was not a demonstrative woman. 'Fine, fine, you look fine, *bach*!' was all she said as we walked down the hill to our cottage.

'Your Dad would be proud of you, *bach*.'

'How is he, Mam?'

68

'He's at sea now. The last letter was from Durban. He wrote he couldn't say where he was bound, but he quoted a poem . . . Here, I have it.' She reached into the pocket of her cloak and brought out Dad's letter, written on blue paper. 'See . . .

> 'April, April,
> Laugh thy girlish laughter;
> And the morning after,
> Weep thy girlish tears!'

'. . . now what do you make of that, *bach*?'

'It means he's expecting to be home in April,' I said. I knew Dad well enough.

Angharad wanted to know if I had seen the Princesses Elizabeth and Margaret Rose, and seemed disappointed that I had not.

The first thing I did, inside the cottage, was go upstairs to my room and change into my old civvy clothes. They were too small for me now, but I didn't care. All I wanted to do was forget HMS *Ganges* and all it stood for. I looked out of my bedroom window, down to the foreshore and the Irish Sea. I saw a long line of barbed-wire barricades stretching all along the sands to the headland in the distance. It all looked so impermanent, as if a gypsy tinker's caravan had traipsed along the shore and left its litter. It wouldn't—couldn't last. If the Germans never came, the sea would eventually beat it all down into the sands. If the Nazis wanted Llangareth they'd better hurry, or we'd have nothing to defend it with, except the sea—the angry Celtic Sea—and if they beat that they would earn all they might gain, the hard way, just as we had, ourselves. I could get away from *Ganges*, but I couldn't get away from the war. That was here to stay, so the sooner we got on with it, and got it over, the better. Then for the tropical islands . . .

Later that afternoon I ambled down to the foreshore as far as I could before the barbed wire stopped me. Goodness Gracious Jenkins' stone boatshed had been turned into a Bren gun post. One Bren gun, it seemed, defended the shores of Gwynedd. It poked its dull-blue muzzle out of Goodness Gracious' window and glared out towards the Irish Sea, 'like a flea menacing an absent elephant', as Goodness Gracious said.

That first evening at home, Cei Powell, my best friend in civvy street, turned up with his brother Gwrtheyrn for supper. They lived in a cottage down the lane towards the sea. Cei was older than I—about seventeen and a half. I was disappointed to see that his sister Branwen was not with him but she was at college in Aberystwyth. It was a pity—I would have given anything to see her face when she saw me.

'Where's your uniform, then, Tristan *bach*?' Cei asked as he grabbed my arm.

'I hung it up—don't want to wear it out, see.'

'Keeping it for the Victory Parade, are you? Ah, come on, let's see you in your uniform, *bach*!' Cei insisted.

And so they cajoled me until at last I crept back upstairs, donned my Number Twos, blue jersey, best blue collar with three white stripes, white dickey, jumper with red badges, black silk neckerchief and white lanyard—bell-bottom trousers and boots. Then I grabbed my round matelot's hat and, feeling a bit ridiculous and proud at the same time, I marched down the stairs and rejoined the company in the kitchen.

Cei grabbed my hat. 'It only says "HMS",' he said. 'What ship are you on?'

Gwrtheyrn looked at me with intense admiration, as I enunciated slowly, '*Ganges*.'

'What is it?' asked Gwrtheyrn. 'Is it a cruiser?'

I couldn't tell them the truth. Instead I said, 'No, she's a battleship, anchored on the English East Coast, off Shotley peninsula.'

'Does it go to sea?' asked Gwrtheyrn. 'Have you seen any U-boats yet?'

'No, battleships don't go after U-boats,' I replied. 'They're kept in reserve ready for the big stuff. We're waiting for the Jerries to start their invasion, then we're going out to clobber them.' I thought of the wind-swept parade ground back at *Ganges*. I tried to imagine it steaming out into the North Sea, all guns blazing. I must have smiled.

'When will you be ready to sail to fight the Germans?' asked Angharad.

'The skipper's waiting till I get back. They can't sail without me. I've got the keys,' I said, keeping a straight face.

Mam turned from her cooking at the stove and, smiling, silently shook her head at me.

Suddenly Cei said, 'I'm joining the RAF in February.' This was a blow. Since Dad had left to join a ship in South Africa (its pre-war captain had been German-born) Cei had looked after the heavy chores around our cottage. I looked over at Mam. She must have seen the dismay in my eyes.

'We can't find anyone to do the work,' she said. 'Everyone who could have done it is being called up, or already gone.'

'What will you do? Maybe I can get leave . . .' But even as I said it I knew that was a hopeless wish. The Andrew did not let go of anyone that easily. Only dead men and incorrigible skates were listed as 'Discharged', until their time was up, and even a dead man was not listed 'discharged' until the last stitch of the hammock needle was through his nose.

Mam said, 'No—Angharad and I are going to stay with Aunty Lowri and Uncle John in Manchester.'

'But what about all the bombing?' I asked her. 'They're getting further north all the time. Look at Coventry.'

'Oh, Uncle John wrote that it would be all right. They live outside the city, see, and the Avro aircraft works near where they live have guns all around to protect it.'

'Some naval guns, too,' said Cei. 'They won't get past that lot.'

It didn't occur to me to wonder why or how naval guns would be at Manchester, nor that the Avro factory was a prime target for the Nazis.

Then we talked about how Mr Jeffreys Geography, our erstwhile teacher at the one-room school, had landed a 'cushy' job with the Ministry of Information, and, naive as we were, dismissed our qualms about aerial strategy. After all, Cei was our air force expert, and if anyone should know if Manchester was safe, he should. How ignorant, how innocent, we were in the ways of war.

Mam insisted that I wear my uniform when I visited the town. A few Civil Defence people wore their blue air-raid suits, the bobbies carried steel helmets, and a few elderly men were in the uniform of the Home Guard, and medal ribbons galore, otherwise there were few signs of war in Dolgellau. Apart from the railway station and the town jetties, there was very little, it seemed, that the Germans could wish to waste bombs on. The town seemed to be crowded with civilians, mostly old people and children, who had been evacuated from the big cities of England, and many a peacetime tourist boarding-house was doing quite well on their lodgings, paid for by the government. At the cinema and in the café by the waterfront, I found myself the only lad in naval uniform. Little old ladies made a fuss of me, while old sailors and soldiers stopped me and rambled on and on about their years in the navy and army during the Ashanti, the Boer, and the First World Wars. I even met one old man who had been at Rorke's Drift with the South Wales Borderers when they had won twenty-two Victoria Crosses in one night during the Zulu War. In the café, the lass whom we knew as Liverpool Lou made a great play at me, her eyes flirting all the while, but Cei and I talked loudly about soccer and so I kept 'out of trouble'.

For the rest of my leave, cold and rainy as it was, I donned Dad's oilskin coat and rambled the hills, sometimes with Cei, sometimes alone.

Gwynedd was soft green under the winter sun. The trees were stripped and bare, so that they looked like young warriors ready for battle, their flowing garments cast aside. I walked on and on under the Caeder Idris and realized the fine stark severity which lies beneath all natural beauty. I jumped the rain-puddles under a clouded sky, without any especially happy thoughts—there was *Ganges* awaiting my return and after that almost fourteen more years of the navy—and yet I enjoyed a perfect exhilaration, such as only a boy can know. I was joyful to the brink of dread. It was as though every eye of everyone in Welsh legends was upon me, watching.

I think the only time I felt depressed on that leave so long ago was when I visited the grave where Caradoc, my pony, was buried. It was down at the end of the garden in the tall grass, beside the brook which wended its way down to the foreshore, over the sands and into the sea. It wasn't so much the memory of Caradoc or his death that affected me so; I remembered the last time I had seen my Dad, when he was walking to the stable to put the pony out of his misery, and I wondered when I would see my Dad again. He would very likely be home in April; but I was due to join a ship in February . . .

Once or twice I went out fishing with Goodness Gracious Jenkins—a sad man now. His eldest son, Tomas, had gone down in the aircraft carrier, HMS *Courageous* when she was torpedoed by a German U-boat just after the war started.

Over 500 men went down, and many of them were from our part of Wales, including the captain, who had, it was said, followed naval tradition and elected to go down with his ship saluting the ensign.

The New Year came around much too quickly. January —the month of empty pockets. It was time for me to return to *Ganges*.

'We won't move to Aunt Lowri's until Cei joins up,' said Mam. 'Then Cei's Dad is going to look after the place until the war's over. He says it shouldn't be more than another few months at the most. Then we can all come back, see, and your Dad will be home again . . .'

Almost everyone from Llangareth came to Dolgellau to see me off on the train. Mam and Angharad ('If you see Princess Elizabeth do you have to salute her?'), Cei, of course, and Gwrtheyrn—who had been hanging about me much more than he had when I was a mere civilian. Goodness Gracious Jenkins came, too. 'Give them one for Tomas, *bach!*' he murmured as we shook hands. The steam engine hissed and puffed. Acrid smoke blew into our eyes and made them watery—and then everyone was gone. I was on my way back to England and duty. I sat miserable in the carriage as the hills and valleys slid by all too quickly. I watched the last Welsh cottages under the wintry sky as the train crossed over the border into England—and then Wales, too, was gone. I didn't know that it was the last time I would be ashore in my country for thirty-seven years.

The first signs I saw of the hell ship *Ganges* were on Snow Hill station, Birmingham. It was late evening. I had to wait until early morning for the train to Harwich. Down the platform were two crushers obviously returning, too, from leave. In their shoes and long raincoats that hid their badges, they seemed almost benevolent. I found myself, while avoiding them by hiding behind a column, somehow thinking of them as 'family'. Their faces were familiar—in a strange way, afraid as I was of them, I felt a sort of affection for them. The way to a boy's heart is through his familiarity, and not, as many would have it, through his pocket.

Gradually, singly, in twos and threes, I was joined by more *Ganges* boys, until there was a knot of us, sitting on our cases, dozing away the cold night, or trying to put a brave face on our misery.

Just after nightfall—a clear night—a dangerous night in early-wartime Britain, the steady sinister moan of the air-raid sirens in the city wailed away, a long, steady blare of 'Attention'. The red-caps on the station platform marched up and down in the darkness, shouting at all servicemen to take 'shelter' in the open—at the ends of the platforms, away from the buildings, all blacked out. 'And no bloody smoking,' ordered the sergeant, 'or I'll stick yer fag up yer nose . . . !'

One *Ganges* boy with me—I think he was Scots— wondered how a Jerry airman would see a fag-end glow from a couple of thousand feet up in the sky. Just after we'd all wondered about that the first bomb hit the station marshalling yard, only a short distance down the tracks. Whatever it struck went up with a mighty flash and seconds later the blast-wave hit us, not very strong by then but still hot enough to be frightening. Then other bombs hit, and all hell was let loose as incendiary bombs landed on the station roof, and high explosives shattered the streets and water mains outside the station. Soon, all of us, even the red-caps, and civilians too, had formed a water-bucket chain, and were passing the buckets from a water tank above the lines, up the platform, to auxiliary firemen, who did their best to quench the flames. The actual bombing occurred in a short time—no longer than about ten minutes around the station, but it seemed like hours as we passed bucket after bucket up the platform.

Then, suddenly, it started to rain, and it seemed to be all over. There was still the now muffled crump of bombs striking, but it was from somewhere away from the station, on the outskirts of the city, and we had the fire under control by the time the undulating wail of the 'All clear' sounded.

There were a couple of deaths in and around the station that night—some people trapped under a bridge—and some wounded by flying glass and shrapnel and a few firemen badly burned. They were carried away on stretchers and shoved into ambulances in the station courtyard. After some confusion in the darkness, now that most of the fires in the station had been quenched, emergency lighting—oil and gas lamps —were lit, and the work of cleaning up the station got under way, with everyone lending a hand. In the travail and dust everyone was dirty. Some of the soldiers had removed their forage caps and jackets to move more easily; some of us sailors had gone so far, in the excitement, as to shove our hats back on our heads, the more securely to balance them. When the last of the firemen rushed off to fight blazes elsewhere —when the last of the salvage-rescue teams roared away in their trucks to dig someone else out from under the blasted rubble, the red-caps—now joined by naval policemen—all ramrod straight and regimental still, strode around and brought order once more out of casualness and seeming undiscipline, which I learned later is the true hallmark of real warfare. 'Get your hat on straight, lad. Where do you think you are—Bertram Mills' Circus?' This from a grizzled Petty Officer with a bandage around his head and his peaked cap balanced atop, and a dark trail of blood down his left arm, over his three good conduct badges, his crossed anchors and their crown.

I got my hat on straight. The Petty Officer harrumped and strode on. He noticed a couple of nozzers sitting down on the platform, resting after four hours of strenuous bucket-

passing and stretcher-bearing. 'You boys there! Get your
bloody asses vertical! What the . . .' He stood, both hands on
his hips, and glared down at them as the two miscreants
scrambled to their feet. 'Where the bloody hell do you think
you are . . . ? A bloody holiday camp? What do you think
these bloody squaddies will think of the bleeding Andrew?
Bloody *Ganges*, eh?' By now the two boys had unscrambled
themselves and were busy dusting down their filthy uniforms. 'Bloody nozzers . . . !' The PO started to stride away
down the platform, towards the distant glare of an obstinate
fire at the far end of the station. 'Christ . . . when I was at
Ganges . . .' was all I could hear of his comment as our train
at last pulled into Snow Hill, seven hours late.

We must get back to war . . .

'Old Jerry's got it in for Brum,' said a matelot in the train, as
we pulled out of Snow Hill. All across the city incendiary
bomb fires burned with a deathly glow. Anti-aircraft guns
flashed in defiant anger.

'The bastards are after the BSA factory,' said someone
else. 'They make small arms there, machine guns and such.'

'Yeah, and Lee-Enfield bloody rifles,' said another voice.

'Lee-Enfields, eh?' said the first voice. 'Then bloody Jerry
can have it. I hope he blows the buggers to smithereens!'

So did we all, as we remembered hefting the heavy rifles up
and down Faith, Hope and Charity at the double, arms
stretched right up vertical over our heads. So did we all hope
that BSA would be blown to hell, only some of us wished it
was us who were doing it, and that the BSA factory was
German.

Before we went on leave we boys had been instructed to
return via Harwich jetty, to wait for an Admiralty steam
harbour launch, which would ferry us across the river, back
to *Ganges*. I knew the town jetty, of course, having warped in

there once or twice on board the old *Second Apprentice*. As we turned the corner from the railway station I eagerly looked for her, but there was only one of the *Everard* barges in port, and I knew no one in her. If *Second Apprentice* had been in port, I was in half a mind to board her and hide away, but I guessed that neither Tansy the skipper, nor Bert the mate, would have let me stay with them. They would know only too well how long the arm of Royal Navy justice was, and that sooner or later I would have had to return to the Andrew.

The weather that morning in January was miserable. A freezing sleet was driven in from the estuary by a wind all the way from Siberia. But regardless of the weather, any returning-from-leave morning on Harwich jetty would have been woebegone to us lads. As it was, we huddled ourselves in small groups out of the wind and sleet, and silently stared through the drizzle across the river, at the small buildings, dirty red and grey, at the signal tower, reminding us of Faith, Hope and Charity, and at the mast towering above all.

As the steam harbour launch, puffing smoke and steam from its brass funnel, pulled up neatly alongside the jetty there was still jocularity among us lads, tired as we were, but it was stifled as the boat hissed and bobbed its way across the river and the mast grew higher and higher. Half way across the River Stour there was an almost tangible stiffening of everyone's attitudes, even the boat's crew, and we changed from being individual beings living and breathing under the grace of God into a mass of parts existing by miserly granted privilege and bawled command, as per King's Regulations and Admiralty Instructions, by direction of My Lords Commissioners of the Admiralty, and God help any stragglers.

I doubt if there was ever anywhere in the world where the extremes of elation and despair were so patently obvious as in the boy seamen's mess in HMS *Ganges* on the day they returned from leave. Elation at our being back again with our 'oppos', laughing and joking and taking the mickey out of each other, comparing notes on girl-friends and soccer teams, and despair at being back again under the iron fist of Royal Navy discipline. But even so our despair was leavened by the prospect of our being drafted to proper barracks in two months' time, from where we would be sent to ships and the sea. Then we would be real sailors.

PART TWO

The Anvils

She's a tiddley ship,
Through the ocean she slips—
She's steaming by night and by day;
And when she's in motion,
She's the pride of the ocean—
You can't see her ass-hole for spray!

Chorus: Side, side, . . . ship's side;
Jimmy looks on it with pride;
He'd have a blue fit if he saw any shit—
On the side of the . . . ship's side!

Lower deck ditty, sung to the tune of 'This is my story'
(Salvation Army hymn). It was used for any ship.

5. Cameroon

Goodbye Shotley, soon we'll be in clover,
One more 'Charlie', then the training's over,
Leaving Shotley won't make us forlorn.
As with the dawn, Draft Day will be born,
So cheer up . . .
Goodbye Shotley, draft will banish sorrow,
One more 'Charlie', off we go tomorrow,
Life's a pleasure, there'll be lots of leisure,
Goodbye, Shotley, Goodbye!

One of the very few *Ganges* ditties which were not obscene. It was
sung to the tune of 'Goodnight Sweetheart'. In its own way, it was,
it turned out, far more obscene—truly obscene—than all the
'dirty ditties'.

I was drafted, along with another hundred or so ratings of
different branches, to HMS *Cameroon* towards the end of
February 1941. Chatham Barracks parade ground was
crowded with a thousand men of different ships' drafts all
milling around, under the watchful, jealous eyes of gunnery
instructors, who looked as if they were smouldering at the
thought that we would shortly be out of their domain, that
they would no longer be able to taunt and bully us.
    The parade ground was about an eighth of a mile long, set
between a raised roadway on one side and the barracks parade

shed on the other. All was worn, clean brick, except for the bronze lamp-standards with their diving dolphins and the granite fascia whereon was mounted the golden legend: FEAR GOD—HONOUR THE KING! Beneath the roadway, beneath the golden legend, were archways which led to air-raid shelter tunnels under the road. On the other side of the parade ground the barracks shed windows and doorways were protected from bomb-blast by piled-up sandbags, and the windows were blackened with paint and strips of tape pasted over the panes to prevent glass splinters from wreaking havoc in case of a direct hit. It had happened once during World War I, when a Zeppelin had dropped a bomb which landed directly on to the roof of the shed and killed dozens of men drilling below.

Soon the different ships' drafts were in some semblance of order, drawn up in ranks three deep, each man with his kit-bag and hammock set alongside of him, and his gasmask over his left shoulder. There was no band—no bullshit. The order to 'shoulder kit-bags and hammocks' was given. 'Left turn! Quick march!' and we were off.

'Here we bloody go again!' murmured a two-badger alongside of me. He must have done this a dozen times in the past.

'Any more for the Skylark?' called a Cockney voice on the other side.

'You'll be sorree!' came the traditional catcall from a few barrack stanchions loafing in one of the shed doorways.

'Silence in the ranks!!!' bawled a GI. Even though he was not in charge of us, he could not forgo this last chance to yell at us.

'Bollocks! Shit in it!' muttered everyone within hearing range of me.

We joined the ship in Southampton, where she had been converted hurriedly from a merchant passenger liner to an armed cruiser. We stepped out of a make-work mad-house into a place where real labour seemed to be performed.

In Southampton, ahead of us, and all around, dockyard cranes loomed into the winter sky; the sounds of pneumatic drills and portable diesel generators ripped and rent the air. The ships alongside for repairs and refits looked like gigantic heaps of so much rusting scrap iron, crawling with yellow-overalled dockyard mateys. The gangs of working men hardly looked down at us as we passed them and crossed over the lifting-bridges that led over the entrance to a deep dry-dock. Far below in the dry-dock, a hundred feet below, we could see a destroyer sitting low and dry in what looked like a waterless open grave. At first she seemed to be under-going an ordinary refit, until we could see her far side and the great gash where a torpedo had blown her starboard bows half off. The one-inch steel was peeled back like a sardine-tin lid, and we could plainly see the blistered white-painted bulkheads inside the ship.

'She got pasted, Stripey,' I said to the two-badger.

'Right, son, she got her after funnel blown off, too. The poor bastards down the after boiler-room didn't stand a chance . . .'

With her bow guns cocked up and her anti-aircraft Oerlikon pointing up at the sky, too, the wounded ship still looked defiant. By now we had crossed the bascule bridge, and soon the operational ships came into view—destroyers, mine-sweepers, frigates, corvettes. Southampton was not a naval port. I already knew that from having seen the ships come and go up and down Southampton Water from the deck of my old ship, *Second Apprentice*. Now bundled up in an oilskin coat about twice my size, with a kit-bag and hammock over my shoulder, the world of *Second Apprentice* seemed a million miles away, yet I knew she might be lying in the river, awaiting cargo, only just outside the docks. I felt suddenly that all I was doing seemed futile.

As we stumbled now under the weights we were all carrying, and tried to avoid the muddy puddles in the cobblestoned road, Stripey said, 'Well, Wings, there she is—home from home!'

I looked over in the direction to which his chin was trying to point and saw a great lump of dark grey painted hull. She was a converted merchant ship, with sides like cliffs. I saw she had been fitted with eight anti-aircraft guns and a bow four-incher. 'There she is, Nozzer, HMS *Cameroon.*'

We came to a halt at the foot of the ship's gangway. Even as we halted the air-raid warning sirens blew.

Those of my readers who have ever boarded a liner know of the hurly-burly which usually accompanies them from the gangway to their cabins—but they can have no idea of the seeming chaos when a hundred and fifty odd matelots, all strangers to the ship, boarded *Cameroon* against the rushing flow of dockyard mateys struggling to get down the gangway to shelter from the coming air-raid.

Slowly the line of matelots, all with their kit-bags and hammocks a-shoulder, clambered up the steep gangway against the yellow overalled rush coming down.

'Let's get off her, Jack!' shouted one skinny civilian in a peaked cap. 'They've already clobbered her twice!'

'Who have?' grunted Stripey, as he struggled to maintain his balance against the descending herd.

'The bleeding Jerries!' wailed another dockyard matey.

'Well, ask a silly question . . .' started Stripey.

'Keep that line moving!' shouted the voice of the ship's cox'n. 'Next man who stops goes on jankers!'

The peak cap matey shouted back to Stripey, 'Better you than me, mate; the Jerries are marking these buggers out. They know that we might be on to a good thing . . .' Then his voice wailed off under the new blast of an 'All clear' siren. The raiders had passed overhead. By now Stripey and I were at the head of the gangway. It was the only occasion when I stepped on board and didn't salute. I couldn't, not with sixty odd pounds of gear on my back . . .

When I left the ship I didn't salute either; but we'll come to that later.

We were greeted by an able seaman Quartermaster in his long ankle-deep blue coat, with a bosun's pipe chain dangling around his collar. He was about twenty-one; his mate, I saw to my relief, looked even younger than me. His little baby face was almost drowned in the navy blue watch-coat collar pulled up around his ears. He could have been no more than sixteen. By this time the tide of dockyard mateys had reversed and they were pushing their way back on board, silently abashed, it seemed, now that the danger had temporarily passed.

The Quartermaster and his mate were being watched by the Petty Officer of the Day, a veteran of about thirty, and beyond him the Officer of the Day, a sub-lieutenant in his late teens.

'Steady theah!' called the OOD.

'Draft fall in on the fo'c'sle!' shouted the PO.

'You'll be sorree,' someone called from somewhere aloft.

'You'll get used to it!' added the Quartermaster, with a grin. Then he seemed to recognize the Stripey. 'What ho, Nobby!' he called. 'Come to get some sea-time in?'

Nobby shortly greeted him and passed forward. I followed him.

'You'll be sorree,' muttered the QM's mate to me as I passed him. '*Ganges?*' he whispered, grinning.

'Not bloody much!' I replied, and already felt better at joining this strange ship. Already I had come across 'one of us'.

'You stick alongside of me, Wings,' Nobby shouted over

his shoulder as we clambered over hoses and cables strewn haphazardly over the deck. 'I know the score. We'll get ourselves stuck in the after mess.'

'Right, Stripes,' I replied. I saw again in my mind's eye the blown-off bow of the destroyer in the dry-dock. The two-badger knew what he was about, all right.

'You call me Nobby, Taff,' he muttered, as we joined all the other draftees on the fore deck of *Cameroon*.

'Right, get fell in, lads,' a Petty Officer hailed us. It was a shock to me to be addressed in the least bit so civilly by anyone over the rank of Leading Seaman. The PO's voice was almost gentle, and there was a welcoming gleam in his eye. He was dressed in his Number Three blue serge uniform, but unlike the barracks bullies', his was worn and greasy in patches, and his shoes looked as though they had hardly ever been polished. The badge on his cap—the crown and anchor—was tatty beyond my belief. His face—he was no more, I would guess, than in his middle twenties—was, like his cap and uniform, worn and tatty. He looked as if he had not had a good night's sleep in weeks. He noticed my two-badge friend. 'Wotcher, Nobby!' he grinned.

'Wotcher, Soapy!' replied Nobby.

'That your winger?' asked the PO. His face straightened as he inspected me. Then to me he said, 'You from *Ganges*?'

'Yes, sir,' I replied.

'Sir to me?' said the PO. Both he and Nobby laughed. 'Sir to me?' he repeated. 'You'll be saying bollocks to the Skipper next!'

Nobby said, 'Yeah, Soapy, stick him in my mess. It's his first ship.'

'Right, my son,' the PO gently took my elbow. 'You fall in with Nobby. I'll put you in fifteen mess, that's Knocker White's . . . he's the killick of that mess. He needs someone to empty the gash bucket, see?'

Then the Officer of the Day appeared, and trailing behind him the First Lieutenant, and everything changed again to naval discipline and formality, until we were all down aft in our own mess.

But first of all the new draft of men on the fore deck were separated into bunches of their own branch; the stokers, who always seemed to belong in a world of their own, to this side, the seamen to that, the communications men to the other. Next we were separated by rating, the Leading Hands and the Able-Ratings being tallied off for their watch duties and action stations. Then we lower orders, the ODs and the nozzers, were lined up and shouted at by the buffer: 'Right now, you lot. You're lucky that you're in an armed merchant cruiser and not in a proper cruiser. There they put you nozzers in your own mess and you have a crusher breathing down your neck from dawn to bloody dusk.'

The buffer noticed some lad who seemed perhaps surprised. 'Ho, yes, they've got boys' messes in the cruisers all right, and in the battlewagons, too, and they go through the hoop, I can tell you, and I know, 'cos I just left *London* and the crushers on board wallops them from asshole to breakfast time. You lot are lucky, 'cos we ain't got a crusher, only a jaunty, and all he's doing is waiting for his pension. They're all too busy hiding behind the bloody barracks wall, see? So you lot are going to be messed with the real men, see? But you still come under me, whatever, and I won't say this again,' his voice lowered half a notch, 'woe betide any of you little bastards that even so much as thinks of coming the strop or skiving, I can tell you, 'cos those of you whose voices have already broken will suddenly find themselves talking in a very high octave indeed.' The buffer strode up and down in front of us, trying to glower under the expressionless gaze of the Jimmy. 'Ho yes, indeed,' the buffer repeated, staring at us one by one as he intoned, 'the very least infractions of KRs

and AIs or ship's standing orders and . . . I . . . will . . .
personally . . . cut . . . off . . . your . . . balls . . . any . . .
one . . . of . . . you . . . and . . . make . . . you . . . eat . . .
them . . . for . . . *breakfast!*'

The buffer then handed us all our station cards and listed
us for messes, parts-of-ship, action stations, divisions, duty
watches, leaving-and-entering-harbour stations, dress-ship
stations, emergency stations, abandon-ship stations; every
station, it seemed to me, apart from the one I wished I was on;
a railway station, waiting for a train to take me up the line.

To everyone's relief it started to rain during our first
muster on board. Thick rain. Nice, murky black clouds,
black as a guardsman's boot. Just right for hiding Southampton from any Jerry planes which might stray overhead
from their track on the way to bomb the Midlands. We were
wet and cold, stood out on deck most of the afternoon and
early evening, but we didn't care. We were well hidden, and
that's all that mattered.

Later, below on the after mess deck, as we stuffed our
tropical white uniforms and sports rig and easy shoes into the
bottom of tiny seat-lockers, well out of sight and mind, and
found space for our ditty-boxes atop the seat-backs along the
cork-insulated ship's side, and found our own hammock
spaces, it was again 'Knocker' this and 'Wiggy' that, and
there wasn't a 'Leading Seaman' or 'Petty Officer' to be heard
of. This was the real Andrew. This was home.

I little realized that here, on board a merchant ship converted to an armed cruiser, there was much more room for us
on the mess decks than there would be in later ships, and
especially the destroyers, although the set-up was very much
the same. Once the Admiralty got their hands on a ship their
prime intention seemed to be to make life as uncomfortable
and rough as they could for the matelots, a little less so for the
Chiefs and Petty Officers (who had separate, enclosed mes-

ses), while at the same time providing accommodations for the majority of the officers which would compare very favourably with first-class cabins on the most modern ocean liner, and a wardroom for their social hours which would not, in most ships, shame any yacht club on earth.

The Chiefs' and Petty Officers' messes each had a messman to wait on it. Each officer had a runner—a 'yeoman'—to run and fetch for him. The wardroom had its own separate galley and cooking staff and stewards who served the officers their much finer food than the general run of the pig-swill dished up to the lower deck. The wardroom had its own bar steward, even, to serve pink gins and Scotch at most times.

All through this tale, these differences of worlds must be borne in mind, just as they were by the vast majority of matelots, always. The conditions varied in different ships —from bearable to vile—but generally the appearance of the messes was the same in most ships.

If Jack served well and honourably in battle, in circumstances that are almost impossible to describe, in the stink and foul air of crowded gun turrets in the cold, freezing Arctic nights, in the unbelievably hot, sweaty boiler rooms, I honestly believe that he did so mainly because he knew—he experienced—on board no other conditions, or conditions which were only slightly better, when he was *not* at action stations. If accounts of battle from the officers' side have been so appalling: hours on the bridge, in the open air, after the comfort of the cabins and the wardroom, then how much more cruel and torturous was the average matelot's existence, with no relief at all from—I use mild words here—absolute discomfort at all times?

To me, or to any other comparative newcomer to the ways of the Andrew, it was a wonder how soon everything fell together and was organized on the lower deck. This was because ours, like most drafts, was composed of a good leavening of 'old hands', who knew exactly every facet of the routine, every snag that might crop up, and every dodge around it—and especially the most completely unnecessary snags which Authority implacably and incessantly raised before us to make life more difficult than it already would have been.

It was astonishing to me how soon the crowded mess deck was orderly; how quickly things worked out. It was amazing how rapidly men, in that spartan open space between two steel bulkheads and two steel ship sides, cornered their own little territory, and how space was divided unspokenly between 'private' and 'public' ground.

The mess deck was one deck below the upper deck, and was painted mostly grey. It extended half way across the ship. It was about twenty feet wide and thirty feet long fore and aft. The 'roof' or deckhead was about twelve feet above the deck, which was covered with dark brown linoleum-like material, the joints of which were hidden by brass strips. All across the deckhead, this way and that, ran grey pipes for the salt-water fire-main, the fresh-water supply, pneumatic air, hydraulic oil for the guns and the after steering system, steam to the capstan aft, and a dozen other commodities, liquid and gaseous. Between the pipes, grey electric-cable channels, some as wide as three feet, wended, dipped and rose their way forward and aft. In between them, above each of the two messes, grey ventilating trunks carried a weak stream of air, which was vented into the mess deck through little directional louvres, slightly bigger than the ones you now see over the seats in airliners. Thus the headroom was diminished by about two feet. In one corner of my mess, on the starboard side, was a huge grey-painted electrical fire pump, twice as bulky as a big man, which alternated duty with its opposite number forward in the ship. Every other twenty-four hours we were subjected to its high-pitched scream, all day and all night. In both messes large, grey encased fans pumped air into and out of the ventilating system. They ran all the time with a low roar. The ship's sides had two small portholes, each side, each one with a steel armour-plate scuttle over it. The porthole was just about big enough for a full-grown man to stick his head out through it. On the shelf below each porthole was a used cigarette can, open at the top, which was used as a urinal, when the porthole was open in harbour. These piss cans were always in place, except for Captain's Rounds on Saturday mornings, when they were hidden in the nearest locker, while the highly polished best mess-fanny was displayed for the Captain's benefit. Otherwise the best mess-fanny never saw the light of day. It was treated like the Holy Grail.

Above the grey scuttles, the speakers for the ship's broadcasting system—the Tannoy—were situated. Over these speakers came the orders—the 'pipes'—which governed practically every minute of our day and night.

Over each mess, and by the hatch, too, there were red-bulbed lights, which were automatically switched on when the main, white lights went off at 'pipe down'. These cast an eerie scarlet glow over the scene of dozens of men asleep in their swinging hammocks at night.

There were wireless speakers, too, which piped the BBC down to us, and which we might hear when the fire-pump was not running. Over these, in later ships, the appalling 'ping' of the Asdic signal was piped, day and night, when we were sub-hunting, so that the sound of our searching death and destruction never left us for one moment.

Each mess had a bare wooden table, about ten feet long, which was strapped to the deck with iron rods to stop it falling about in rough weather. The mess table was scrubbed every morning by whoever was 'cook of the mess' for that day. One side of the table, against the ship's side, was a row of seat-lockers, with thin canvas cushions set atop. The lockers were about eighteen inches wide and fourteen inches deep. In one of these we were expected to stow all our seven uniforms as well as other gear. This we achieved by tying everything up separately in a tight little knot—jumpers, pants, underwear, the lot—and, mostly, leaving it there for the entire time we were on board. We knew that we probably wouldn't need it again until we were ordered to muster our kit while under punishment or upon arrival back in barracks. Thus, each man's locker was crammed, and there was no room for his writing pad, cigarettes and personal gear. These he kept jammed under his hat in his ditty-box—a round, black, tin box, which was stowed atop the backrest of the seat-lockers in harbour, or suspended from the hammock rails at sea.

In this space which I have just described, an average of forty men lived, slept and tried to relax. Here they ate, slept, drank their tot of rum, wrote their letters home, played cards and simply existed. The conditions would make a modern-day prisoner in the average American or British prison blanch. Many and many a time I would have given my right arm to have been locked up in a cell on my own, just for one night—or for a hundred thousand.

On the grey bulkheads fore and aft were rows of thick hooks, each set about eighteen inches apart from the next hook. From these the lashings and netting of the men's hammocks were suspended. Each man had a sleeping place of precisely eighteen inches wide by about seven feet long. In harbour or at sea, when the hammocks were occupied by all the men off-watch, we could only escape the proximity of other bodies and the sense of foul air by withdrawing completely into our own little worlds.

The whole of my time in the Andrew I rarely was in a mess

with enough hammock space for all the men at sea. Mostly, there were men sleeping on the sea-lockers, and even on the bare wooden benches ranged fore and aft along the tables away from the ship's sides.

There was, too, the hammock netting, which is where the men's hammocks were stowed when not in use. These were steel rail pens in the middle of the mess deck, which took up about an eighth of the total deck space, and in which the 'pits' were stowed standing upright on one end, all lashed correctly with seven 'round turns and half hitches' as per King's Regulations and Admiralty Instructions.

The men generally changed their pits every week or so, and scrubbed the dirty one, but there were some men—usually ex-*Ganges* boys—who changed and scrubbed their pits daily, so that they were snow white and perfect in their virginal purity and somehow, at least to me and a few kindred spirits, sinister-looking . . .

> Dhoby, dhoby, never go ashore . . .
> Finish up at the sick-bay door . . .

Although cleanliness may be next to godliness, excessive cleanliness, and having a fetish about it, is a bit close to insanity. This was proved time and again.

At the head of each mess table, fixed on the bulkheads, were two small cupboards about the size of the average kitchen cupboard ashore, and made of steel; painted grey, of course. There the knives, forks, spoons, plates, mugs and rum measures of about twenty men were stowed shipshape in between meals, except during Captain's Rounds, when they were all polished up and laid out on the table for inspection in fancy whirly patterns, mostly with a sense of showmanship which would have made the parade of girls in the Ziegfeld Follies look like a line-up at a welfare office.

The only time that it was possible to feel what civilians call 'comfort' at that period was in the evenings in ports in Britain, when a few of the matelots went ashore, if they had any money, or if there was a baron in line to be strangled. The rest of the time, and especially at sea—which was most of the time—there was no such thing as 'comfort'. It did not exist. It was not in our vocabulary; it hardly ever entered our minds—the regulars among us, that is. Even I, who had known the hard life of a boy in a sailing barge, and her spartan fo'c'sle, had difficulty, at first, in becoming accustomed to the squalid crowding in the mess decks of His Majesty's Ships. What it was like for the 'Hostilities Only' men, the HOs, most of them used to home life, the small but steady comforts of life in British working-class homes, I can only start to imagine today, forty years on, now that I have had a little taste of what that strange word 'comfort' means.

There were subtle occupations of territory. The best hammock berths depended on inclinations, outlooks and other facets of character. For those who sought some bit of privacy, alongside the ship's side was good. There they would have other men only on one side of them, plus the added advantage in harbour of being somewhere near to an open port if the weather was fine in the daytime. At sea, it was a different matter. There hammocks bumped the ship's side every time the ship rolled—say a thousand times an hour. Also you were more likely to hear the sea crashing on the ship's side in bad weather, but worst of all was the incessant thought that if a torpedo or a shell came into the ship we'd had our chips. Even if the explosion was yards away there would be no chance of reaching the hatch through the milling mass of dying, wounded or panicky men trying to get topsides.

The next favourite place to sling hammocks was as close to the hatch as possible, regardless of all other considerations. This was where most of the wily old hands would be grouped, dreaming of how to wangle a barrack stanchion's berth as soon as they got off this ship.

The thin, scrubbed, bleached hammocks of the health fanatics would be found slung as close to an air-vent as possible, usually right in the middle of the bunched hammocks.

The most senior hands in the mess slept, as a rule, on the cushions. They were the best berths in spite of the risk of rolling off in rough weather, or being splashed by freezing water sloshing around decks. These were the best because the lower you are, in crowded conditions, the better the air. The more the chance of escape, too, in case of explosion.

It was in these conditions, then, that I was to learn, along with a dozen or so other boys and HOs, the lore of the Andrew; and was to listen, at first almost continuously either revolted or amazed, at the time-serving matelot's modes of expression, at his rich lode of stories, true and imagined, and at his always-underlying respect for his fellow sufferers.

'So there I was,' a two-badge AB recounted from his pit, 'on the fucking trot up the Dilly, back in '36. I'd had a knee trembler with a bird outside the Heffelent and got a nap hand . . . and I went adrift 'cos I didn't want to be in the rattle for the next bleeding ten years, and I was skint, not a bloody penny to my name, and this here hatter—a real toff he was—comes up and pushes the boat out for a few jars. Well, one thing after another, and I clews up living at his place until his fucking skin came down and chucked me out of his gaff, and I got nicked. A right bleeding gigolo I was then, wings . . .'

There I was to learn all about 'Hawsepipe Harry' and the golden rivet, and muff-diving and how the snotties were mostly all prats, and how to strangle a baron, and phantom flippers and ass bandits and Aggie Westons and fanny rats and chew bosuns and whose old lady was in the pudding club and peacetime runs ashore in Hands, Knees and Bumpsa-daisy; how to polish a can spanner; whose mate had gone for a Burton and how to load a Costain gun; and how six annas made one rupee, and how 'Handsome is as handsome fucking *does*', dodging pigs and ignoring the Hope-and-Glory bosuns and the only other place to be was either 'up the line' or in 'Lily Langtry's Yacht'.

There I was to learn to yaffle train smash and pavement pounder, and take a round turn and two half hitches on myself when I felt like crying, and cackleberries and kye, bangers and Spithead pheasant, underground pheasant and doctor's chum, and keep my bobstay and shit-kickers clean, and watch where I put my plates when I hopped out of my pit into the crowded mess.

There I was to hear tales from Danskers, where the poufs lived in the trees, and Haggisland, and Aussie, and Yankee-land, which seemed to be very close to the end of the rainbow, and the Gold Coast and Capers and life among the camel-bashers and runs up the Gut in Bells-and-Smells, and chasing the apes in Gibbo, and exotic evenings in Trinco and Hon-kers, brass monkeys and sons of guns, pier-head jumps and canteen cowboys, Rose Cottage and Pompey Lil, prick tobac-co and swinging the hook, and, the holiest of all, *Nelson's Blood* . . . and *fuck the begrudgers* . . .

The first thing we all did that evening on board *Cameroon* was stake out our own hammock berths. Nobby lashed my pit to the hook next to his before he went on watch. His was directly by the hatchway—mine was outboard from him, almost under an air-vent louvre. On the outboard side of me a bloke of about twenty strung his pit. He was of medium height, fair, with thin blond hair, staring blue eyes and a large forehead. Very unusually in the Andrew then, he wore spectacles when he read, which I noticed he did most of that first evening. Along with most of the others, up to an hour before 'pipe down' at ten-thirty, he was down to his under-wear and swung into his pit.

'Right, Taff,' he said, as he nestled down under his blanket. 'All time not spent sleeping is time wasted,' he quoted what Admiral Nelson, according to lower deck legend, is supposed to have said about the matter.

'G'night, mate,' I replied.

'My name's Harris,' he said. 'But you can call me Prof.' He smirked over the top of his blanket and winked. 'That's what these fakking enimals' (so much for his dialect) 'down here call me. You might as well, too.'

His voice was cultured. It had a cynical tone. I looked over; his eyes were shut. I turned over again as the red glow of the night-lights replaced the white glare. He's a strange bloke, I thought to myself. Might be a pouf. Then I fell asleep.

6. *Maiden Voyage*

I was walking through the dockyard in a panic,
When I met a matelot old and grey.
Across his shoulder was his kit-bag and his hammock
And this is what I heard him say:

Oh I wonder, yes I wonder,
If the Jaunty made a blunder,
When he made this bloody draft chit out to me?
For I've been a barrack stanchion,
And I've lived in Jagoes Mansions,
And I've always said good morning to the Chief;
GOOD MORNING, CHIEF!

Oh, a million miles I've travelled,
And a thousand sights I've seen,
And I've always said good morning to the Chief,
Oh I wonder, yes I wonder,
If the Jaunty made a blunder,
When he sent this bloody draft chit round to me?

'Oh I wonder . . .': This ditty was popular in the Andrew during
the Second World War. I think that it originated during the First
World War. 'Jaunty' originates from 'Gendarme' and means
'Master-at-Arms', a naval non-commissioned policeman,
responsible for issuing 'draft chits', orders to proceed to a ship. A
barracks stanchion is someone who is evading sea-duty, and thus
becomes a permanent fixture in the shore barracks. 'Jagoes

Mansions' is the lower-deck name for the Royal Naval Barracks, Plymouth. Sung to the tune of the hymn, 'Oh I wonder, yes I wonder, if the angels way up yonder'.

Although discipline seemed, at least on the surface, to be more relaxed on board *Cameroon* than it was in *Ganges* or in the barracks at Chatham, it was still there, an underlying threat every second of the working day and at night, too, outside the mess. Every time a matelot left his mess to go to his part of ship he passed by huge notice boards displaying the ship's standing orders and the King's Regulations and Admiralty Instructions, written in their cruel-looking early eighteenth century script: 'Any man found guilty of treason or of burning down any part of His Majesty's Dockyard shall suffer death or any other punishment hereafter mentioned . . .' The list went on and on. Sodomy with man or beast was punishable, with about another fifty crimes by 'seven years hard labour' and no appeal. The list of punishments 'hereafter mentioned' were enough to make the average person's skin crawl. It was there on the day we joined the ship, and it was still there when she went down a mass of scorching flame. It was probably the last thing to burn.

Reveille, now played by a real marine bugler over the ship's Tannoy, was at six. As the bugle blared so the duty QXPO clattered down the steel mess deck hatch ladder and, back bent, skittered among the swinging hammocks, banging them with his flashlight. 'Come along, my lucky lads . . . Come along, me hearties! Wakey, wakey, rise and shine! The morning's fine, you've had your time! The sun's burning out there fit to burn your bloody eyes out! Let's have you, me lads, hands off cocks and on to socks! Wakey, wakey, wakey!' The PO was under the hammock of a man who had been ashore the previous night and who did not stir. 'Out you get, mate, let's see you move or I'll have your card and you'll be dancing the Enfield jig.' The sleeping man stirred as everyone else slung themselves out of their hammocks and, in a flurry of flailing arms and shifting underpants, lashed their hammocks with seven half-hitches as per the KR's and AI's.

As soon as all hammocks were stowed it was up on deck, with our pants rolled up to our knees—thus the reason for bell-bottoms—to scrub the deck with hard brooms and salt water flushed out of the fire-main outlets. As QX division, our first job was to scrub the quarterdeck which was the 'ossifer's turf', and this we did, all forty or so of us, for a good half-hour, even though it had been spotless when we had first trooped on to it.

While this was going on the men who had been detailed off by the killick as 'cooks of the mess' had got breakfast ready. There were two systems of messing in the Andrew in those days. One, recently introduced in some new ships, was 'general messing', where a Supply Officer drew up a list of meals and supplied the food to the crew's galley, to be collected by the messes. The other, which was usual in older and small ships and converted ships, such as ours, was 'canteen messing'. Here the messes were allotted so much money per day, and the killick of the mess 'bought' the mess's food out of the supplies available on board, usually the day before it was to be consumed. Then the cooks of the mess prepared the food on the mess table and took it to the galley to be cooked, and collected it when it was done. There was an advantage to this system: any money left over in the 'mess-fund' at the end of the week, could be shared out among the members of the mess. The disadvantage was that if the killick in charge of the mess-fund was pyso, then, although you might end the week with a couple of shillings extra in your pocket you would also be permanently hungry.

But it was a wonder, in some messes where the old hands took over as cooks of the mess, how all kinds of good, nutritious meals, pies and pastries, roasts and stews were turned out, all made on the mess-deck tables, even despite conditions of crowding and lack of space which would make the average shore-side cook either throw up his hands in despair or his previous meal in revulsion.

The reasons for this 'canteen system' might seem incredible to the average modern observer; it saved the Admiralty having to provide the professional cooks (and their accommodation and wages) to feed the men. It was a direct throwback to the days of fighting sail. It allowed fiddling and creaming off profits all the way down the food chain in the Andrew, from the suppliers ashore through (in some cases) corrupt supply officers and their underlings ashore and in the ships, all the way through bent tankies and killicks of messes, who starved the men to line their pockets. On the big ships, such as *Cameroon*, it was easy for corrupt men to do this; on smaller ships it was not so easy. Generally, food was better the smaller the ship, because the supplies and the money for them could be monitored more accurately by the matelots. This was one of the main reasons that men preferred, begged for, and wangled drafts to small ships, even though the prospect of death in action was, in most cases, greatly increased. There was little thought of 'gallantry' as mooted in officer poets' pæans to small craft, in Jack's way of thinking. So far as the average matelot was concerned, there was little romanticism about the preference for frigates, destroyers, frail E-boats that could be blown up with one well-aimed cannon, and submarines, those breeding grounds of TB and madness. It was simply a matter of better food, because it was more difficult for the occasional middle-men shitehawks of the Supply Branch to get their fat fingers on up to a third of the matelot's shares.

Our first breakfast in *Cameroon* was 'herrings in', which now was vastly different, in harbour in a canteen messing ship, to what it had been in *Ganges* or would often later be at sea in destroyers. The tomato sauce was hot and the herrings were tasty. But then, I suppose that anything would have been tasty after fifteen minutes drawn up on the cold windy quarterdeck and then thirty minutes barefoot scrubbing it with freezing sea-water.

The mess tea was made in a huge tea pot, about eighteen inches high, highly polished steel on the outside, black with encrusted tannin inside. The inside was never cleaned—that was supposed to preserve the flavour of the tea. The tea supplies were kept in the mess, in a big old biscuit tin, and were about two ounces a day a man, although I couldn't swear to that.

Then, at seven-thirty it was 'Hands fall in part of ship'. That meant falling in line again on the quarterdeck and being detailed off by the PO in charge of the quarterdeck division for the work to be done that day. As *Cameroon* had just finished her conversion, in our case it meant cleaning up after the dockyard mateys removed all their tools and gear, and polishing brass tallies on valves, armoured doors, and the bronze tampons on the muzzles of the four-inch guns which had been fitted in open turrets aft. This went on until ten-thirty, when 'Stand easy' was piped over the Tannoy. That was a ten-minute break, when the cooks of the mess brought a steaming hot fanny of tea around to us, as we were not allowed to go down below to the mess, even though it was pouring with freezing rain. Then it was 'Out pipes' and we turned to again until eleven-thirty, when 'Hands to dinner' was piped, and we could at least head for the bathroom to scramble along with fifty other men for one of the six washbowls so we could wash our hands before our midday meal. The officers, of course, were by then at *lunch*.

As the matelots clattered down the ladder to the mess for dinner, Wiggy Bennett, the killick of the mess, waited before the rum-fanny, to dole out to each man over eighteen his tot of one third rum, two thirds water. This made a total of about a third a pint of 'two and one' per man. It was measured with an old, dented, brass measure, into a variety of mugs, cups and stolen beer-glasses from ashore. Then the day's debts and bets were paid and taken in Nelson's blood and there was a sense that this, and not midnight, was the main division between one day and the next, in the Andrew.

Dinner was ladled out by Wiggy. That first day it was toad-in-the-hole, spuds, and cabbage, wet through and truly soggy. This was the way that the vast majority of the matelots —all from working-class homes—liked it. We sat, twenty men or so in the mess, each side of the table, with Wiggy at the head on one side, and the next senior man, Nobby, on the other. I sat at the far end of the table from them, next to the gash bucket. Meal scraps were scraped into the gash bucket by each man after he finished his meal. On canteen messing there were not so many leavings as there would be later on in general messing ships.

It was gospel that there were several reasons why the rum ration was doled out by the Andrew to matelots. One was to give the men appetites to scoff the otherwise often inedible food. Another was to make alcoholics of them by the time they were thirty, more or less forcing them to sign on for another ten years after the first twelve years were finished in order to assure their supply of rum. Third, to rot their insides so that they would not live too long after discharge to draw their pensions. This was first explained to me by Prof, as we ditched the gash over the side straight down a foul-smelling garbage chute—no thought of pollution in those days—and into the harbour water, grey and greasy, where it was instantaneously seized on and devoured by gannets the size of young pterodactyls. 'Listen, Taff,' said Prof, squinting through his spectacles in the pouring rain, as we waited for our turn at the rusty gash-chute. 'You listen and you'll hear half a dozen different versions of the story about the matelot who finished his time for pension, walked out of the barracks gate, and collapsed on the pavement outside and died, with his liver and kidneys rotted away with rum.'

We turned-to again at one-thirty, to our parts of ship, to polish brass for another three hours, with a ten-minute break again at two-thirty. My oppo on the brass-polishing detail was Prof, who had been on board *Cameroon* ever since she was taken over by the Andrew, and knew his way around all right. He was an HO, from Hampstead, in London, and his father was a playwright, a well-known one, by all accounts, while his mother was a poet of some distinction, from what I could gather. Prof's god seemed to be George Bernard Shaw, and he was for ever quoting the Irishman. Prof was the first honest to goodness Socialist that I ever met. He was the first person I ever met who expressed how he saw the world mostly in Marxist terms.

Prof also introduced me to the writings of George Orwell —*The Road to Wigan Pier, Down and Out in Paris and London, Homage to Catalonia*—and told me that Orwell was one of the very rare products of the middle class who were improving with age. Prof said that Orwell had gone through the 'revolutionary bullshit' and was realizing that there were bullies on both ends of the political spectrum and anywhere in between—which we matelots knew all too well. Prof lent me Orwell's books; they opened my eyes as to what was going on in the world outside the ship, at that time, as no other books did. I'm not saying that Orwell was popular in the Andrew—the average matelot read a western or two, and perhaps an adventure or detective book now and again, for variety, but that's how I first found Orwell. His work left a mark on me which has never left—or, I should say, brought out a flow in me which was already there, for I suppose I was born with it. Although Prof used Marxist terms, he was not a Marxist, because he knew and said all the time that material improvement without spiritual improvement was a waste of time, and that excellence in either one, alone, was futile. In this way I think he went back to the old British Whigs rather than the European Communists. Thinking back, in many ways Prof—probably prodded by Orwell—was pointing out what we have had to find out the hard way, that mere material well-being is not enough, and that is true in either a Socialist or a Capitalist society. In short, what I learned from Prof and from Orwell's writings was that people are more important than things. It is so simple, and yet year by year the trend of societies the world over is to lose sight of that one plain simple fact. Now, as we approach the real 1984, the Capitalists are hooting that Orwell, in his *1984*, was forecasting only for Socialist societies. But of course he wasn't—he was forecasting for all. *Animal Farm* is just as possible a representation of Washington and London as it had been (and still is) of Moscow and Peking. But back to sea in 1941 . . .

As we shuffled in our oilskin coats in the rain from one brass valve tally to the next to polish it—I put the polish on with my rag, Prof wiped it off with his—always under the eagle eye of a Petty Officer only yards away, Prof opened my eyes to the ways of this wicked world, and especially in the Andrew. He must be an expert on the matter, I told myself; he was eighteen and a half, and had been in the Andrew for five months longer than I.

Unlike most matelots, Prof rarely swore, except when he was riled badly, which was not often.

'One thing, Taff, this is an imperialist war,' Prof was expounding again. 'The Capitalists in Germany want to get rid of Communism, so they backed Hitler.'

'Then why have the Russians signed up with the Nazis, Prof?'

Prof scoffed in his own particular way. His large forehead jerked up, his hat almost fell off. He snorted. 'Pah! That won't last for long, you see. Old Joe is getting territory between him and the Jerries. All he's doing is waiting for Hitler to invade us and take over, then, while he's snarled down here Joe will invade Germany, see?'

'But why should Stalin do that? We're Capitalist, too, aren't we, Prof?'

Prof sneaked a vicious look around through his spectacles at the Officer of the Day, standing by the gangway, a tall pimply youth in a long Burberry raincoat and a cap that seemed far too big for him. 'They are, not us lot,' Prof said, as though it were gospel. 'And Joe knows it, too. He won't leave us in the lurch, you watch. He'll be in this war as soon as Hitler takes the plunge and starts to invade Blighty.'

'But what will he do if Hitler doesn't invade us?'

'Then Old Joe might just be in trouble,' said Prof, mysteriously, even as a Petty Officer barked, 'Pipe down and get on with it!'

'What will you do if the Jerries take over, Prof?' I asked, quietly, later.

'Buy the first one I meet a pint!' he replied. 'They're just like us, you know, I mean the ordinary Jerry. They're mere pawns in a big power game, that's all. I'll have him in the Party before he knows where he is!' I knew Prof had a twin sister. 'But what about your sister, Prof?'

'If he wants my sister he'll have to learn English first. She's too thick to learn German!'

'So what are we fighting for, Prof?'

'The Empire, Taff. Markets, that's what. The Jerries want to unload their stuff on to India and Africa and we won't let them. But it's stupid, anyway, because we're going to lose the

Empire regardless of whether we fight or not. It's historically inevitable, whatever anyone tells you, and it will be the best thing that could ever happen to us.'

I was non-plussed. This went against everything I had ever been told in the past sixteen years of my life, except by my mother, who, while no Marxist, had simply been anti-Empire. I was thinking fast and deep by the time 'Secure' was piped over the Tannoy and it was time for tea. I was in the duty watch that night, so I saw little more of Prof until the next day. Duty watch hands fell in for muster at five, and again for fire-drill at six, and again for muster at eight, and to clean the passageways throughout the ship, and again at ten for Officer-of-the-Day's rounds, and I finally turned in at ten-thirty, aware that I was but a tiny, tired part of a machine which was spread unevenly all around the globe and never stopped ticking and grinding, day and night. It was a daunting prospect for a boy of sixteen from the coast of Wales. That, sketchily, was the day's routine for a seaman in the Andrew. 'Action stations' were something else.

Cameroon sailed shortly after I joined her. By the time we were ten days out I was fairly efficient in all my duties and used to the peculiar routines of the Andrew. I had been drilled on the Oerlikon guns for at least an hour a day, and on the four-inchers for about half-an-hour. On several occasions we had used live ammo. Our job was to meet a convoy of merchant ships and escort it to—we didn't know where, but we guessed either off Newfoundland or Yewkay. Of course we hadn't known until after we sailed where we were bound, so there was general satisfaction all round when the buzz was (we were rarely told anything about a voyage by Authority) that the destination on that first trip was Canada.

'Get some of those new-fangled nylon stockings, I will,' said one hand on the mess. 'My party told me about them. If I don't get a bit of the other for them, my prick's a bloater!'

Mostly, the officers on board *Cameroon* were a bit like the Gods on Mount Parnassus—they were distant and left us alone, and the Chiefs and POs, being mostly men finishing their time for pension and called-up reserves, were quite civilized compared to the ones we had encountered ashore. Some of the Chiefs and POs were ancient. PO Gilly Gilmore, who was in charge of our action stations at the starboard aft ack-ack guns, had been in the Boer War at the turn of the century. He was a quiet, yet firm, man who looked about sixty, but was probably younger, and who usually, when there were no officers around, patted our shoulders and called us 'son'.

We had four ack-ack mountings aft, each surrounded by a circular steel casing, which enclosed almost all the mounting. Each mounting had two Oerlikons, each capable of firing about 500 rounds of 20mm fused high-explosive shells per minute. Our Oerlikons were for use against planes flying at about 300 miles an hour and up to 1000 yards aloft. For the low flying bombers and torpedo planes *Cameroon* had four twin mountings of Bofors guns, made from a Swedish design. They fired about 120 rounds a minute, but, having more punch, a hit by a Bofors' shell pretty near ensured a kill.

We worked the Oerlikons and the Bofors by hand, and my job, at first, was to see there were no snags in the run of the ammo belt. The gun-layer, Sweeney Todd, Able Seaman, aimed through open, 'cartwheel type' sights, and he was good. He proved it at practice when he shot a flying drag-target out of the sky and received a week's Number Tens for his pains from 'Scranbag'.

There's usually a son-of-a-bitch, everywhere; ours was a sub-lieutenant of about twenty who was in charge of our part of ship. He was often unshaven in the morning, with dirty, overlong hair and uniform, filthy shoes and even holes in his socks. How he got away with it we could never fathom. Prof said he was 'probably the Skipper's bastard son'. He had appeared on board in Southampton, stopping men from going ashore on short leave because there might be a flick of dust on his shoulder—that kind of thing.

When we turned up at action stations, in Number Three blue serge uniforms, woe betide anyone who hadn't his tapes tied properly in front of his jumper, or his boots polished. Scranbag would be certain to be reported to the Jimmy.

We called Scranbag that name out of his range of hearing, of course. Gilly thoroughly detested him, but being one of the old school he would never have dreamed of standing up to him, despite the difference in their ages. Scranbag was an officer—that was enough for Gilly. That meant that Scranbag's word came only just a fraction of an inch after God's, as far as he was concerned.

I had learned very early on, in the first few days in *Ganges*, that, in general, the higher the rank of a naval officer the more humanely he tended to treat matelots, and this rule held pretty well in *Cameroon*, too. We saw the Captain only at Sunday divisions and on his rounds; as a rule I can't remember when he wasn't attended by a junior officer or a runner. When we did encounter the Skipper he always greeted us, either by rating or by name. How he managed this was always a mystery to us because sometimes he couldn't see our badges. Prof said that the junior officer who trailed behind the Skipper was a psychic, but more likely the Skipper looked up some names in the parts of the ship before he stepped out of his cabin. We never saluted officers when we encountered them on board the ship, except the Skipper on first passing of the day—then we stood to attention for him—and when we were dismissed from a charge after being at the table. Also, of course, every time we stepped over the brass strip which marked the edge of the quarterdeck. Being quarterdeck-men meant we saluted that length of wooden deck over steel plates about fifty times a day. Prof said we'd be saluting the shit-house every time we stepped into it when we got back 'Up the line'. The only time I didn't salute the quarterdeck when reaching or leaving it was when *Cameroon* was going down—but about that anon.

The other officers, except Jimmy—who, as far as we were concerned was a Lloyd's registered twenty-four carat bastard, and Scranbag—were distant but decent to us. From one or two officers, in the supplies and medical branches, we might even get a smile and a nod as they passed us. Prof said they were probably poufs.

The First Lieutenant—what the Americans call the executive officer and who we c█████, by tradition, Jimmy, was a lieutenant-commander as ████ as a rake and as hawk-faced as a vulture, with beady bla██ eyes that seemed to penetrate right through us when he passed by. He walked with a stoop, his hands behind his back, and looked as if he was going to pounce on someone at any minute.

Jimmy's relationship with all on board who were under his direct aegis—that included practically everyone but the stokers' branch—was a continual war of nervous attrition. Nothing was ever good enough for Jimmy: the paintwork was always too dirty, even though it was scrubbed day in, day out; the brightwork was never polished highly enough, even though we polished until our elbows felt as if they were ready to seize up; the timing at gunnery practice was never fast enough; the matelots never smartly dressed enough.

Prof said Jimmy was like that because he was peacetime navy and resented being in a converted merchant ship and not in a battlewagon. Nobby said it was because he was 'bloody born that way—his old mum was frightened by a bobby with shiny buttons when she was having a knee trembler with his old man in an alley off Wardour Street'.

Prof said the Jimmy got his stoop from being born in a pusser's hammock.

President Roosevelt had made a speech early that year —1941—and he had called for the Four Freedoms; freedom of speech and expression, freedom of religion, freedom from want and from fear. 'He forgot the fifth,' said Prof. We were in the mess, studying an old newspaper. Several other matelots were sitting around, studying Prof. He was their guiding light in worldly matters and politics by now. A couple of them grinned and nodded. I was puzzled. I fell right into it.

'What's that, then, Prof? I mean the fifth freedom?'

A Liverpool voice piped up, from the end of the table, 'Freedom from fucking naval officers like Jimmy, you Welsh cunt!'

I didn't take umbrage. Scouse never meant ill in the mess with his language. Ashore was a different matter . . .

Our destroyer-escort for the ocean crossing was HMS *Hayes*, named after the town, not the president. And for days we ploughed in company through the grey Atlantic waters, thankful for the bad weather, which usually, said the old hands, kept the U-boats' heads down, and made spotting by the German Blohm and Voss long range reconnaissance planes very difficult, if not impossible. Rumour had it that the Nazis' friends in Canada and Iceland were informing them about ship movements, and there were even said to be secret Nazi plane bases in Labrador and Iceland which supported the spotter planes. Whether these rumours were true or not I have never been able to ascertain. The ones about Canada are doubtful to me, but about Iceland I would not be at all surprised if they were true. We had invaded that country the previous year, and it was now occupied by the Royal Marines. We'd had to; Iceland was a jagged splinter aimed right at Britain's jugular vein, the North Atlantic passage.

The Anvils

As our ship, huge by naval standards, lunged and plunged in the wild Atlantic seas, we caught glimpses, now and again, through the thick grey rainstorms, of *Hayes*. It was the only time while I was afloat in the Andrew that I didn't regret not being in a destroyer—a 'real warship'. *Hayes* was like a wild animal in those seas. First her skinny bow came up, up, up, until half of her keel was clearly showing, then it slammed down, sending heavy seas right over the destroyer's bridge. It was a wonder to me that her boilers did not dowse, with the amount of spray flung over her funnels. It was difficult to see which was spray and smoke. Spray and smoke . . . When she came close to us, to pass signals by semaphore lamp, we could plainly see the lookouts on the bridge and the Skipper, in his brown duffel-coat, and the four-inch gun crew closed up behind their open gun, with the ocean swirling all around them, and them lashed to the gun to prevent themselves being washed away.

Life at sea was much better, for the average matelot, than it was while he was ashore in the clutches of the Andrew. Despite the long hours at action stations in foul weather—in my case the after starboard Oerlikon guns, and then the increased misery of normal working stations—polishing brass in a teeming rainstorm, brass which we knew moments later would be under a Niagara of salt water, and despite the miserable conditions on the mess deck, with no relief from crowding, and despite the petty depredations of Scran-bag, life was still better. For a lad of sixteen it was good to know that I was doing a man's job among men, and that to an extent their lives depended on me as much as mine did on them.

About the fourth day out we caught a glimpse in very bad weather—it must have been somewhere off the south coast of Ireland—of a Nazi spotter plane. The alarm went off and the port forward Oerlikon shot off a few rounds at the ghostly shadow in the sky, but that was all the anti-aircraft action we saw.

So the days passed, ordered, crowded, full of life—and the thoughts, sometimes—of death. The inevitable routine of the Andrew took little account of where the ship was or how close the enemy might be. It had been refined and honed over the centuries for the fast frigates and the ships of the line, and what had been good enough for Jolly Jack Tar in the days of Vernon and Nelson, was good enough for us. Thus the gospel from above in His Majesty's ships.

Off watch, in the mess, life became more amenable, as we became more and more accustomed to one another's presences and foibles. Friends and antagonists had sorted themselves out, and managed to rub along together without any major friction. The movement of the ship, in rough weather, was sickening. This was surprising, because I had thought that in a big liner the movement would be gentle. This was not the case. *Cameroon* didn't slash and slide and roll, as *Second Apprentice* had done, and as I was later to learn, destroyers did. She waddled agonized, hesitated and *hefted*. She started her roll, slow and ponderous, and we waited for a few seconds, expecting it to change back, but no. Over and over, and over . . . she rolled ponderously, and then everything that had been left loose on the mess deck went scattering helter skelter all over the deck. Then, when she had reached an almost impossible angle of heel—about thirty-five degrees—she started to roll back, up, up, up and *up*, then down, the other way, down and down, until all the loose stuff was skittering back to the other side of the mess deck. Shooting an Oerlikon gun—or any kind of gun in those days before stabilizers—with any kind of acceptable accuracy, was almost impossible, yet it was expected, because My Lords Commissioners of the Admiralty did not accept the impossible. To them it did not exist.

The Anvils

One forenoon, early in April—it must have been about a week out—the radar lookouts sighted a vessel and we closed to sight her. She turned out to be HMS *Brooke*, a destroyer, heading in the opposite direction, east. I know it was a Sunday, because the fire burst out just after we had finished Sunday divisions and prayers, about eleven-thirty. I had fallen out with the RCs, along with anyone else who had the wiliness to get out of the cold wind and rain.

7. *One bloody thing . . .*

Way down in Gay Paree,
For ten francs you can see,
A young tattooed lad-y,
Tattooed from head to knee.
Now she's got tattooes by the score,
There isn't room for any more,
And on her back there's a Union Jack,
What could you ask for more?

And on her starboard knee,
Is a full rigged ship at sea,
On the left cheek of her arse,
Is a map of the Khyber Pass,
While just below her kidney
Is a bird's eye view of Sydney,
But what I like best,
There upon her chest,
Is my home in Tennessee!

'Way Down in Gay Paree', sung to the tune of 'My home in Tennessee': this ditty probably originated in the 1920s. There are several slightly different versions. This was the most common in the Andrew.

I am still not sure where the fire started, or why, but I think it was just forward of the forward boiler room, where there was a fuel stowage compartment. I don't know—no one could tell me—if it was a tinfish or if it was the result of the hurried preparation of the ship. There seemed to me to be two explosions, one directly after the other. If it was tinfish there must have been a very fast and able German submarine crew.

The God-walloper had just wrapped up prayers in a thin voice in the wind on the quarterdeck. We 'RCs' in the shelter of the after gun could only just hear the muttering of the matelots. 'Hypocrites, the lot of them,' said Prof, who had also chosen the Roman Catholic religion as a temporary wartime measure. 'That sky-pilot will be back in the piggery within minutes, knocking back pink gins all afternoon along with the Jimmy—' and just as he said that there was a loud, dull thump from somewhere forward. The ship was on the rise from a deep roll to starboard. Even before she rolled back one degree I thought there was another thump. It is strange how deceptive are senses when something expected for a long time eventually occurs.

For a few seconds there seemed to be comparative silence in the ship, then all hell broke loose. Over the Tannoy system came the loud booming voice of the cox'n: 'Hands to action stations . . . !' Then a moment later: 'Belay the last order! Hands to damage control stations!' I was already on my way up the after screen ladder, to my station at the Oerlikon guns. It was only when I arrived there, along with six other puffing, excited but calm, white-faced men, that I wondered why we'd bothered. The sky was thick with cloud. The rain was pouring down. There would be no chance of sighting anything like a U-boat periscope. Soon Scranbag came huffing up the ladder, as supercilious, officious and pompous as ever and as scruffy. We were all still in our best Sunday Number Two uniforms. There had been no chance to change, of course. We had managed to get the anti-flash hoods, gloves and our steel helmets out of the lockers by the guns. Most of us had managed to don them by the time Scranbag appeared. Only Duffy from Kildare still had not his helmet on and the strap fixed properly.

Scranbag stood for a moment, looking as if he did not know which way to turn. His face seemed to turn green. He stared up for a couple of seconds at the great pall of smoke and flame coming out of the funnel, then his bird-like head pointed at Duffy. 'If you haven't got that helmet on in one second you'll be on First Lieutenant's report!' he screamed. 'Always adrift! I've drilled you . . .'

Duffy didn't wait to hear the rest of it. He looked at Scranbag straight in the eye. 'Ach, get knotted—sir!' he said.

There was not time for me to wonder whether or not I had heard aright. Immediately Duffy said that, the pipe was made: 'All hands to fire stations!'

There was a quick rush past the struck-rigid Scranbag to the forward after-house ladder, and then down into a milling crowd of men on deck struggling with hoses, axes, and mobile fire pumps, great lumbering diesel-run autonomous pumps, trying to get them forward. My fire station was aft, on the starboard side, and I fell in there, awaiting orders to move wherever I might be wanted. Now the ship was drift-ing, beam on to the seas.

'She's lost power,' said one of the killicks.

'Fucking great,' said someone else.

By now the upper deck was a throng of blackened men, mostly stokers. Some of them were very seriously burned and blistered and lying on what stretchers were available. Others were more lightly burned, with their overalls torn away by the sick bay tiffies to expose patches of blistered flesh. Now flames were shooting high from the funnel. It was eerie then, without the pulse of the engines under our feet and smoke everywhere.

Suddenly someone came running aft. He was black from

head to foot. His clothes were a smouldering mass of tiny flames. He threw himself over the guardrail and disappeared over the side. We fell out and rushed to the guardrail. Duffy flung himself over and we saw him flounder towards the man. Then the someone heaved and turned over face down and Duffy disappeared. That was the last I saw of them.

I turned inboard again, not knowing what to do, waiting for someone to tell me. I stared about me. Many others did so, too. A killick stoker grabbed my arm. 'Steady on, mate,' he said. 'You wait here.' Even as he said this the pipe came: 'Hands prepare to abandon ship.' Now the ship was listing heavily to port.

'They say that *Hayes* is coming alongside,' said the killick stoker. 'You stand by. She'll send Carley floats over from her stern on lines. When one comes alongside you hop into it. Right?'

The cox'n came aft then, shouting: 'All hands help with the wounded! Come on, look lively! Get them into *Hayes*'s Carley floats! Take the standing cases first! Lower them down the side ladders!'

I headed for a group of standing wounded. Some of them were in a very bad way, burnt from the waist up and neck down by scalding steam, it seemed. One was behaving like a drunken man under the effects of the morphine which the sick bay tiffies had given him. He was singing his head off, his eyes glistening in his scorched, blackened head. I think he was a stoker, but I could see no badges on his scorched overalls.

'. . . Show me the way to go home . . .
I'm tired and I want to go to bed . . .'

I could hardly believe my ears. Some one shut him up with more morphine.

The ship was still rolling as badly as before the explosions, even though she was well down now in the water and listing over at forty degrees. It must have been about five o'clock. I went to grab the now quiet burned stoker, to take him to the ship's side and guide him down the ladder. 'Don't touch that man!' came a voice behind me. I swung round and saw the chief sick berth tiffie glaring at me. He shook his head. 'Don't touch him, son. You don't know how badly he's burned. Looks like his arm's got it bad.'

'How will he make it down the ladder, Chief?'

'He won't,' the Chief said very quietly and passed on to another burn case. The burnt stoker now was trying to crouch. I gently took hold of one leg and helped him to ease down to sit on the deck.

'All right, Stokes. You stay there a minute,' said a seaman killick who was on his way aft with a fire hose to fight the spreading fire below. 'You, Boy, help me.'

I followed the killick, down into the forward main passage-way, a smoky shambles, but there was nothing we could do with the hose. The firemain supply of salt-water had failed. From the hydrants came only a mocking dribble of water. Bodies lay all about.

The port main passage was a wreck, with most of the paintwork burned and blistered—all except the ship's notice board. It was still, by some miracle, pristine, and I clearly remember reading, as if in a daze, the heavily printed '. . . *shall suffer death by hanging or any other punishment hereafter mentioned . . .*' It is strange how in times of stress certain images impress themselves on the mind and memory. I suppose I ought to have remembered more the appearance of the dead men, about whom the dirty water sloshed, all black and blistered with their eyes staring out of their heads, and their hair, in many cases, completely burned off. I ought to remember more the shouts and screams of the men too injured to be moved. But no, I see it clearly now, that appalling sentence on the brown varnished poster in the glimmer of a handlamp as men tried their best to fight the encroaching fire with buckets of water scooped up from the deck, and the darkness and smoke, and I clearly recall wondering if one of the punishments hereafter mentioned was burning to death . . .

When we got back on the upper deck, I saw that men were crowding into *Hayes*'s Carley floats—six men per raft—and were being pulled to the destroyer over the almost mountainous seas. The destroyer, all the while, was rising and plunging like a wild thing. As the men in the Carley floats reached the destroyer's stern some of them jumped too fast and fell into the oggin. Some were recovered, but many of them were not. I'd just made up my mind to hold on to the Carley float whatever happened until I was dead sure I could make it to the destroyer's side nets, when another ship appeared, grey and ghostly at first, out of the thick weather. She was the destroyer we had passed earlier that day, HMS *Brooke*.

By now things were breaking loose on board *Cameroon*, and some were sliding over the side into the violent sea: pumps and ammunition lockers, things like that. I didn't see any men fall over the side, though, but some may have done, on the other side of the ship. We were heaving opened drums of oil over the side in hopes that the leaking oil might calm the sea between us and *Hayes*, but I think all it did was blow all over the destroyer and make a fine mess for her dabtoes to clean up when she was clear.

As we sand-scratchers were busy throwing oil drums into the oggin, *Brooke* started to pump oil into the sea between us and *Hayes*—thick, black, oozy fuel oil. She had a close call. In the heaving seas she almost got herself crushed between the two ships and only got away by the skin of her teeth. As she slid out from the deadly passage between us, now even lower in the water, and the bucking tossing *Hayes*, I noticed men on the Carley rafts, looking like insects on the huge grey slopes, waving to *Brooke*. It seemed a cross between a deadly nightmare and a Keystone Cops comedy.

In our ship, by now, there was no semblance of separation by branches, all the seamen and stokers, the cooks and stewards, the signalmen, everyone was mixed up in the abandon-ship parties. Only the men too wounded to be moved, and the dead, had been sorted out and separated. The waves were, it was agreed by all who survived, about sixty feet from crest to trough. We were all mustered aft. There was nothing we could do but wait to be rescued, if that was possible.

I noticed Scranbag on the poop. He was white-faced and silent now, with nothing to say for himself. I never saw him again.

Brooke then came up on our leeward side, away from the wind, and cast a Carley float into the sea. It drifted up under our stern and AB 'Shiner' Wright, a close oppo of Nobby's, climbed down into the raft. As he heaved himself over the rail he cried, 'Any more for the Skylark?' Then we saw him get into the raft—and be pulled right under *Cameroon*'s pounding stern. The heaving line from the destroyer had caught around our propeller shaft. The destroyer men had pulled on the line, Shiner had been pulled towards our propeller just as our ship, with an almighty crash, had descended. We never saw Shiner again.

Prof turned up aft just as Shiner went missing. He sought me out in the crowd of men on the after deck. 'Thank God we don't have a marine band on board, Taff,' he said. 'I can't stand 'Abide with me!' It reminds me of all those money-grubbers grabbing the lifeboats on the *Titanic*!'

Brooke fired her costain gun, and missed. The long line

drifted away to leeward of our ship. *Brooke* steamed right up under our stern and, after several near misses as she heaved up and down in the seas, she managed to land a heaving line on our stern. Someone out of our milling crowd grabbed it and wrapped it around a stanchion. *Brooke* sent over a thick grass line which we all pulled over to our ship on the end of the heaving line. The grass line was secured on one of the burning *Cameroon*'s bollards and we watched as *Brooke*'s dabtoes passed one of her Carley floats into the heaving sea, then signalled us to pull it in. A couple of our own seamen, in a frenzy of effort, pulled the float over to us, against the heavy wind and sea, but when it was alongside there was no chance that anyone would ever be able to get into it, or if he did he would not last long in that moving mass of foam and wind.

Then, probably in reply to our own Captain's semaphore signal—he was now also aft, with his chief signals yeoman by his side—*Brooke* started to head straight for our ship's side, so that we might jump directly on board her.

I have written that last sentence in the calm light of day, at a steady desk in semi-tropical weather, in a reasonably comfortable room, which does not move. As I write I remember many things, all in a rush, with extreme vividness; I could try to set down in words the rush of the sea between the ships, the grinding rumble and screech as *Brooke* scrunched her hull alongside *Cameroon*; the shouts of the men, some jocular now, some crying in their despair and fright, as one sickening lurch and crash of both ships, one against the other, followed the previous one. It will not do. So that you will clearly understand what happened I must write down what followed in cold, precise phrases, just as, when I try to dissect my memories, they come to me like frames in a fast-moving film suddenly stopped for a few seconds. It is only thus that I can write what followed *Brooke*'s sacrificial gesture. The facts are visible, tangible to me; part of my senses, part of me, keeping their place in space and time, in part of my life. They needed only a U-boat or two, a 1,000-ton destroyer and a converted liner of about 20,000 tons, an Atlantic gale, a raging fire, about one and a half thousand men and about three and a half hours before and after dusk. These facts made a whole that had facets galore, a complicated series of menacing events that could be seen in glimpses by the eye. But there was something else besides. Something invisible, a directing spirit of comradely essence, a willingness to lay lives down for the sake of friends. Here, now, my writing is slow . . . slower than it has ever been, and yet my mind flies round and round faster and faster, with images surging up before me, as though to cut me off from all the modern shoreside world about me and everyone else in it.

The facts were plain. *Brooke* ground and smashed in that raging sea alongside of the sinking *Cameroon* for three hours, and saved the lives of 180 men.

It is difficult to give an impression of the risk of jumping from a ship's deck in the screaming wind over mountainous seas, one minute forty feet above the upper works of a destroyer, able almost to look down her funnel, and the next moment fifteen feet or so below the destroyer's upper deck. The slightest misjudgement in the moment to jump, the slightest hesitation when the moment came, the slightest weakness in grabbing on to the destroyer, and we were, any of us, with no doubt at all, dead.

Those who have never seen two ships in a heavy sea-way, close to one another, should imagine being in a huge factory building which is burning, and also canted over forty degrees or so on average, while rolling and pitching heavily at the same time. Then another, smaller factory building, rising up and smashing down three or four times a minute, approaches and touches the bigger factory—and all the while, all around,

125

the moving seas threaten, grey and ominous and loaded with sudden death.

I remember clearly that the first group to jump from *Cameroon* were nine sand-scratchers from our QX division. I was standing by the rail, aft, with Nobby's arm around my shoulder and Prof telling me that the two Captains were probably related, or that ours owed the skipper of *Brooke* a gambling debt—I can't recall his exact words, but they were something of the sort. Of the nine men who first jumped as *Brooke* rose so fast on a sea, four landed safely on her fore deck and five landed on her 'B' gun deck, about twelve feet above her fore deck. As the nine landed they immediately stumbled off aft in the destroyer, out of the way of the main action. From the way they ran they were obviously all right, although the very heavy rolling of the destroyer made it almost impossible for the men crowding her fore deck to keep their footing.

The second lot to jump were six men. Of them only three were all right, the others were injured when they landed on *Brooke*'s deck, and were carried aft by some of the destroyer's crew.

Then the destroyer pulled away from our ship's side and we thought she was going to abandon us to take our own chances in that sea. But no, she crashed back, took off another 'flight' of men, then pulled away again. This she did again and again, about two dozen times. Two dozen times the Captain of *Brooke* put his ship, and the lives of everyone in her, in danger of foundering in those rough seas, until everyone who could jump had been taken off *Cameroon*.

By the time I jumped it was almost full night. I recall watching one man drop between the ships even as the destroyer crashed alongside, and me gauging *Brooke*'s rise, and Nobby at my side, holding me steady.

I recall Nobby shouting above the roar and the cries, 'All

right, here she comes . . . two . . . six . . . *jump!*' And then I
crashed on the destroyer's flag deck, two decks above her
upper deck, splayed on the deck itself. I had banged myself
against some obstruction—probably the ladder—but I felt
that I was unhurt. The rolling of the destroyer was much
more violent than *Cameroon*'s had been, and it took me a few
moments to become accustomed to it after one of *Brooke*'s
bunting-tossers dragged me to my feet. 'Nip down aft, mate,'
he told me. I did, and as I went I looked back to see that
Brooke had rigged floodlights on her fore deck now, so that
our lads could see better that dark, dizzy boiling gap as they
jumped. Floodlit, it looked like some ghostly terror-film set.
I remember feeling, while I hesitated at the bottom of the
bridge deck ladder, as if I were looking at something that was
going on in a different world, at a different time, in a different
life. All the action and men up on the fore deck and on board
the still heaving *Cameroon*, dying under her blood-red pall of
smoke and fire, looked as if they were somewhere far away in
time and space.

Soon the men injured during the transfer were being
brought aft, on board *Brooke* and some of the injuries were
grim. One man was completely impaled through the shoulder
when he fell on to a guardrail stanchion. There were many
broken arms, legs and ribs.

As the night drew in so the wind and sea worsened, until by
the time the last men were jumping it was a roaring, boiling
inferno, and certainly, as we stared and squinted aghast in the
spray, the last two of all were lost over the side, between the
grinding hulls of the destroyer and the dying armed cruiser.

Brooke stood off *Cameroon* all night and we watched her red
glare a mile or so away through the gale. By midnight or so
the fire in *Cameroon* reached the rockets on her bridge and
they took off with a display of fireworks rarely exceeded in
brilliance anywhere ashore. Great red and white blossoms of

light all over the sky and the heaving sea to accompany the dying on their way to Valhalla, and then the small-arms ammo went off, first one or two here and there, then in machine-gun rattles, then in a full-blown roar, which lasted for several minutes, with bullets and cannon shells whizzing overhead as we in *Brooke* all cowered behind steel protection. She finally sank with a great hiss just before grey dawn, and took hundreds—the exact number will never be known—of dead and dying men with her to her resting place on the ocean floor. There and then, I learned what real prayer is.

The destroyer was crowded, with twice as many men in her as her already overcrowded wartime complement. I was sent down into one of the seamen's messes forward, and fell asleep under the mess table on a blanket which a friend of Nobby's had lent me. Prof sat on a seat in the corner of the mess, holding forth about it all being a plot to wear down the working class, until someone—probably off watch and trying to sleep—muttered from his hammock, 'Shit in it, mate.' Then Prof was quiet, after he had commented, to anyone left to listen in the dull red glow, 'Well, we've only got about a thousand miles to go, and probably fifty U-boats to get past, and we'll be home in no time! I'll bet Jerry's having a good old laugh—' Someone else threw an empty mess fanny at Prof, and all was comparatively quiet after that.

As I dozed off, I made up my mind never to sail in a big ship again if I could possibly avoid it, and I remembered that my father might be at home on leave. Perhaps, if I got leave, I might see him again?

Down below, on the doubly-crowded forward seamen's mess deck of HMS *Brooke*—I think there must have been well over a hundred men crammed into a space of about thirty feet by twenty—the talk among us survivors was mainly about dead and wounded friends, and how we would probably get leave on our arrival at Liverpool, and how everyone was going to avoid being sent back to big ships. Nobby intended to volunteer for E-boats, and Prof said he would go up the Dilly and find a short-timer who would give him a dose of siff so he could stay in the barracks hospital in Chatham for six weeks—the war would be over then, and he'd be safe. I decided to volunteer for destroyer duty. They were fairly small, fast ships, heavily armed for their size, and I'd seen that, as *Brooke* had risen out of the sea time and again, they did not draw much water—say fifteen feet. The chance of one being torpedoed was much less than for a cruiser or a battlewagon—and it came home to me how very different this all was to what I had expected while I was in *Ganges.* There we had imagined big fleets steaming out to sea to meet the enemy and blow him to bits: battleships, cruisers, aircraft carriers, and all their escort ships; destroyers, frigates, corvettes, protecting the bigger ships and being safe under their guns. No one had mentioned ships slinking out in ones and twos to slide hopefully through the U-boat gauntlet, on the way out to meet slow convoys of merchant ships to bring back again through the shoals of murderous Nazi submarines.

I don't remember ever trying to compare life on board *Brooke* with life ashore in Wales, in the quiet coastal country-side, or with life on board the old *Second Apprentice.* If I did, I must have been content that I was helping in a struggle for things and places and people I loved. But I doubt if I did—boys are not like that.

8. . . . After Another

Oh I don't give a fuck for the Killick of the Watch,
Or the Chief of the working party;
I'm watch ashore at half-past four,
I'm Jack me fuckin' hearty!

I've been ashore since half-past four,
I've chased three matelot's parties
I've drunk two beers and slogged three queers,
I'm Jack me fucking hearty!

Now back to Chiefy I must go,
The gangway's waiting for me;
I'll straighten up and sober up,
I'm Jack me fucking hearty!

'Jack me hearty', sung to the tune of 'The girl I left behind me'.
The concept of the jolly, hearty sailor, as imagined by the
shore-side sentimentalists, was genuinely detested by RN ratings.
The 'wild rover' ashore was generally ineffectual on board, usually
fairly unintelligent, sometimes a menace to the lives, limbs and
peace of mind of his messmates. Ashore, he'd have two pints of
beer and be looking for an argument or a fight. Other names for
him were 'Jack Strop', 'Jack-me-tickler tin' and 'Gangway Jack'.
This is a sardonic comment on his attitude.

We had a rough trip back to Liverpool. Most of the time we *Cameroon* survivors stayed down below in the heaving, rolling, stuffy mess deck in *Brooke*'s fo'c'sle. All the way back, for about a week, the weather was heavy and the destroyer pounded and rolled incessantly. We were, most of us who weren't injured or wounded, willing to give a hand at any odd jobs in the destroyer, but the crew had been on board since before the beginning of the war, and they preferred us not to get in the way. Prof said they had a union going, but I doubted that.

We were welcomed like heroes as the ship pulled into Gladstone Dock in Liverpool. The dockyard mateys crowded the sea-wall to cheer us in—the Captain of the Port had delayed us steaming in until their lunch break—and then again on the march from the docks to Lime Street station civvies crowded the pavement to cheer us home. They, too, didn't know why they were cheering. News of the sinking was kept secret. I certainly didn't feel as if we were heroes at all, just very lucky, but we all grinned and made a brave face of it in our oilskins as we swung along. We wore the oilskins of the *Brooke*'s crew, because many of us had nothing decent to wear, what with burns and rips and tears.

The train journey to London took all night—about ten hours. We were transported across London in grey double-decker buses with white-painted windows, so we couldn't see out and the civvies couldn't see in. The train to Chatham was delayed for seven hours during the night as a recent air-raid had blown away viaducts and temporary ones were being built. When at last we passed over the new bridges, the workmen, bobbies, and Civil Defence people in their blue coats and steel helmets and the soldiers on guard mostly cheered us, and waved their rifles and picks and shovels. We all waved back and grinned, of course, but we felt abashed about it. As Prof said, it was us that should have been cheering them. He leaned half his body out of the carriage window as we slowly pulled over the timber baulks of the rebuilt bridges, and shouted 'Up the workers!' until a Petty Officer in the next compartment also leaned out and told him, 'Shit in it, you bloody Bolshie, or I'll have your cap as soon as we get to Chats.'

'Fucking fascist,' muttered Prof as he sat down.

On the march from Chatham station to the barracks, right through the middle of the town, hardly anyone looked up from what they were doing as we plodded along. Ship-wrecked crews were obviously nothing new here. One or two people called out, 'What ship, Jack?' but we had been forbidden to talk at all about the loss of *Cameroon*, or even mention her name. This was, so we were told by our former First Lieutenant, 'because it was best if the enemy were kept uncertain as to which ship had been lost'. That made sense enough, but it was hard not to talk about it, and especially to people who might have relatives who had died with the ship. 'They will be informed in due course,' said the Jimmy, 'and by the proper authority.'

Once inside the prison-like walls of Chatham barracks we were all marched into the drafting office, manned mainly by Wrens, with a sprinkling of chiefs, old POs, barrack stanchions, and a few officers. I was amazed at their attitude to us. It amounted to almost plain callousness. We were kept waiting, those of us who had not been dealt with by tea time, from three-thirty p.m., until the duty watch came on at seven. Then we were kept standing for hours in line, with no supper, nothing to drink, being recorded and issued chits for missing kit, and station cards and new paybooks and all the other paper paraphernalia with which the bureaucratic squadron-leaders made their private little empires and with which the officers and Chiefs and POs managed to make themselves indispensable so they would not be sent out to sea. Being in front of a counter, only three feet or so from a Wren, was the closest that almost all of us matelots had been to a woman for months. For them, the ones in that office in Chatham, we might just as well not have existed. Men who were reporting from their second or third sinking in the past eighteen months were treated like unwanted intruders, and made to stand silently in line, forbidden to smoke by a big notice in six-inch letters on the yellow-painted wall, while split-ass mechanics, maybe twenty or so, puffed away at their Black Cat corked tips and re-touched their lipstick in little mirrors they kept in their desk drawers. I'd managed to stay close to Prof the whole of the dreary way through the barracks. 'I wonder what else they keep in their drawers?' whispered a voice from the back of the line.

'Probably pink gin on ice,' replied Prof, mentioning the officers' favourite drink.

'You don't mix gin and ice,' said another.

'They do, when they mix with the pigs,' replied Prof.

It was mostly the same throughout the war, but with blessed exceptions, where the Wrens were concerned. It never ceased to amaze us matelots, who were by no means the stupid people we might have appeared to be when on parade, how a few of the transformed shopgirls and some of the jumped-up office-secretaries could suddenly be stuck-up stars, behaving as if they had, as Nobby put it, 'never been for a shit in their lives'.

There was a glaring discrepancy. Officers and men could never mix socially ashore, yet Wrens and officers could—but the average Wren didn't even want to know Jack. If the Wrens made the excuses perhaps that the matelots were a little beneath them, that they were 'common', that their accents were not 'right', that they could 'do better than a mere sailor', then they would have been speaking the truth as they evidently—all too clearly—demonstrated it to us. But they hid the real truth—our truth—which is that it was their attitude, their very disdain for matelots, some of whom had been through things unimaginable, that made us matelots behave as we sometimes did, in self-defence, with a butch crudity that would have made Primo Carnero look like a wilting lily. To a man who has been through the gates of hell and back, a mere smile from a female—or anyone else—can work wonders. There was very little wonder-working in Chatham barracks. There, what supposed females were around had the whole male field to themselves, and they showed it with no holds barred.

I could not have cared less how the Wrens treated us, but I heard time and time again the talk of other matelots, and what I am writing now is what they felt and said then. As for me, each time a Wren or a barrack stanchion Petty Officer looked down his nose at this mere stripling who, they seemed to think, had no business in the Royal Navy anyway, each time I was called up to their little corner of the British Empire, there to be kept waiting perhaps on my aching feet for another ten minutes while a cup of tea was fetched to them by a flunkie and slowly sipped while last night's score of dancing partners or pints of beer was again tallied and gloated over, I remembered that leave was due to me. I would soon be home again with my family—or at least my Mum and sister Angharad, in their new home in Manchester.

I see even now the patient looks of disgust in the eyes of some of the older matelots as they stood and waited yet another hour! We were finally trooped out of the joining office to the divisional barracks at one o'clock in the night, just as an air-raid warning sounded and we were diverted by bullying-voiced GIs to the shelter tunnels, there to spend a night on the cold concrete floor under one thin blanket.

Whenever I recall Chatham barracks I always wonder at the seemingly ox-like patience of some of the HO matelots, who themselves had been men of some position in civil life—a few had been office and bank managers, works foremen, artists, writers—and the older I become, the more I wonder at the downright courtesy of those men in not jumping over the tables and murdering the barracks staff —many of them—and strangling them to death as they sat there so self-importantly.

In the shelter tunnel I slept well enough, despite the crumping outside in the distance. Jerry was giving the Medway towns a hammering. I had my draft-chit, and to a destroyer, too, HMS *Eclectic*, and I had my railway warrant to go home on leave for seven days before I joined her in Scotland in Scapa Flow. Prof had the same ship, and so had Nobby and a few other *Cameroon* survivors. We made arrangements to meet at Manchester, Prof and I, on his way north. I think no one can imagine the half of the delight with which a boy of sixteen, almost seventeen, anticipated being out of the clutches of the Andrew, away from the orders over the Tannoy, and watches and drills, action stations and working parties, and the machinations of every pusser-faced bastard within sight, for a whole seven days of glorious liberty.

There was a sudden explosion, louder than the rest, away in the distance, outside the tunnel.

'Jerries after the Short's aeroplane works,' someone said.

'That pilot will be in the rattle when he gets back to Jerryland,' said Prof. 'It's the workers' houses they're supposed to be clobbering. Old Krupps'll do his nut when he finds that their lads have been breaking the windows in his mate Short's works!'

'So long as they hit the fucking factory and not my house I don't give a monkey's tit—my missus lives only half a mile from Short's,' said another voice in the gloom.

We were up most of the night, standing by in case the Medway Towns Civil Defence needed hands to dig out bodies from the rubble, or to mend broken fire-mains and the like. That meant standing around in our oilskins, waiting. By the time we went to breakfast, after the 'All clear' sounded, not many of us wanted the train-smash that was offered up, cold and greasy, on tin trays. We still had all forenoon to wait, until we could go off through the gates, but we went without eating. We could, we knew, get good scran, like meat pies, on Victoria Station, from the WVS van.

London, as we crossed it in daylight, looked a weary mess with gaping holes in the rows of buildings everywhere.

'Bloody bastards!' someone muttered.

It took eighteen hours to get from London to Manchester by train—a distance of about 180 miles. This was mainly because the train was diverted around Birmingham, which had again been bombed by Jerry the night before. There was ruin and muck, chaos and cheery acceptance everywhere. It was quite clear that if Jerry was going to bomb us into surrender he would have his work cut out. The most common British characteristic is to have a heart more like a sponge's than a lion's. The more it is stabbed into, the more it gives, but stays beating and defiant, all the same. Even though most of the rail tracksides were scarred with bomb-craters—even out in the open countryside—it was clear that Jerry was not doing as well as Lord Haw Haw claimed in his broadcasts from 'Jairmeny'. We all concluded that if Hitler was going to bomb Britain into submission, he would have to crater every acre of the land, all at the same time, because what got flattened here was going to pop up there again in a very short space of time. The land was becoming crowded with 'shadow' factories. That was the general consensus in the train, among us matelots and soldiers and what few civilians there were.

But the generally unspoken thought, at least among us matelots, was that when the bombing failed to achieve what Hitler wanted, he would turn more and more to the thing that *could* win his aims, and he was closer and closer to doing it all the while. He would increase his U-boat stranglehold, and put on the pressure with more and more U-boats, until all our warships were sunk—and us with them—and he then would have the merchant fleet at his mercy, to allow the country's food and supplies to pass, or not, at his whim. We knew what his whim would be all right. He would starve Britain into surrender, and then, once she'd packed in, starve her to death. None of us, I believe, had any doubts at all about what was in store for us if the Nazis won the sea-war. Sometimes we were given pep-talks by officers which gave the impression that we matelots did not already know what was at stake in the battle for the Atlantic, but we knew all right. If a mere lad of almost seventeen knew, it is pretty certain that all the others did, too. I was by no means an exceptional person, and never thought of myself as such. I was one of the lads the whole time, and I wouldn't have wanted to be anything—or considered as anything—else. I was a matelot, and proud of it. It was not British naval tradition that made me feel that way—I felt that way despite it.

The centre of Manchester, as I saw when I left London Road station, was another bombed mess. It was raining, naturally, and noisy from screeching, grinding tramcars which shook and waddled their way over the cobblestoned streets. Many of the buildings showed scars and gaps from the heavy bombing the city had endured the previous Christmas. But the Mancunians had a good reputation for friendliness, and they certainly showed it to me as I waited for the tram to Harpurhey, one of the inner city working-class districts. That was where my family was now lodging with my Aunt

Lowri and her English husband, John, a railway guard. It was early evening when I arrived and the sirens had not yet sounded. Probably Jerry was delayed in getting to the North Country through the thick weather, everybody at the tramstop agreed.

'Eeh, well, ir'll gi' oos a chance ter goa hoam,' commented one stout elderly lady with a shopping bag. The bag looked empty, but I knew she probably had her week's food ration in it. It took me about ten minutes, standing in the rain with my hat pulled down as tight as I could manage and my Burberry collar turned up, to begin to understand the local dialect, even though there had been a few Lancashire lads in *Ganges* and *Cameroon*. As I figured out an interpretation of what the lady had said: 'It'll give us a chance to get home', three men appeared at the tramstop. They were manual labourers, as I gathered from their flat peaked caps and boots, and obviously half sozzled from the way they walked with their arms around each other's shoulders. One of them, a small, dark, gypsy-faced man of about forty at a wild guess, left his companions, reaching into his pocket as he came at me. He staggered slightly as he ambled up from the back of the queue. Then he thrust a quart beer bottle at me. 'Tetley's Ale.'

'Ere thee are, Jack, 'ave a drink on uss lads, eh?' His voice was thick and he leaned towards me and slapped my shoulder. 'Wheer art from, lad? Eh? Hast t'a been ter sea, then?'

I took the bottle from his unsteady hand and grinned at him.

It was the first time in my life that anyone had ever offered me a drink ashore. It made me feel much more like a man. I'd been given tiny sips of bubbly on board for little favours I had done, but this was the first time I'd ever had booze ashore.

'Cheers, mate,' said I. 'I'm from Wales, but now I'm in . . . destroyers.' It wasn't strictly true; I hadn't joined

Eclectic yet, but it sounded much better than 'I'm from a sunken armoured merchant cruiser'.

'Oah, th' art a Taffy, then, eh, lad?' The man stepped back and inspected me, as if he were about to present me with a gold medal. Then he shouted to his comrades, 'It's a bloody Taff we 'ave 'ere, lads!'

As soon as he said that just about all the dozen people in the queue claimed Welsh descent, as the beer-giver started to chant:

'*Soons o' the seeeaa,*' he hiccuped,
'*All British bawnnn,*' he waved another bottle of Tetley's,
'*Sailin' ev'ry ooshun,*
Laffin' fooes too scawrn,' he hiccuped again and winked at
me.

By now his mates had taken up the song, and soon one or two elderly ladies, and even a respectable looking gentleman in a bowler hat, who carried an umbrella at the 'slope arms' position over his shoulder, joined in at least humming the tune.

Over on the Piccadilly pavement, about ten yards away, two matelots passed, each with a young woman holding on to them. They stared over at me through the rain as they passed on. I felt a real idiot. One of the matelots shouted, 'Get some sea-time in, Jack!' The other called out, 'Bloody ODs!'

I merely waved the still full bottle of beer at them and grinned as broadly as I could. I said silently to them, 'Fuck you, Jack, you might have the women, but I've got the free beer!' Then the tram came along, and I pushed my way into the hot, jam-packed lower deck where there was still standing room.

As the tram accelerated, ground and swayed and bowled along, I found myself pushed up hard against a young woman. She must have been about nineteen. Of course at six-teen, three years is an eternity, so I had no mind to beat up to her. In fact I was thinking, as I somehow opened my oilskin coat, how very different it was to be crowded with civilians from what it was with matelots. Matelots could be jammed together in the same way, and yet still be somehow cool and distant, each with the others. Civilians seemed to be soft and cuddly, and of course nature took its course as I was pressed against the young woman and the tram swayed and my erection hurt in my tight Number One pants. I must have been going red in the face and wanting to apologize to the young woman, who was pretty, but demure looking. Inside the tram now, with the windows shut against the pouring rain outside, it was hot and stuffy. We bucked and swayed and grinded along the unlit streets even as the air-raid 'Warning' sirens wailed. No one showed any alarm. By now civilians seemed to be becoming accustomed to air-raid alarms, and they knew that a percentage of them were false alarms, and that even if they were real alarms the chances of being hit were very slight, and anyway if you were hit you would know very little about it—and suddenly the young lady turned and hustled, bustled her way round until she was facing me. I could smell her scent and feel her breasts and thighs hard against me as the tram swayed and jerked. Then she smiled up at me as *she hung her handbag on the bulge of my erection.* As she did so she pushed me away slightly and stared down at her bag swinging there, all without anyone else, I believed, being in the slightest aware of what she was doing.

I was so shocked that I stared at her wide-eyed for a full minute, and then avoided her laughing eyes. She reached up and whispered, against the tram-car racket, 'Give us a kiss, Jack, while I touch your collar for luck!'

Of course in the mess I'd heard of similar things happen-ing, but I had always imagined that they were figments of matelots' imaginations. I hardly knew what to do. I'd never kissed a stranger lass before, much less one who had suspended her handbag from the top of my dick. Then in a flash I thought of what my shipmates would say if they could see me now, and I put my arm around her waist—I was surprised how firm it was—and planted a quick kiss on her lips. It was over in a second. As I pulled back half the tramload of people laughed and cheered. The nearest ones, the men, reached over through the packed shoulders and heads and patted my back. Other women, some young, some older, reached over, too, to touch my blue collar for luck. I felt half-relieved that my erection had gone down, what with the embarrassment and all, and half like a spoiled pet. I wanted to get off the tram as fast as I could. I started to make my way to the conductor's platform, all the while half-grinning at the bold lass and at the same time muttering excuses for treading on people's toes, but they all laughed back at me, until I stumbled finally on to the rear platform and scanned the gun-flashes in the sky as the tram came to a halt.

'We don't go any further, lad,' said the conductor, an elderly man of about sixty. 'Not while t' raid's on. Jerry can see t' flashes when t' conductin' rods pass t' junctions on t' wires above. If tha's in a horry tha'd better 'op off 'ere and walk t' rest o' t' way.'

'Aye,' said a man's voice behind me. 'We don't want Jerry to see the flashes, do we? There's been enough flashing already tonight.'

I stepped off the tram and walked on up Rochdale Road towards Harpurhey, about a mile, through the rain, under the sky-wide flashes of the anti-aircraft guns and the fire-glares on the horizon. I still had my little case and the bottle of beer, and the main bombing seemed to be towards the south of the city, towards the big industrial estate at Trafford Park. Harpurhey was on the northern side of town, with only cotton mills around. Surely Jerry wouldn't be interested in destroying them, I asked myself as I traipsed along.

There was very little traffic, except for a few Civil Defence people and policemen on bicycles, and not many pedestrians, either. The policemen and air-raid wardens flashed their dim handlamps on me as I passed along the blacked-out streets. The few cars that did pass showed lights only from very narrow slits in black masks over their headlights. They were mostly Civil Defence vans and fire engines, with a few military trucks.

Some way up the road from where the tram had stopped, in a district where streets of mean-looking little terraced houses, rows and rows of them, led off the main road, the rain thinned out and the clouds above started to clear. 'That's bad, Jack, that bloody sky clearing . . . G'night!' called a bobby as he passed me on his bike and shone his torch briefly over me. He'd seen my round hat.

As I came to a particularly dark corner and watched out sharply for any traffic in the dark, a soft voice hailed me from a doorway. 'Eh . . . Jack!' It was a young woman's voice.

'Hello, hello,' I said to myself. I had seen a few whores hanging around in Piccadilly as I'd waited for the tram, but I hadn't thought I would encounter any this far out of town. I turned. She was close to me now. A car passed and a dim glimmer shone over her. She was pretty and shapely and about the same age as the lass in the tram, say nineteen.

I was flustered for a moment, not knowing what to reply. Then finally I blurted, 'Which way to Conran Street, love?'

'It's up the road, about half a mile. It slants off to the right, Jack,' she replied. She had the same dialect, as far as I could tell, as the people at the tramstop. I won't try to reproduce it here, so as to make the events more clear.

'Thanks, love,' said I, and turned to go on my way. I was not at all sure now that she was a whore. She certainly didn't look like one, if a lad of almost seventeen can tell how one should look. I started off and she hailed me again. 'Just a minute, Jack.'

I stopped and turned towards her again. She looked somehow small and defenceless and beautiful yet pitiable in the glare of the gun-flashes. 'What is it, love?'

'Can I talk to you a minute?' She said this quite calmly.

'What is it? I'm broke.' Then I immediately felt a bit foolish.

'No, I don't want your money, love,' she said. 'I want you to stay with me for a bit . . .'

'What . . . ? Are you afraid? I wouldn't worry about the raid. It all seems to be dropping on the other side of town,' I said, to comfort her as best I could. I liked her. She somehow made me feel older than I was. She made me feel as old as I felt.

'Can I walk with you up the road?' she asked me.

'Of course. I'm on my way home. Been to sea . . .' I trailed off. Women didn't understand things like the Andrew and hard discipline and strain and fear and death and destruction, I thought. Naturally I thought that; what did I know about women?

'I know,' she said. 'There's something about you, even though you're still a young lad . . .'

'I'm eighteen,' I lied.

She turned and looked at me. She had blonde hair and blue eyes and was pretty by any standard. She frowned slightly, 'Are you? I thought you were older than that.'

'That's the travelling,' I said. 'Been up all night last night on the bloody train, see love?'

We were silent as we walked for a few minutes, and the 'All clear' siren undulated near by. The rain had stopped, too.

Suddenly the lass turned to me and grabbed my arm. She

143

squeezed it hard and she felt friendly. Then she said, 'Jack, will you . . ?' she hesitated.

'What, love?'

'Will you . . . make love to me?'

I stopped still in my tracks and stared at her. She had tears in her eyes. 'What . . . ?'

'But . . .' I was nonplussed for a few moments as I stared at her. She gazed at me straight in the eyes. She couldn't be lying, I thought to myself. 'But where shall we go?' I blurted.

'There's an air-raid shelter down a street I know, only no one's around at night, so it'll be all right,' she replied.

She took my arm, more gently now, and walked me towards a dark street, at the end of which sat a squat brick, concrete-roofed air-raid shelter. It was very dark inside the shelter. I lit a match so we could find our way on to one of the upper wooden-slatted beds inside, in the musty air, out of the wind, away from the far off wail of yet another siren warning, the grumbling rumbling thumps, a little later, of death and destruction raining down outside, in the city. Soon there was no more raid, and no more war and no more Andrew and no more grey seas and wind and rain . . . and death. Soon there were flowers floating on the ocean under a blue sky, and the sound of surf on a far-off beach . . .

'Thanks, love,' was one of the last things she said to me as we parted at five o'clock in the morning, just as the 'All-clear' siren blew. We never met again, so far as I know, and yet I never forgot her. I did forget the bottle of Tetley's Ale, though. When I ran back for it to the shelter, it was gone.

It was 6.00 a.m. when I reached the little house where Aunt Lowri lived and where Mam and Angharad were lodged. They were not expecting me—on my pay there was not enough to send telegrams, and a letter would have taken ages, then, if it arrived at all. Telephones were things, ashore, which film stars used to talk to each other in the never-never land which we sometimes glimpsed whenever a film was shown on board—about twice a month.

Aunt Lowri's was a little house in the middle of a row of them all joined on to one another and all exactly alike. At the front were two windows, one above the other, and the house was all of fifteen feet wide. It didn't surprise me. It looked right for Uncle John, and narrow enough for his outlook.

There was a flurry of excitement from Aunt Lowri—her face painted and powdered even at 6.00 a.m.—and Angharad, but Mam never did show much emotion. She was calm as she told me I'd missed my Dad by only two days. It was the only chance I'd had to see him since 1938, and I would never have the chance again, although I didn't realize it of course at the time.

Angharad, the moment she saw me, exclaimed that I was a grown up man now. I wondered to myself if the episode in the air-raid shelter, only a couple of hours before, showed all that much. It didn't occur to me that there might be other reasons for my suddenly looking like a man to Angharad. In my sleep, I still saw the men falling from *Cameroon* being swept away in the boiling seas.

9. Close Encounters

Now you'll take the paint pot,
And I'll take the paint brush,
We'll paint the fuckin' ship's side together;
When Jimmy comes along we will sing our little song;
Thank Christ we didn't join for ever!

'We'll paint the ship's side', sung to the tune of 'Loch Lomond'.
For more lowly ratings in HM ships, many of the routine jobs
were of sickening drudgery. Polishing brasswork, scrubbing
decks, cleaning paintwork, cleaning boilers; but painting the
ship's side was a never ending chore in harbour. In winter, it took
some beating for boring monotony—thousands of square yards of
dull, flat grey paint.

Aunt Lowri agreed to let the Andrew dump me on her for a
week. My food-rationing coupons were of the same value as a
civilian allowance for the same period though that was small
enough, as I saw when my aunt and Angharad brought back
the shopping the day after I arrived. An ounce of butter, an
ounce or two of tea, a few ounces of sugar, and enough meat
per person to perhaps cover two fingers . . . which was fair
enough, as Aunt Lowri admitted, if everyone got the same,
except that everyone knew that 'the toffs were scoffing as
much as they wanted in the posh restaurants in town'; at the
Midland Hotel and Frascati's. If anyone had enough money

they could get practically anything they wanted on the black market, too . . .'

The next time they shopped I went with them. It was a marvel to see how some little shopkeepers were lording it now that they could choose whether or not to serve people. Things like cigarettes and sweets were 'under the counter', and a customer might get it or not—it depended on whether or not the shopkeeper liked his or her face. Wartime shopping in Britain was a revelation as to how certain people make capital out of shortages. It gave me a lifelong aversion to small shops and when I eventually entered my first supermarket much later I was elated that now small shopkeepers would at last get what had been coming to them.

As Prof said, when we discussed this on board *Eclectic*; 'Yes, they're all fascists. All small shopkeepers are, and especially tobacconists. Them and waiters in restaurants. All of them, with no exceptions. Right-wing Mosley-faced bastards. It's because they produce nothing. All they do is handle stuff and put their bloody bite on to the price. They're limpets, barnacles on the hull of society. Bloody Post Office owners [many small Post Offices in Britain were and still are owned privately], tobacconists and waiters. You watch, if Hitler takes over, that lot'll be the first to creep and crawl to the Jerries. It's inevitable. Post Office owners and tobacconists because they place themselves, they think, in a position of power between the magnates and the workers, and waiters because they crawl to a few arrogant bastards, and take on some of their arrogance. They know all about the "high and mighty", and they spend their lives—most of them—imagining that because they've served some bloody film star who's never done anything except pretend to be someone else, or factory boss, that they too, are high and mighty—and what are they really, Taff?'

'Well, Post-Office keepers and waiters, I suppose, Prof.'

'Bull. They're bloodsuckers. They handle and fetch and carry, and they produce not one thing that is of any use to anyone. They are what the French call *fonctionnaires*, *bourgeoisie*; in plain English, parasites. You watch, one day a Post Office keeper's offspring will seize power and then we'll have a little Hitler all of our own, and to hell with the workers!'

He was partly right, of course. I have often since wondered at how the very worst tyrants have sprung from the ranks of the *bourgeoisie*—Hitler, Mussolini, Stalin, Gadaffi, Peron, Amin—the list goes on and on. Offhand I can't think of one who had ever worked with his hands for a living. If, as Prof told me first, Marx wrote that 'religion is the opiate of the masses', then Prof also taught me that violent revolution is the opiate of the middle class, and the scourge of modern times, and he was right; forty-two years ago, he was dead correct.

At Aunt Lowri's, another revelation, now with Uncle John to explain things, was how many men of military age had managed to avoid the draft by wangling jobs in 'reserved occupations' and in the auxiliary fire service. At least that was Uncle John's view. I couldn't see how aircraft could be made, or ships built, or fires fought, if there were not enough men and women to do it, and the youngsters and old people couldn't do it.

That leave I rose mostly about nine—late by any standard. The women, of course, fussed over me but they didn't ask me much about what I'd been doing in the navy. Mostly it was the men neighbours who asked about that, and I told them I'd been on a convoy and that it had been 'a bit rough'. Mam was full of what Dad had talked about; how he was bound for the Far East, to ship regularly between Singapore and Hong Kong. She would, she said, 'feel much safer for him, know-ing he was out of the way of the war.' I agreed with her. There was small likelihood of Jerry submarines getting all the way out there in a hurry or easily. Dad had a contract for three years as Skipper and he intended, said Mam, to retire home after that, and buy a smallholding, perhaps.

Angharad was now fifteen and she had filled out nicely in the way that girls do. She seemed to have survived the change from a small hamlet in West Wales to one of the inner suburbs of a great city reasonably well. She was on the lookout for a job so as to help Mam out, along with my allotment, while Dad's send-home money was saved. She could go into a cotton mill, of course, but neither she nor Mam fancied that. Many of the cotton-mill lasses still wore black shawls and clogs, and looked very hard worked. Angharad thought she could get a better situation in Lewis's, the big department store in the centre of Manchester, playing the piano in the music department. She was a good player, of course, coming from West Wales, and naturally she could sing like a bird. Most Welshwomen do, thank God.

I accompanied her on a tram to Lewis's to see the manager of the music department. I felt very clumsy and out of place in my matelot's Number One rig. The lasses working in the store mostly smiled, and I got a sly wink from more than one. Angharad got the job—there were about a dozen applicants, and the rest were not all that good—but I suspect that she got it as much for her ability as for the fact that the manager, a large, bald fat man of around forty-five, fancied me as much as he did her music. He certainly made more fuss over me than he did her and asked me all kinds of questions, such as when was I going to bring my sailor friends along? I told him next week, to hear Angharad. It was a lie, of course, but in a good cause.

Back on the tram home, Angharad asked me why I'd said that. 'You know very well you'll be gone back to sea?'

I thought there were tears in her eyes. She thought the

world of me. 'Well, *chwaergen* (little sister) Angharad, you got the bloody job, didn't you? It kept him happy. I was only being nice to him. He knows sailors don't buy pianos.'

Other than the trip to Lewis's I didn't go out much, except to a local municipal park when it was fine and sunny, which was rare. I was still too young to be served beer in a pub. One evening I went with Mam and Angharad to the flicks and I recall we saw *The Maltese Falcon*.

Air raids, during the week I was on leave, were always at night, except for one very daring raid on the Avro aircraft factory at Chadderton, only a mile or two away from Harpurhey, and of which I got a ringside view. The factory was where the new Avro Lancaster bombers were being built, so it was a prime Nazi target.

It was Uncle John's day off. Uncle John and I went together to see his relatives (including a surprisingly attractive niece) at their house, quite near the Avro place, which was over a fence at the far end of a dead-end road. As we walked towards the bus stop, Uncle John dashed into a pub for a quick pint. I had to stay outside and wait for him. Moments later a single plane, a long-range Messerschmitt, I think, came hurtling down from a cloud—there was no siren warning—and fired away like crazy with cannons directly at the factory. I was so astonished that all I could do there was stand and stare like an idiot for a second or two, then make a run for shelter, daft as it was, behind a small butcher's van pulled up in front of the pub. As I hurled myself behind the van, I could plainly see, out of the corner of my eye, scarlet and red streaks of the tracer cannon as they flashed past. I had seen that there were women and kids on the road—there was little traffic in that street in those days—and suddenly there was nobody. It was miraculous how everyone dived out of the way so fast. It reminded me of how matelots disappeared whenever the Captain approached on his rounds on board.

Jerry zoomed right down the road and then pulled up in a steep climb before he reached the factory airspace, disappeared into a cloud again and was gone. A minute or two later, as Uncle John emerged from the pub wiping his moustache, the sirens blew the 'Warning'. Everyone ignored it, the bus came along and we went home.

I didn't think much of it at the time, but since then, it came home to me just how risky life was in those days; at sea or on leave, there was little let-up from the outside chance of sudden death. At the time, I suppose because of my age, it seemed the most natural thing in the world. I had hardly known anything else for the past two years. My childhood on the coast of Wales seemed like another world—another life altogether. And yet there had been something different about this experience. I had been in a raid at sea in *Second Apprentice* on a convoy off the Kent coast, and I had spent hours closed up for action stations in *Cameroon*. Then it seemed a 'fair' proposition, to be attacked out of the sky (as if there were some all-knowing referee up there to supervise 'fairness'), but this—two hundred miles from the South Coast, a hundred from the East Coast—this seemed somehow unfair —'ungentlemanly'—a sneak attack by desperadoes. It was only much later that I realized how clever and daring the Jerry pilot had been to have penetrated British air defences that far, evidently without detection. But at the time—in early 1941—it was not easy to wish Jerry pilots any kind of luck.

As with all leaves from the Andrew—especially with the few wartime ones—this one was over all too soon. A week passed like two days. I spent the last night in Aunt Lowri's house pressing my own uniform, much to Mam's disapproval. In the tiny crowded living room we had the radio on, of course, tuned to the BBC, and as I ironed my black silk neckerchief into its seven layers, we heard the announcer speaking about the German invasions of Greece and Yugoslavia. He was using the usual phrases to disguise disasters —'Allied troops have made strategic withdrawals'—that kind of thing. It looked very bad all around. Britain was still, after ten months since the start of the Blitzkrieg, all alone against Germany and Italy, except for the Commonwealth. Those kin-countries had only just started, as far as we could tell, to get into gear for war. Mussolini's invasion of Greece, the year before, had evidently been bogged down. Now the Nazis were driving down through the Balkans. Soon the Mediterranean would be an Axis sea, the Suez Canal would be taken, and then the road to India and the East would be open to Hitler. For the British Army, until now, it had been one retreat after another. Since the fall of France the RAF had managed to prevent the Luftwaffe from totally seizing control of the skies over Britain.

But out in the Atlantic the battle—the life and death struggle for the sea lifeline of Britain—had never, not for one day, ceased since the first day of the war twenty-three months before. By the spring of 1941, the Andrew had been fighting for seven hundred days and nights without let. Even when the U-boats and surface raiders were not in any particular area the patrols went on, and on, and on.

Both Mam and Angharad came to the station with me, against my inclination. I was never one for good-byes. I think they realized that, and they left me in the main hall after I collected my kit from the left-luggage office. They say that misery loves company, but in my case I have always preferred to be alone when my fortunes are at the ebb, which they always were whenever I returned to the waiting embrace of the Andrew. I watched them wend their way through the crowd of people parting—matelots, pongos and erks and their wives and parties and families—in the huge gloomy hall, lit only by small red bulbs here and there as a blackout measure. As I stood a-tiptoe to see them pass out into the drizzle of Manchester, I didn't know it was the last time I would ever see my mother. If I had I would have stepped out with them, regardless of what the Andrew might have done to me. I wasn't brave nor was I callous—I was ignorant; and that, in many instances, is about the same thing.

'Come on, mate!' said a voice behind me. It was Prof, and we turned and lugged our gear towards the train for Scotland.

The train journey from Manchester to Northern Scotland seemed interminable. It took all that first night and most of the next day to get to Edinburgh, where matelots heading further north had to wait over another night, on the cold windy station platform, for another train to Inverness, about one hundred miles as the crow flies. But we were not crows and this was wartime Scotland, so we covered about two hundred miles in twists and turns and diversions, and another day and night in long waits in remote sidings under lonely, heather-covered hillsides. By the time we reached the jetty from whence the MFV left for Scapa Flow, we were practically starving.

On the whole, the attitude among the matelots going to Scapa Flow was cheerful. We were off to join the Home Fleet at a base far beyond Nazi bombing range, where we would be reasonably safe, at least from the sky threat; there was fighter cover at Scapa, so the grapevine said. It was true that a U-boat had managed to penetrate right into Scapa Flow very early in the war, and had sunk the battleship *Royal Oak*, but the chances of Jerry getting past the defences twice were very slim. It looked, said one stripey in our compartment, like we were going to 'sit it out in the 'ome Fleet, wiv the battlewagons, and wait for Jerry to come out wiv 'is big ships, see . . . just like in the last bloomin' lot. Blimey, they was anchored in the Flow practically all the war.'

' 'Cept for the Dogger Bank and Jutland battles,' added his winger, a one-badge killick stoker. 'Then they got clobbered all right.'

The stripey scoffed. 'Yes, okay, but Jerry had a much bigger surface fleet then. What's he got now? Fucking hell, you can count 'em on one hand. Let's see, the *Deutschland*—'

'She's called the *Lützow* now,' chimed in Prof. The killick and his mate the stripey stared at Prof silently for a second, then he went on '—All right, the bleedin' *Lützow* then . . . and *Prinz Eugen* and *Schlesien*, *Scharnhorst* and *Gneisenau*, *Scheer* and *Tirpitz* and *Hipper*, say nine ships that count as 'eavy stuff and what 'ave we got?' Stripey started counting on his fingers, one by one, as he reeled off the names of the British battleships and cruisers in the Home Fleet. '*Kay Gee Five*, *Nelson*, *Prince of Wales*.'

'She's the fastest of all our battlewagons,' piped in the killick stoker, 'the *Pee Oh Doubleyew*.'

Stripey went on, striking the tip of a finger each time he counted off one of our battleships: 'The *Ramillies*, *Rodney*, *Royal Sovereign*, *Malaya*.'

The killick stoker butted in again. 'No, the *Malaya*'s not up here, Wiggy. She's at Gib, along with *Resolution*, and *Valiant* and *Warspite* are both at Alex. I know, I just come off the *Valiant*, and *Duke of York* ain't finished yet.'

'All right,' said Stripey, 'but we still got six battlewagons against Jerry's one new and two old, and let's see, how many cruisers?' He started counting again on his fingers as he and the killick stoker called off the names of the British cruisers in the Home Fleet. '*Dorsetshire*—she's just moved up, I know 'cos I've got a mate on board, and he owes me two tots —*Devonshire*, *Norfolk*, *Sheffield*, *Suffolk*, then we've got the *Aurora*, though the buzz is she's off to the Med, and *Belfast*, but she's still in dock. That still makes six battlewagons and five cruisers, against Jerry's four battlewagons and five cruisers. I reckon that's pretty good odds.'

Prof said, 'Yes, but you're not taking into account their age. Some of Jerry's ships are new. Some of ours are pretty ancient by now, built in the last lot.'

'Well, there's that,' said the Stripey. Then he cheered up again, 'But so are two of their battlewagons, and their cruisers are armed lighter than our battlewagons . . .'

'And there's one of theirs you've forgotten,' continued Prof.

'What's that?' said the Stripey.

'*Bismarck.*'

'Well, I never included the ship we're joining in the tally, either,' he replied.

'Which one's she?' asked Prof.

'*Hood*,' replied the two-badger. 'HMS Bloody *Hood* and she's our ace in the hole. Best of the lot, biggest of the lot, she is, pride of the frigging fleet. She can take on anybody. Right, mate?' He nudged his killick stoker oppo. The killick started from his doze. 'Eh, wazzat?'

'I'm talking about our top ship, the *Hood*,' said the Stripey. 'I'm just telling these ODs she's the best of the bunch!'

'Let's hope so,' replied the killick. 'Let's bleedin' hope so.' He closed his eyes again, and murmured, 'Just so long as she sees me through this bloody war I couldn't give a fuck!'

'Eight fifteen-inch guns,' recounted the Stripey, 'fourteen four-inchers and four tubes, besides Christ knows how many pom-poms and Oerlikon guns. Any Jerry that even thinks of tackling her is going to get fucking spattered!'

'Let's hope the Jimmy ain't a bloody bastard!' prayed a seaman killick, evidently in the same draft as the Stripey and the killick stoker.

The drift of that conversation was then lost as the train

carriage was plunged into the utter darkness of a tunnel yet again, and the draft for HMS *Hood* broke into the 'Lobster Song'. I did wonder, as we rushed out into misty light at the end of the tunnel, what our chances of surviving the war would be. Prof and me in little destroyers, with their small guns and thin armour-plating, compared to these lucky blokes going to the indestructible, unsinkable *Hood*.

I asked Prof about German matelots. He said that they were probably just like ours—all they really wanted was booze, food, and fanny, most likely, and there was a train somewhere in Europe where the same conversation was taking place, probably, only with them the boot was on the other foot, and they thought, most likely, that *Lützow* and *Bismarck*, too, were unsinkable—and they most likely were, just like the *Hood*.

As the train pulled into Inverness, I asked Prof, 'Well, what will happen when the battlewagons meet? Ours and theirs?'

'Oh, they'll just grind up us poor bastards in destroyers,' he replied, screwing up his lips, 'and then steam back home, "flags a-flutter".'

That cheered me up almost as much as did the Scottish rain, as we made our way, about two hundred of us, down to the port and the waiting MFV.

The long arm of naval discipline reached even to Inverness jetty. As I tramped through the dock gate, with my kit-bag and hammock over my shoulder my cap had inadvertently slid back a half inch up my brow. From inside the dark and gloomy, but warm and dry gatehouse came a voice, loud and fierce, 'That man *there*! Get your hat on STRAIGHT!'

I glanced over at the gatehouse door. Sure enough, inside, in the shadows, I caught a glimpse of the white belt of a crusher. They even got this far from the barracks. I grounded my heavy load and pushed my hat back down into its correct

angle—horizontal, and hoped that the effort would somehow
help to win the war. He was the furthest-north crusher ever to
bark at me.

I recall little of the sea-trip from Inverness to Scapa Flow,
except that the weather was roughish and conditions on board
the jam-packed MFV—a wooden boat only about seventy
feet long—were miserable, and that it took, I think, two days
and nights. It seemed that the usual route for drafts to go to
and from Scapa was through Wick, but evidently there was so
much traffic that the Admiralty had decided to open a second
ferry-route, from Inverness, even though it was a good fifty
miles further away from Scapa. But I do recall that as the
MFV rolled and rumbled through the Pentland Firth, between Duncansby Head on the mainland, and South Ronald-
shay, the sun broke out in mid-morning and made the sea
blue and the land green, and made the war seem far, far away.
It reminded me of my days in the sailing barge *Second
Apprentice* and of when I used to go fishing as a lad—I
thought of myself as a grown man, now—with Goodness
Gracious Jenkins in his little boat *Gwenhyfar* in the blue seas
of Tremadoc Bay. Wales was what I was homesick for—not
Manchester. That city wasn't my home; that was only where
Mam and Angharad were lodging. Then I felt better, because
I felt that I hadn't left home—I had come home, to the blue
seas and the driving clouds and the green hills of the islands.
Then the MFV turned around a headland and the great grey
bulks of the ships of His Majesty's Fleet hove into view. I felt,
as I stared at each one of their great powerful grey hulls while
we passed in the sunshine, that if coming home meant that
the Andrew had to be there—so be it. It was our seas which
they defended, these ships, and it was my job—my duty—to
help them.

If anyone considers that it was not likely that a lad of

seventeen could feel so, then they do not know my generation of young matelots—and especially those who had been bred and brought up in the coastal trade of Britain. Anyone who thinks it unlikely that I thought so, and believed so, and would willingly have laid down my life to prove it, makes exactly the same mistake as did the Nazi leaders—perhaps not the Admirals, but certainly the rest. And we felt this way even despite what the iron first of the Andrew could do to us; did do to us.

PART THREE

The Hammers

When Britain first, at Heaven's command,
Arose from out the azure main,
Arose, arose, arose from out the azure main—
This was the charter,
The charter of the land—
And guardian angels sang this strain:

Rule Britannia!
Britannia, rule the waves
Britons never, never never shall be slaves!

'Rule Britannia'. This famous anthem was written at the command of the Prince of Wales. It first appeared in a masque entitled *Alfred* which was performed in 1740. The words are by the poet James Thompson, and the music by Dr Arne.

10. *Brides of Death*

Good morning, Mister fisherman,
What do you have for me,
Have you a lobster
You can sell to me?

Chorus: Singing roll tiddly oh,
Shit or bust,
Never let your bollocks,
Dangle in the dust!

'Yes,' says he, 'I've got three,
And the biggest of the bastards
I will sell to thee.'

I took the lobster home,
Couldn't find a dish,
I put the fuckin' lobster
Where the missus used to piss.

The missus went to piss,
Heaved and gave a grunt,
And there was the lobster
Swinging from her cunt.

Now I grabbed a squee-gee,
The missus grabbed a broom,
We chased the fuckin' lobster
All around the room.

The Hammers

I hit it on the head,
I hit it on the side,
I hit that fuckin' lobster,
'Til the bastard died!

The moral of my story,
Simply is this,
Always have a *shufti*
Before you have a piss!

That's the end of my story,
There isn't any more.
There's an apple up me asshole,
And you can have the core!

'The Lobster Song', a lower deckers' song. I once heard it sung by
the ex-Able Seaman who claimed his picture is the one on the
Player's cigarettes advertisement. The picture was taken in 1885
and he had been paid three pence a day for life by the John Player
Tobacco Co. At the time I met him, in Portland, Dorset, he was
ninety-two years old and still working.

HMS *Eclectic* was one of the first real destroyers ever built.
Before her class had been laid down, there had been built
swarms of smaller ships around the 1900s, known as torpedo
boats. Then, the military mind being what it was (and is),
they had to have 'torpedo boat destroyers', which is where
the name for this class of ships originated. During the First
World War the Allied torpedo boat destroyers had proved
themselves in convoy duties, against German and Austrian
U-boats, but they had been too small and frail to stay at sea
long enough. So My Lords Commissioners of the Admiralty

ordered bigger and bigger destroyers, until they had ships that could stay out on patrol for weeks at a time—and yet were still, at a push, expendable. By the time *Eclectic*'s turn to slide off the stocks had come around, the first war was about over, but My Lords had glimpsed—but only just— the fact that the average matelot was not merely a breathing automaton, but also an animal, and to some extent a human being, too.

The seamen's mess deck was still crammed and noisy, but it had hooks built into the deckhead, so that at sea loose gear could be hung up out of the way, to prevent it sliding around the deck. Also, in the ship's heads, the toilet cubicles (for the Chiefs and POs only, of course) had little doors in them, to hide everything but Chiefy's head and shoulders and lower legs and feet. That, to my readers ashore in the 1980s, may not seem much in the way of comfort, but to the twenty men or so who used the two cubicles, it meant a great deal. At least Chiefy could now shit behind a small door. It was just about the only privacy anyone on the lower deck ever had on board, and so it was treasured—and savoured, as the eternal line of waiting Chiefs and POs testified. For Jack it was still into one of sit-open cubicles, shit and out, fast.

Apart from the heads, though, our other living quarters for the sixty-odd seamen and communications ratings who lived forward in the ship, were a space about twenty-eight feet wide and twenty long, and about ten feet high in between the lower of the mass of overhead pipes.

There were three mess decks—ours, the biggest, up for- ward in the fo'c'sle; the stokers', on the next deck down, just forward of the Number One boiler room, and a small mess deck aft for the after guard—about twenty seamen, stewards, sick berth tiffies and other odds and sods.

We had other comforts in life, too. For instance, just above our mess deck, in the poky passage to the upper deck, and to one side of it, there was a canteen, actually a metal box, run by the civvy NAAFI manager, the 'damager' as we called him. That was about six feet long by seven feet, or less, wide. It was usually crammed with a stock of nutty and DFs and 'goffers'. There we bought our cigarette and sweet rations, and such little luxuries, when we could afford them, as soap and toothpaste.

Apart from that, the only other space where we could relax was on the upper deck in harbour when it was fine (which was rare). But even then, in the Fleet harbours such as Scapa, and Hvalfiord in Iceland, bullshit was the order of the day, and after working hours we had to be in night clothing—blue serge uniform without light blue collar—to go topsides. Most of us stayed below, in any old rig, but with comparative ease of mind. That was one of the reasons for the high incidence of TB in the Home Fleet—Jack was reluctant to get into the fresh air, because of such stupid bullshit as having to be in formal uniform, and with not one non-Andrew observer, apart from the seabirds, for miles and miles around.

The forward seamen's mess deck was divided into two —one table for the port watch, one for the starboard. Each mess consisted then of thirty-one men and boys. They had a space about fifteen feet by twenty in which to eat, sling their hammocks, read, write letters and relax.

Yet despite the cramped conditions, uniforms and gear were expected still to be kept in pristine condition for Sunday divisions and Captain's Rounds—and they were. Somehow Jack transcended the vile conditions and kept himself clean and smart—at least in harbour. At sea it was a different story. Then the bullshit was more muted.

The forward seamen's mess was right up in the fore part of the ship. At sea, anyone who has seen the pitching and tossing and rolling of a destroyer in any kind of weather except the calmest, knows what that means. It was like being on a switchback car running wild. But added to that was yet another discomfort. In those days of riveted ships, the side plates generally leaked, especially in any kind of sea, with the ship working and bashing around, and the side plates up forward, on the bow. So as soon as *Eclectic* worked in a sea, the mess deck was anything up to six inches in salt water —cold North Atlantic water—which sloshed back and forth and from side to side as the ship hammered and rolled, and it was almost as much as the fire-and-bilge pumps could do to keep up with the incoming water. With the water splashing around that meant that no one could sleep on the deck, or, in very rough conditions, even on the benches or the seat lockers, as he would be continually splashed with cold sea-water, yet Jimmy enforced the order that no hammocks could be slung until 8.00 p.m., so men who had been on the night watches were forced to doze sitting until then, with their feet hunched up clear of the cold water streams.

Destroyers on active service were known for their less rigid discipline and friendlier relations between the lower deck and the officers, and in some instances—most instances—this was true, but there was usually a bastard in the duff. In *Eclectic* it was the Jimmy.

It seems that our Jimmy had made a professional mistake at some time in his naval career—the buzz was he had been on watch in a cruiser as OOW when she hit a sandbank. That was in the piping days of peace and, of course, Jimmy had been passed over for promotion. He was a big man, saturnine and handsome in a bitter way, and he was in his mid-thirties and still a lieutenant—and he took it out on any one of us matelots who gave him the slightest excuse. We got to know him well on the trip from Scapa to Iceland.

'The fucking Yak' was the common matelot's sobriquet for this Jimmy. 'Yak this, yak that, the pusser-faced bastard never stops yakking,' one OD complained, after Jimmy had just dished him out a week's Number Tens for not being in the formal rig of the day at 10.00 p.m. in a stormy night at sea. Jimmy had been a big-ships man all his life, too, and that did not improve matters. He tried to impose battleship bullshit on men who were living in conditions which would make a Devil's Islander blanch.

I do believe that the only reason that there was not a mutiny on board *Eclectic* was because of the 'gentlemanliness' of the other officers, and because the Chiefs and POs, as a whole, tried their best to put themselves between us matelots and Jimmy. This put a considerable strain on the bosun and the cox'n, for example, and they were two of the most harassed men I ever saw at sea. It was quite obvious, from the moment I stepped on board *Eclectic*, that the crew considered the Jimmy to be a far greater enemy than any German. As I recount the outward events of what occurred during my first trip in *Eclectic*, bear in mind the bitterness, almost amounting to hatred, which existed between Jimmy and the matelots of the ship, as well as practically everybody else, including, I suspect, most, if not all, the officers, although there was no way for me to know that, of course. Even on a ship as small and crowded as ours the officers somehow managed to live in a world of their own.

Imagine a world of metal and asbestos, of clanging doors, humming machinery, oil smells, sudden pipes and shouted orders on a tinny loudspeaker system, cooking odours, and dozens of men crowding in the messes and the darkened passageways, and at action stations all day and all night, four hours on, four off, each day and every day, at the ack-ack guns, the torpedo tubes, the main guns, the engines, the boilers, the Asdic compartment, the radar cubby-hole half way up the skinny mast, in the cold North Atlantic weather and all the men eager and willing to do their level best for their mates, for the Skipper, for the ship, and for their family and country—and parading through the midst of this, appearing instantly and almost always unexpectedly, his shoulders crouched, as if to spring, his dark eyes glowering from under black eyebrows, his hands clasped behind his back, Dartmouth style, a martinet who should by rights have been on a parade ground, or in a mental hospital.

I had been on board about three weeks when we sailed from Hvalfiord in Iceland. I had the morning watch—from 4.00 a.m., and at first it was not light enough to see much until about seven, but later I saw that we, along with other destroyers—about a dozen, I think—were escorting practically the whole of the Home Fleet out to sea, in a northerly direction, as I could tell from the rising sun to starboard over the land. There was the Eighteenth Cruiser Squadron, *Norfolk* and *Suffolk*, each with three funnels, horizontal on top and somehow stately. Beyond them, a picture of power and arrogance and majesty, were *Prince of Wales*, way out on the horizon with her attendant destroyers, and *Hood* much closer to us, no more than two miles away. I could plainly see the people drawn up on *Hood*'s quarter deck. Someone told me it was her marine band parading for morning colours. Then it was my watch below and I was 'cook' that day, so I saw little more of *Hood* or the other ships when I was not at action stations. It was a strange feeling, though, whenever I saw the two battleships. It was a feeling of utter safety, of pride, of tremendous invincibility. I know we all felt it, at least the matelots with me down aft. 'Fucking sight better than convoy duties,' said one hooky. 'At least with those two bloody great buggers around there won't be no trouble!'

A few days later we were up in the Denmark Strait, north of Iceland, still in company with the other destroyers. The two cruisers and *Hood* and *Pee Oh Doubleyew*. I remember it was a couple of weeks after my seventeenth birthday on 8 May, so it must have been about the 22 May, and we were closed up to action stations. There was generally nothing unusual about this: there were continual reports, some true, some false, of U-boat or plane sightings. But somehow this one was different. Word got around among the matelots that even Jimmy was smiling. There must be something big on. A while later the buzz was that the German ships *Bismarck* and *Prinz Eugen* were not in their usual hideaway in Bergensund, Norway. They might be out on the loose. They might be trying to force their way through the Denmark Strait out into the Atlantic Ocean.

Looking back, it was amazing how very often the rumours —'buzzes', which flew around the lower deck somehow instantaneously—were such highly accurate synopses of what the situation was within the higher echelons of command on board or even outside the ship. Buzzes seemed to generate on their own, like busy fruitflies in a ripe melon. One minute no one knew what was happening, who was involved, or where the ship might be heading. The next minute the buzz flew and it was all clear to the tacticians and strategists, of which each mess boasted a fair number. Still looking back, it is clear to me that some of these 'buzz-kings' would have been far better employed in the War Room of the Admiralty. In many cases their prognosis turned out to be far more accurate than those promulgated by My Lords Commissioners at such great expense to Britain, and later to her Allies.

'Tovey's going to bait the bastards with *Norfolk* and *Suffolk*,' said one lower deck strategist. 'Then, when Jerry bites the hook, he's going to trap them between the battlewagons and the ice-cap, and once they're there they have to fight or surrender. There's no other way out for them. They can't steam north, and they can't go back to Norway or Adolf'll have the Jerry admirals' guts for garters.'

The next day, in the evening, one of the sparkers who had

been to the mess earlier for sippers for his birthday and was a
bit garrulous, told us that *Suffolk* was tracking *Bismarck* on
her radar and that *Norfolk* was joining her. Shortly after, I
closed up to the after Oerlikons.

It was a typical Arctic summer night—half day and half
gloaming, and the sea was not too rough. We all stared to the
north, beyond *Hood* and *Prince of Wales*, but we could see
nothing beyond the empty horizon until an hour had passed.
Then there were smudges of smoke, the merest traces.
Nothing else. We steamed on and on. Obviously *Hood*—she
was nearest to us—had closed up for action. There was not
a soul out of her ship's company of fourteen hundred to be
seen on deck, even at the distance, which was about four
miles.

Suddenly, our engines speeded up to a howl and *Eclectic*
began to race and pound through the seas. Something was
up. We looked in silence at the two battleships, and all
around the horizon ahead. As we all stared around, someone
in our port ack-ack crew shouted, 'There they are!' I turned
and stared hard, and sure enough, way out on the northern
rim of the sea were two grey shadows, which materialized
soon into ships, and even though they were like toys at that
distance, they were like immense toys. At first they looked,
too, like innocent toys. My eyes went back to *Hood*, which
had also speeded up and was now about seven or eight miles
from us. Suddenly there was the flash of her morse signal-
lamp. A killick nearby said, in a low voice, but above the roar
of our machinery below, '*Hood*'s ordered "Open Fire"!'

Almost immediately a great flash of orange fire and black
smoke belched from *Hood*'s forward guns. Then, a moment
or two later, *Prince of Wales* belched forth smoke and flame
from her forward guns, too. We could see it all plainly, as if
we were observers at some great water-sport arena or some
hellish tennis match. We all turned to watch if the enemy

ships showed any sign of being hit. There was none. Still they
steamed, grey and low on the horizon, in stately procession.
Someone said he had seen a spout of water just astern of the
first German ship. 'That must have been *Bismarck*,' everyone
agreed. Even as we watched, as if hypnotized, the first
German ship opened fire, with the same kind of flame and
smoke belching from her as from the British ships, except it
was from all her guns. We could actually hear, even at this
distance from the enemy, the shells roaring through the sky,
British and German. They sounded like trains in tunnels
heard from a long way off along the lines.

The killick of our watch, Dusty Miller, was half way up the
little aftermast to get a better view; the subby in charge was
too excited to curb him. He shouted to us, 'Jerry's just fired!'
as if we needed telling with that strange roar in our ears.
Prince of Wales was now firing her forward main armament,
the fifteen-inch monsters, like mad, salvo after salvo, and at
the same time Nazi shells were causing sea-quakes off her
stern where they were falling short. Over both British battleships the German HE shells exploded with bright shocks,
like lightning.

'Cor, fucking hell, they must be getting a real dose of
bleeding shrapnel!' shouted Dusty, even more excitedly.
'Just look at those buggers bursting over *Pee Oh Doubleyew*!'
Then suddenly he gasped very loudly—we were all, I think,
still gazing at *Prince of Wales* and the bursting lightning
flashes above her—Dusty gasped not words, just a long
moan, very low. As he slid down the aftermast I turned round
to look at *Hood*. I stared and stared. I could not believe my
eyes. There was a clearing pall of smoke hanging over the
sea—I could see right underneath it clear to the horizon
—and *Hood* was no longer there! There was only smoke . . .

Everything else was practically the same. The destroyer
under my feet was racing through and over the self-same seas,

and *Prince of Wales* was still firing salvo after salvo, which seemed to be still falling short of the German ships, which were still racing across the horizon ahead, and I was on the self-same deck I had been standing on only moments before, holding on to the self-same Oerlikon gun, and the faces around me were all the same, but everything had changed —for ever.

Hood was gone. A great symbol of British naval might and power, all the more than 42,000 tons of steel, and the eight fifteen-inch guns (imagine, guns with muzzle-openings fifteen inches wide!) and the fourteen four-inchers and the four tubes—and the Stripey on the train, and the killick stoker, his mate, and the killick seamen who had been with them—and over 1,400 men . . . *Eclectic* was racing now, over the scene of *Hood*'s disappearance. One thousand, four hundred and eighteen men—and we got closer and our ship slowed down, and we stared and stared like madmen, everyone on deck now, because there were *no men*. Only three survivors, we were later told, were picked up by one of our destroyers. They were an officer and two ratings.

It seemed in the days after, as we raced south escorting the ships chasing *Bismarck*, much more than merely a ship and fourteen hundred lives had been lost. It was as if the whole of the old Andrew had been sunk, to most of the men on board *Eclectic*, and especially the older regulars, and evidently the officers, too. They had, some of them, served in *Hood* between the wars. They had cruised all around the world, they had 'shown the flag' all over the globe, and the matelots had strung coloured lights around her quarter deck in exotic tropical ports for officers' dances, and they had seen her, proud and arrogant, in a thousand different anchorages off five different continents. She stood for all that the old Andrew had been. She was the symbol of all that had been gained at and handed down from Trafalgar. Now there seemed, to hear some of the old matelots talk, to be only odds and sods left.

'The bastards. The bloody fucking bastards!' moaned one three-badger. 'Now they've bloody well done it, by Christ!' That seemed to be the prevailing sentiment on the mess decks for the next couple of days, until it was clear that the Admiralty also wanted blood—any blood—just so long as it was blood, and especially German and preferably from *Panzerschiff Bismarck*. Even on board a small ship, in the lowly seamen's mess, it seemed as if a mother wolf was howling in her lair for the guts of a predator who had killed her young. The order reached right through the Fleet, from the Commander in Chief to the lowest of the low—the Boy Seamen. It was posted, it was quoted day and night, it was passed by radio, by Tannoy and by word of mouth. It was an order of three words only, loud and clear. It was an order direct from the First Sea Lord, or seemingly through him, from God: '*Sink the Bismarck!*'

Bismarck had to be destroyed, whatever the cost. We knew, even at the after Oerlikon guns in *Eclectic*, that eleven of our convoys were out in the Atlantic Ocean—say three to four *hundred* merchant ships—and the only protection they had from the Nazi battleship with her immense firepower were older, smaller cruisers and a few frigates and destroyers. If *Bismarck* got loose among that lot it would be the biggest sea-slaughter ever in the history of nations; the war, for Britain, would be lost—it was that simple. She had to be sunk.

By now we also knew—from buzzes and from post-mortems by some of the older hands, who were no dummies where naval warfare was concerned—that the reasons *Hood* was sunk so quickly, so tragically, was that she had no proper upper-deck protection from dropping shells, that *Prince of Wales* had a forward gun turret out of commission, that she still had dockyard mateys on board to fix it, and that the two British ships had steamed headlong, bows first, at the Germans, and so masked their after guns, depriving themselves of half their firepower, while Jerry had been able to blast away with all of his. In other words *Hood* had let the Nazis 'cross her T', and that spelled disaster to any sailor worth his salt in those days—and not only disaster, but plain stupidity.

What we didn't know at first—what we couldn't know, of course—was that *Prince of Wales* had scored hits on *Bismarck* and damaged one of her fuel tanks. Later, our sparky killick told us that a minesweeper, forlornly searching for *Hood* survivors, had sighted an oil trace heading south, and it might be from *Bismarck*.

Later that night, as we raced after *King George V*, heading south—always south as we could tell from the moon's path above us—a report came through that *Bismarck*, like a wounded animal had snapped back at the cruisers *Norfolk* and *Suffolk*, who were tailing her at about twenty miles or so out of sight and just within range of her fifteen-inch guns, but no damage had been done.

All this time it was difficult for us to see outside the ship, except when the clouds cleared the moon. All this time our ship plunged on through the sea-darkness broken only now and again by rapid flashes from the signal-lamp in *King George V* which had now joined us and was away to our starboard aft horizon. The whole time, until *Bismarck* finally went down, we were closed up at action stations for four hours on, four hours off, in the stuffy, madly-moving forward mess. The fresh-water supplies on board were cut off except to the galley, so as to save water in case we should be at sea for weeks, and food was cold, served direct from the galley. Chocolate (kye) was served each watch to the gun crews, and I supposed that the stokers, in their separate, brilliantly lit, warm world down below had their share, too.

Every now and again, from the after housing, we saw puffs of bright red sparks stream into the night sky from our after funnel. Stokes was changing sprayers, and we envied him, warm and independent and out of the way of the officers.

Around us, on that first watch, ships came and disappeared quickly under the patches of moonlight, and sometimes we saw the ghostly grey shadow of a ship, or the phosphorescent wake of her screws at full speed on the rim of the dark world.

As we watch keepers wended our way down below at midnight, along the pitch-dark upper deck and through the screen door into the red-lit port passageway, a voice called out over the crowd of men 'They hit the bastard!'

'Who did, skurs?' shouted a chorus of tired men coming off and going on watch.

A bearded bridge messenger, in his dufflecoat, appeared in Number One boiler room flat. 'The fucking Fleet Air Arm!' There was a profound silence, except for the humming of machinery and the distant grinding of the engines and propellers. '*Vicky*'s come up!'

We all knew he meant HMS *Victorious*, our biggest carrier.

Down in the mess a killick seaman said, 'So they've brought *Vicky* up, eh? Christ, they must be bloody chokka —she's been in Gib for ages—well, in Force H. They must be pissed off being up here with the real bloody war, eh?'

Contact with *Bismarck* was lost then for three days. Three days of steaming, closed up all the while at action stations, at full speed round and round the *Kay Gee Five* and all heading full pelt to no one knew where . . . south . . . south and then south-east . . . south-east. Then Jack knew all right what was happening. *Bismarck* was trying to sneak away to safety in France, and the chances were she would make it. The buzz was humming all through the ship by the second night after *Norfolk* and *Suffolk* had lost her on their radars.

'She's making for Brest,' said Prof. 'She's got to be.

Look . . .' he pointed with a grubby finger at the mess's
school atlas, left there by some soul the commission before,
evidently; no one knew who it belonged to. 'Look,' said Prof,
'even a bloody idiot would see that Brest is her best bet, with
all this load of iron out looking for her.'

'But what if she isn't?' asked a young AB on our same
watch. 'What if she turns around and clobbers *Kay Gee
Five*—and then the bloody *Pee Oh Doubleyew* and then,
Jesus Christ, the bleeding *Rodney*? Just like she did the
Hood.'

There was a silence for a minute or so, then the AB went on:
'Cor, fuck the Pope of Gozo! If that bastard got loose among
our lot and sank the fucking battlewagons there'd be nothing
—*nothing at all*, to stop her steaming around at thirty knots
and making sodding mincemeat out of the whole fucking
Andrew . . . and then her mates *Prinz Eugen* and *Scharnhorst* and the rest of 'em come out and mash up the merch.
Use your loaf, Prof. If *Bismarck* ain't going back to fucking
France . . . if she's laying in wait, it means the end of the
sodding war, cocker, and it's you and me for the oggin, old
mate. Either that or a fucking salt mine!'

Prof looked up at him and screwed up his lips. 'Can't stand
salt,' he said. 'I'm allergic.'

It was the first time I'd ever heard the word 'allergic'.
Whenever I hear it or read it now I think of Prof and the battle
for the *Bismarck*.

So it went on for three days, with the ship hammering
through the seas and everyone aboard wondering how long
the oil fuel would last out, and the food and the fresh
water—and then, as I helped the other duty-cook clear up
after breakfast in a mess full of exhausted men, a great cheer
came roaring down the hatch. At first it was difficult to
understand what the garbled row was about. Then it came

175

out: *Ark Royal*'s Swordfish planes had scored two certain hits on *Bismarck* and the Nazi ship was now steaming round and round in circles, evidently not able to steer.

Everyone was excited. The relief in the foul mess-deck air was tangible. It could have been cut out, wrapped up and sent home to Mum. It was a happy thing. It was a tremendous thing. The Nazi bastard was now in Tovey's clutches. We could catch up with her—even meet her—the word later was that she was steaming slowly west. We could surround her, trap her, out of range of most Nazi planes, and kill her: *King George V*, *Rodney*, *Victorious*, *Ark Royal*, and *Dorsetshire*, *Suffolk* and *Norfolk* and two flotillas of destroyers.

All that night the Fourth Destroyer Flotilla, led by our Captain Vian, attacked with torpedoes and, starting at eight in the morning, choosing his time, Tovey moved in for the kill.

King George V and *Rodney* blasted the wounded *Bismarck* with their fifteen-inch shells for two hours, coming ever closer and closer to her. By 9.00 a.m. we could plainly see her from our after gun station, a black, smoking blob on the grey horizon, eight or nine miles away, still firing, but slower now. By 10.00 a.m. she was only six miles away, alive with blood-red flames and firing with only one turret, it seemed. Certainly the red flashes and the cloud of smoke indicated that. By ten-fifteen she was clearly on fire all through her hull and there were no more big gun flashes, although some of her smaller guns were still firing.

By now *Eclectic* had moved away from *King George V* and towards the cruiser *Dorsetshire*, which was obviously steaming in closer to the flaming Nazi ship for the coup-de-grâce. As we roared toward *Dorsetshire* we watched as she fired torpedoes—I think there were three salvos of six each, at *Bismarck*—and after a few minutes the great German ship suddenly but gracefully heeled over, further and further, until she looked like a gigantic dying whale, with men. scrambling over her upside-down bottom, and finally, with a great gasp which many of my oppos said they had heard, she sank, and there was now silence, from where we were positioned, except for the roar of the machinery down below, the clicking of our radar and the whistle of the wind.

Suddenly there was nothing left to fight except the hidden menace of lurking U-boats, always with us. *Dorsetshire* moved in towards the spot where the *Bismarck* had gone down. It was too far for me to see, but a bridge lookout AB later told me that there were hundreds of Germans in the grey seas, but the seas were cold and rough in that wind, there would be small chance of more than a few dozen being picked up; hypothermia would soon finish the rest—and there was always the threat of U-boats. Here, among this gathered British strength, they could have mighty pickings—the best day in the history of U-boat warfare—if we stopped long to seek survivors.

The skipper even spoke to us on the Tannoy. 'Well done, chaps,' he said. Just that.

'Fuck 'em. They took their chances, they paid the price. Just like the lads on the *Hood*,' one two-badge killick said, and he spoke, I think, for all the matelots, then.

I may be imagining it, but it seems to me that in the few days after *Hood* went down and before the *Bismarck* was sunk, the Andrew took a spiritual beating, and in part the old Andrew seemed to have died. But a new one began to flex its legs, at least in smaller ships, and there was a lot less stress on bullshit after the battle for the *Bismarck*. But that is purely my view of the matter. As far as Jack was concerned the demise of the old Andrew was no loss at all. It was the loss of the men that hurt. I was never to be in a British warship during all the years to follow without meeting someone who lost someone, a relative or an oppo, on board *Hood*.

The Hammers

In the days that followed the sinking of *Bismarck* Jimmy was in his element. The Skipper was too preoccupied with the strain of keeping up with the chase after *Bismarck* to constrain him much, and he had a field-day. By the time the chase was over, and we were back in Hvalfiord, he had a good half of the seamen on board under punishment of one kind or the other, and usually on such trite charges as being out of the rig of the day, or being a minute late for a muster, or failing to salute the quarter deck.

But, even though we knew we had not won the war, we were certain we probably would not lose it to Nazi sea surface power now. It was a great step forward.

'One down, only eight to go,' said Prof.

11. A Visit from Winston

When the HMS *Hood* went down in the deep,
That was the news made two thousand mothers weep,
She was fighting for England her country, so proud,
Now she's below, with the sea for a shroud,
But the boys are in heaven above; the boys are in heaven above.

Then came the day, one day in May,
When the *Norfolk*, the *Suffolk*,
With their guns in full play,
The *Ark Royal*, the *King George*, the *Rodney* as well,
They found the Nazi bastard and sent her to hell,
But the boys are in heaven above; the boys are in heaven above.

'The *Hood*', sung to the tune of 'Silent Night, Holy Night'. This
song was never very popular. However, I did hear it sung on
different ships at different times widely apart. It is ironic that it has
a German melody.

It is incorrect, as the officers were continually telling us, to say
'*the* HMS . . .', which is probably why we matelots always said it
that way.

All that summer of 1941 it was one convoy after another
—usually escorting one out to Newfoundland or Nova Scotia
and bringing one back from there to the dispersal area, which
was a rough strip of ocean known as the Minch, off Western

Scotland. *Eclectic* was based in Lough Foyle, in Ulster, to the north of Londonderry. She usually stayed there only long enough to take on fresh water, fuel and supplies; then it was off again to patrol the ocean to the north-west of Ireland, or to join a convoy escort and head out and back across the Atlantic.

On very rare occasions the ship was at Lough Foyle long enough for each watch to be given an evening's shore leave in the city of Derry. There we could, if we had the money, stuff ourselves on good Irish steak smuggled across the border from the Republic, and perhaps buy a pair of nylon stockings for our lasses back home. Otherwise it was a few beers, to celebrate our God-sent relief from the crowded mess decks, smelly passageways and dreary, cold action stations on board. The difference between the crowd of men who went for shore leave on the MFV which ferried us to the city and the mob of bleary-eyed stragglers who returned, had to be seen to be believed.

On one occasion Prof and I went ashore with Sunny Beame, an AB who fancied himself with the ladies. Sunny dragged me to a dance held at the city hall. The place was crowded with servicemen—mostly matelots from the destroyer flotillas up in the Lough—it was one time when two or three flotillas were all in port at once. Then there were squaddies and erks, too, but they were mostly with girls already. Despite the number of servicemen, they were still outnumbered by the lasses about three to one. There was a beer bar and I had a couple of Guinnesses to give me the courage to try my hand at a waltz or a foxtrot, and I clearly recall that every one of the dozen or so girls I asked to dance, politely of course, replied by first asking me if I was a Catholic. Of course the first couple of times, being still wary of Church of England services on board, standing around for hours on a cold, rainy after deck, I said yes automatically, without thinking. Then the girls—some very pretty—shook their heads and turned away. I soon twigged that move, of course, and at first after that I was so dyed-in-the-wool Protestant that alongside of me John Calvin would have seemed like he was up for election to Pope. That seemed to please the girls, and I took a few home. Over a few runs ashore in Derry I found I wasn't scoring at all with the Protestant girls, so I changed my tack and stuck to being Catholic. I didn't get many dances, but by God the few girls that did accept my invitation made up for the lack of hopping around, once we were by their homes in the Bogside. The conversation nearly always turned to religion—but it is a poor matelot who can't field that particular play. A few nods of the head are worth the return of a world of affection and a mite of warmth and tenderness.

I was still under-age. Officially I was supposed to be back on board by seven in the evening, but the POs in *Eclectic*, and most of the officers, too, turned a blind eye when I got back at eleven—and sometimes later if the MFV had to call at other ships first to drop their libertymen off. Then it was back down to the mess, quietly, to dodge around in the red light under the gently swaying hammocks of sleeping messmates, to my own pit, already slung for me by an oppo in the port watch. I would do the same for him when he went ashore. What a feeling, to be woken at six the next morning—sometimes earlier—by the Tannoy blaring 'Hands to stations for leaving harbour!' and with the memories of the sights and sounds of the pub and the lasses and the civilians ashore, and the grass and trees and the hills and city wall of Derry all still in my mind, to blunder my way up on deck. There we stood to attention on the after deck, just forward of the flapping White Ensign, abaft 'x' gun, between the depth-charge racks, and watched it all slip away, the city grey or blue in the distance, and the green hills of Ireland, of Donegal, so close that it seemed I could have touched them if I'd been allowed to reach out my hand. We all knew that, all the time, we were being watched from the Republican shores, and reported to the Nazis in Kiel, but that was worth the steak and butter which came to Derry from over the border, at least if we didn't think about it too much.

We had several Irish matelots from the Republic on board, and although their proudest boast was of how easy it would be for them to have it away on their toes across the border, none of them ever did desert, and I never heard of any from other ships doing it, either.

The action, during the summer of 1941, was hot, frequent and strong. Almost every day now we had U-boat alarms, and bashed this way and that, for hours on end, in the rain and sunshine, calms and storms, pinging away with the Asdic set in the hopes of a contact. It was during this period that the idea got around that if the 'ping' was broadcast over the ship's Tannoy, someone in the ship's complement might hear something that had perhaps been missed by the Asdic operator in his little dog-kennel below the bridge; some slight change in tone or duration of that appalling 'piiiinnnng! . . . piiinnng!' which persisted day and night, day and night, for a whole escort duty. Even as I write this I can hear it: 'Piiinnng!' But after a while we almost became accustomed to the continual racket, which could be heard everywhere —even down in the engine room over the roar of the turbines.

On several occasions the tone of the ping changed and we knew we had a 'sighting' of a U-boat. At that time ships still worked on their own against the U-boats: it was search and search, until either the contact was lost—and this might happen if there was a wily German skipper to play cat and mouse with—or we went in to a depth-charge attack. It was fascinating, watching down from the after deckhouse, as the depth-charge crews rolled the drums of high explosives down the rails and the Chief Torps pulled a lanyard and sent them tumbling, one slowly after the other, into the sea. Then we waited, in seeming silence, for the underwater flash and crump and the pillar of spray which shot up, sometimes far higher than our own mast. Then we wondered what Jerry was thinking and feeling, the German matelots we were trying to kill, and somehow I felt a bit sorry for them.

Twice we scored the longed-for oil gush, a big black blob of liquid spewing up through the grey waters from the spot where the depth charge had done its job. There was nothing else.

'Poor bastards,' said one voice at the guns.

'Sod 'em. Serve 'em right. The buggers bombed my street last month,' said another. But mostly there was little rejoicing among the lower deck. We left that to the officers. They had more room, and infinitely more amenities for it, than did we. All I remember thinking on such occasions was what Prof had commented the first time: 'Well, one more down—only another five hundred to go!'

It was strange how there developed a friendly feeling between us matelots on an escort and some of the Johns on the merchant ships which we were escorting, even though the chances were one in a million that we would ever meet face to face. We would see the crewmen on some ships, as they went about their business, and after a while we could recognize them as old acquaintances, and give them nicknames. I remember one young man, tall and thin, on a Norwegian tanker we accompanied for a few days in the north-west approaches. We had been close enough for us to see his face. He was blond, and wore an incipient beard such as young men do. Prof named him 'Skywegian Bumfluff' and made up stories, as we stared over the guns at his ship wallowing along. Prof told me how Bumfluff's mother had been scared by a village postman wearing skis, and that's why Bumfluff had such big feet—things like that. Several nights later, in the dark, Bumfluff's ship exploded in a blaze of golden light that lit up the whole convoy. There were no survivors. There rarely were from tankers.

The ships of the convoys were of many nationalities, as many of the merchant ships of the invaded countries had avoided capture by the Nazis. After a while we could almost always tell which ship was of which nationality—there was a certain air about them. The Dutch, of course, and the Norwegians, were always clean and very businesslike-looking, so that we *knew* that their captain's logs were slap bang up to date to the last minute. We spent hours inventing personalities for the ships, as we kept a sharp lookout for Blohm and Voss spotter planes. These—generally there was only one at a time, circling round and round, low on the far horizon, out of reach of any of our guns—were becoming more and more frequently our steady company. Only when they approached a bit close did we bang away at them, and once or twice other ships scored and brought the Nazi voyeur down in flames or smoke.

But in those earlier days, before the war in the Arctic rose to a crescendo, the spotter planes were not all that frequent. When they were around, they made the watches pass quicker. Some of them, after they had circled around us dozens of times, flew off into the clouds. It was a bit like losing sight of an old friend.

When the sun came out—which wasn't often in those latitudes—it brightened up the whole convoy. Of course there were none of the gaily painted funnels of peacetime, the vermilions and yellows and blues of the house colours, but there was a *sense* of colour about those ships, in their sober North Atlantic colours of black and grey, and all the varied colours of the ensigns—the red of Britain; red, white and blue of Holland, Norway and France; and the blue and white

of Greece: these were continual reminders that we did have
Allies, even if their countries had been overrun, and of how
lucky we were that ours hadn't, and wasn't going to be,
either, if we could help it.

Then there were the names of the ships on their sterns
which we could read as we steamed under their wakes:
Cornbrake, Highland Lassie, Karen Helgerson and the Greek
ones that only Prof could read, with their funny letters. On
they plodded, at no more than about ten knots most of the
time, row upon row of ships—sometimes as many as eighty
—sometimes as few as a dozen. Going west they were mostly
riding high and light, but coming back east, to Britain, they
were low in the water, with their decks loaded with tanks and
trucks, crates and fighter plane fuselages. Then they were
prize targets, sitting like ducks in a row for Jerry to take
potshots at whenever and wherever he wished to.

On we went, day and night after day and night, over calm
blue waters at times, but more often amid the rearing grey of
the Atlantic, which at times was rough enough to make even
My Lords Commissioners of the Admiralty appear to be,
after all, *friendly*, at least to a limited extent.

Then, on stormy days, after struggling along the open deck
and up the ladder to the after guns, I dreamed of what I was a
part—the sky and the sea and the beating tides—and it
seemed to me even then that no flowers would spring from
my clay, that I would always be made of grey-painted steel
and that my blood would one day be issued out at eleven in
the forenoon from a rum-tub enscrolled 'The King, God
Bless Him'. No flowers—but what would spring from me
would be, like the sea, strange and cool and yet already within
all, and of all, and offer sippers all round, for it is always the
birthday of the world on every day that you wake and every
night that you lie down in your pit to sleep. That's the way
lads feel at seventeen.

Even now I feel *Eclectic* shuddering as she bows and kneels
to the solid water, and feel the ocean's anger through my
thighs, and I wait, I pause; and spray stings and zithers over
the after deck as I crouch and shield Nobby's binoculars
—he's gone to the heads, ostensibly, but actually is slyly
sliding down below—it is tot time. Down she plunges and
the foam noisily leaps aside, wild and free, marbling the sea,
and the moving, ever moving sea hesitates, for one split
second, to let us see the calmness from whence springs an
irresistible life-force. Above, in the lines of the main mast,
the wind sings a song of untrammelled liberty and I wonder if
it sounds the same to the Nazi navigator in the conning tower
of the nearest U-boat? Liberty from what? From life? From
death? Then, and then, *Eclectic* starts to lift, and her hull,
seemingly as free as the petrels that cry around her tattered
ensign above my head, like a live body, answers to the swell.
And all the while I remember—I must remember—that her
and our purpose is to murder German boys my own age, who
feel as I do, who dream, too, because if we don't murder them
they are going to murder us.

Prof comes puffing up the ladder. He has a small fanny of
steaming hot tea. 'Got this from Twinkle-toes,' he says.
'She's screaming blue murder in the sick bay. The cox'n
wants her to muster all her gear this afternoon for a check on
stores. He's down there now. She slid this out for Nobby, but
he's away on his toes for his tot—so we might as well get
stuck in, Taff.'

I tasted the hot, sweet tea and thanked God that someone
on board thought of the after gun's crew freezing in this cold
wind and sleet. Of all the men in positions to pass any kind of
small comforts on to the matelots—the supply ratings, the
cooks, the officers' stewards, the sick berth attendants—only
the homosexuals, generally, did it. The rest, mainly, waxed
fat and rich on what we did without. This was true in

practically every navy ship in which I served. And before anyone jumps to any conclusions, it was not for any kind of sexual favours—it couldn't be, in ships where not one waking moment was ever spent in privacy and where the minimal punishment for such activity was seven years hard labour and no appeal. It was because they, unlike most of the others, recognized the *humanity* in us matelots, and if they wanted us to know that they recognized it, and were willing to demonstrate it, who were we to deny them that? It was a strange, unspoken thing, but it was there.

Young newcomers on board might scoff at the queer matelots, and try to do a big butch number about it, but that didn't last long. The moment they started trouble with someone just because he was homosexual (there were very few of them) then the troublemaker himself was in deep trouble, especially with the older hands, who understood such matters far better than ODs. 'Gay liberation' is nothing new. It was more the rule in Royal Navy ships, and especially in the cruisers downwards. It was almost impossible to be a bastard with someone whom you had seen at action stations, in the cold and misery and later in the blood and guts, up to his elbows in it, and yet still maintaining a strong, cheerful humour.

There were extremely few homosexuals among the seamen, stokers, torpedomen and such—I can remember only half a dozen in all the ships in which we served. They were most likely to be found among the stores and supply ratings, and officers' stewards. I don't believe that was because they were so much attracted to that kind of work, as that it gave them a niche on board where they could make themselves indispensable, and so be to some extent protected, even from the more pusser-faced officers and chiefs. It is hard to criticize someone who lifts his little finger when he drinks his tot, as long as he's keeping the lads well fed, or bandaging the wounded. Our lives might depend on him at any minute.

That summer (oh the boys of summer!) *Eclectic* was part of a convoy escort out to Nova Scotia. We left the convoy at sea, without calling in for re-storing, and joined a homeward-bound convoy off Newfoundland. It was a huge convoy; an immense array of ships of all kinds, tramps, tankers, passenger ships, troopers crammed with Canadian soldiers. I counted the ships and remember there were over seventy. It was after the Nazi invasion of Russia, and a great part of the stores being carried by the inward convoy were, we were told, destined eventually for the aid of that country. 'That is,' said the Jimmy with a smirk, 'if the Germans don't take Murmansk and Archangel first.'

The German invasion of the Soviet Union in June, 1941 had taken almost everyone on the mess deck but Prof, by surprise. Out came the school atlas and the immensity of half of Asia and Europe was inspected almost as minutely as it probably was back in London at the War Room.

Shiner Wright pronounced the majority verdict about the situation. 'Well, if that bloody lot caves in, we'll really be in the shit!'

Prof maintained that Uncle Joe would fall back until he was good and ready to really hammer the Nazi armies and destroy them with the aid of the Russian winter.

When we were allocated our convoy-guard duty, we took our place as rear escort, steaming across and back over the wakes of the armada, on the lookout for U-boats which were themselves watching for straggling prey. Suddenly, out of a mist bank, a great battleship came steaming straight for us. At first several of the newcomers on board thought she might be the *Scharnhorst* or the *Gneisenau* and almost shit themselves where they stood. The older hands (and that included me by now, though not in age) laughed. We recognized her all right—HMS *Prince of Wales*—majestic, huge and grey and powerful, her guns all of forty feet above the sea. Who can ever forget the sight of a battleship at full speed? She came straight at the convoy and steamed right up the centre lane at a good twenty-five knots to the merchant ships' eight. As we watched and wondered, all of a sudden, and from all the ships as she steamed past them, a mighty roar rent the sky—the sound of men cheering. Roar after roar, ship after ship, and the *Pee Oh Doubleyew*, advancing at speed with her White Ensign shining in the sun . . . And then someone on the bridge hailed down, 'It's *Winston!*' It was typical of Churchill. He always seems to have been a showman.

Of course we all—most of us, anyway—lifted ourselves to give the old bugger a wave of our tin-hats, for luck. Only a Geordie AB, whose old man was a miner, sat tight and scowled. We could understand that. Churchill was generally detested among miners, because of his actions against them to break the General Strike in 1926.

Even Prof raised himself up on his Oerlikon seat and waved a dirty canvas flash-proof glove. 'Well, you've got to give it to the old sod; only he would jeopardize the whole convoy by steaming around at full speed in a forty-thousand-ton battleship right slap bang through it!'

But Prof should have waited a while. When *Prince of Wales* was clear ahead of the convoy she turned and steamed away to port, then headed once more for us and the rear of the armada. Once again, as dusk fell, she and Winston Churchill steamed at full speed right through it. By then there was no one, not even the Geordie, who was not shouting like mad and waving the V-sign at the chubby figure in a duffle coat on *Prince of Wales*' flag deck.

Nobby commented, as the battleship raced away from the setting sun into the gloom ahead of the convoy and its forward escort, 'Yes, you've got to give it to him. I'll bet if it was bloody morning he'd steam up and down the convoy all fucking day!'

And I'll still bet that Nobby was right, too.

Years later I learned that Churchill had, on that occasion, been to meet President Roosevelt on board the USS *Augusta*, in Placentia Bay, Newfoundland. It had been their 'Atlantic Charter' meeting, their last meeting before the USA was attacked by Japan, and war was declared on them by Hitler.

12. Ups and Downs

Verse: Now my ma and my pa were an elegant pair,
(mincing) And they often went out for a trot,
         Our pony and trap were the best in the land,
         We paid five bob for the lot,
         Now we've travelled this wide world both near and far,
         And if you don't know us, then here's who we are . . .

Chorus: We're the twins, ting-a-ling-a-ling,
(sturdily, We're the twins, ting-a-ling-a-long,
in gruff Me and St John and you know where we're from;
voice)   When we're out,
         There's no doubt,
         We're so much alike in our figure and height;
         As we stroll along and the bands they play,
         On the beach and on the prom;
         People say when we pass, 'There go two feeds of ass!'
         Me and my brother St John!

         In the summertime up to the seaside we stroll;
         Where the air is so free and so bracing,
         And then after dark we chase boys in the park,
         They hardly know which way we're facing!

'The Twins'. Surprisingly, or maybe not, there was very little
evident overt homosexuality in the ships in which I served.
Mention of the subject in Naval songs is rare. This is one of the few
exceptions. I have forgotten the subsequent verses of this ditty,
but what is here gives the flavour. It probably originates in the late
1800s.

All that late part of 1941 *Eclectic* hardly stopped steaming, and most of the time, it seemed to us matelots, she was steaming at full speed on the track of U-boats. Day and night, night and day, the deadly game went on, in good weather and in storm, in rain, hail, sleet and sunshine. It went on and on, until it seemed that we in our ship were but mere parts of her, as if her steel soul entered into ours, as one day followed the same as the next. The long, grinding monotony of the ship's routine was broken only by mad spurts of action firing at spotter planes, or watching, enraged and helpless, as yet another merchant ship was torpedoed and blew up in a great pall of smoke and flame. The sinkings were now so many —sometimes a good third of a convoy—that we were trying to inure ourselves against the always present, full tangibility of sudden and awful death which was flung at us almost every hour of the day and night at times.

By now there was little sympathy left for the German matelots in the U-boats. As ship after friendly ship was destroyed, and as their crews were killed or rescued—their chances of survival were about fifty-fifty—so our attitude to the enemy became more and more callous. By the end of November, when our chummy ship *Obdurate* scored a definite kill and we all watched the U-boat's jagged, torn upper hull shoot up through the surface, somehow foul-looking and obscene, and then immediately plunge again, to disappear in a welter of spray, we were all cheering like loonies. There were no survivors, even though three warships steamed slowly for an hour around the site of the killer's grave.

As we stared, sore-eyed, through the deepening gloaming on the lookout for bobbing heads, Nobby commented, 'If I get hold of one of those bastards and there's no pigs around, the sod is going straight over the side again.' Later, in the mess, swinging in my pit, I thought about that, and the full evil of war came home to me. Late 1941 was not the time for sentimentality, so I tried to hide my secret thoughts, and joined the others in their attitude of bloody-minded resentment against Jerry—at least while he was bodily out of sight and trying to kill us twenty-four hours daily.

We saw American naval ships rarely until about September. The first ones were US coastguard cutters on 'weather station' duty somewhere to the west of Ireland. They were kept brilliantly lit at night, with their white hulls gleaming, and looked like beacons of well-being and sanity in an otherwise bloody world. Then, later, we passed a US destroyer in broad daylight and everyone who was on her deck waved and cheered at us, while we blared 'Auld Lang Syne' over the Tannoy at them.

'They're after our bubbly,' said Shiner Wright. 'Yanks don't get no tot, see? Cor, stone the bloody crows, what a navy! No bloody bubbly! Might as well join the bleedin' Sally Army!'

'Reckon they'll join in the war, Shiner?' said Nobby.

'Bloody well have to if they want sippers from me,' grunted Shiner.

We watched as the American destroyer heaved and pounded past our own heaving, pounding ship. Somehow she looked less fancy than our destroyers. I stared at her for a while and then figured out what it was: she had no brasswork on deck, and everything was painted the same colour, yet she was efficient looking. Then I saw her name as she turned her stern to head north, away from us: USS *Kearny*.

About twenty miles astern of the *Kearny* another American destroyer steamed over the horizon, also heading north. She was carrying big crates on deck.

'That's their Coca-Cola supplies, see?' commented Shiner, as the ship showed her name: USS *Reuben James*.

'It must be fucking marvellous to be as safe as those Yanks are,' said someone.

When we arrived at the anchorage in Heflavik about a week later we were told that both the US ships had been sunk by U-boats off the south coast of Iceland. Most of *Kearny*'s crew were safe but there had been heavy loss of life to *Reuben James*.

The older hands discussed the turn of events in the mess. 'The bloody Yanks have to come in now,' said one.

'They'll wait until next year, to see if the Russkies are holding the Jerries,' said Prof. 'Then they'll step in and grab the pickings—what's left—before Joe does.'

A Geordie piped up, 'Well, then we might see some decent shooting, when they get the gangsters and the cowboys up against Jerry.' Most of our younger matelots had been weaned on Hollywood's presentation of America. It was not our fault.

'They've got washing machines on their ships,' said Shiner, pensively. 'I know, my mate Jock McTavish was over in Brooklyn Navy Yard last year. Reckons you can't move on their ships for grub and washing machines. If they come in I'll get them to do my dhobying when they're alongside.'

Everyone laughed at the idea of Shiner having his clothes washed by a machine in someone else's ship and little they guessed how correct Shiner was—except that it wouldn't be his dhobying, because he'd be dead by the time the American fleet finally appeared.

'Can't stand their Yankee fags, though,' reflected Shiner. 'It's like smoking old rope.' The Tannoy blared 'Hands to action stations!' and we knew, as we rushed for the mess deck ladder, that yet another U-boat's shark-shape had been picked up by our ever-watchful, ever-probing, ever-'piiinnnging!' Asdic set, and that we would be closed up at the guns again for another interminable wait in the wind and rain. How we envied the stokers going about their own, then to me, mysterious business, in clean overalls, down into the warm independence of their boiler rooms.

I often went down below to dry my dhobying, to hang it up on wire-lines alongside the boilers. Then, in the heat and roar of the boilers, I looked down through the iron gratings and saw Stokes calmly going about his business. The stoker POs were usually humane and friendly, with very little disciplinary bullshit about them. Often, if things were steady and quiet, the PO would be reading a cheap paperback under the forced draft fans, and his mate, the stoker, would be making cocoa or tea. They appeared to be completely isolated from the world we knew topsides, and the most comfortable ratings in the ship, with no officers to oversee them directly. They certainly seemed the most content, even though they and we knew that only a quarter of an inch of steel plate stood between them and sudden, excruciating death. If a torpedo struck a boiler room their chances of survival were about nil; the superheated steam escaping from the ruptured pipes would consume them as fast as flaming paper.

The stokers usually joshed the boy seamen, and called us 'Skin' and things like 'Wiggles' and 'Chubby Cheeks' and such, but both they and we knew very well that it was all a big joke. We knew that if we were ever in trouble ashore, perhaps with a fist-fight brewing, Stokes would be the first to our side, and woe betide anyone who so much as laid a finger on us. It was very much a big-and-little brother relationship.

All the time, as I studied the differences between the seamen and the stokers, I determined that if the opportunity arose I would transfer—but only when the war was over. The thought of being able to read a book sometimes when I was on watch was the overpowering factor in my decision. That and to be warm and reasonably dry most of the time. There was also the attraction of perhaps having some kind of trade when I finally left the Andrew. There was very little demand for a

The Hammers

good ack-ack gunner outside, but a stoker—well, he could find a job practically anywhere, and put himself in a niche where he might become indispensable, perhaps, to a school or a department store, and where he could earn his living and improve his own education at the same time. In the seaman branch that was practically impossible. Although matelots like Prof, who read serious books were tolerated, there was a certain embarrassment at the other dabtoes' reactions, at least until he had been in the mess for a longish spell and had become accepted as eccentric but harmless. There was also the dreary drudge, if you were at all read, of having to continually prove that you were good at everything else, too. The main topics of conversation in the mess, apart from ship's business, were women, sports—especially soccer and boxing—booze and grippo-runs. It took a while—several weeks—for the two main factions in any mess—the 'Jacks' and the 'Square-eyes'—to come to terms and become accustomed to each faction's mental world. Yet it was done, and men came to cross the lines more and more, from one world—of dreams of action—to another, of dreams and ideas. Those few who could continually pass from one mental territory to the other, and transfer original ideas along with them, were the most successful and in many respects the most popular. Kipling hit the nail on the head in this matter when he wrote:

> Or being hated, don't give way to hating,
> And yet don't look too good, nor talk too wise.

I didn't know Kipling then. I'd seen his poem, 'If', posted up in the gym at HMS *Ganges*, but it hadn't meant much to me. I took it all with a grain of salt as yet another example of officer-inspired bullshit. I wasn't old enough then to know the difference between wheat and chaff, and had no idea how to sort them out in my own mind. Later, when Prof and I got round to reading such things as *The Odyssey* (!) he explained to me that the sailors who voyaged with Ulysses probably mainly talked of women, sport, booze and grippo-runs.

I think that was the first inkling I ever had of the importance of literature in forging the continuance of human history; of giving us a reflection to inspect, so that we might try to change ourselves for the better; of showing us a star by which to steer. By the time I was seventeen and a half I didn't merely want access to knowledge—I wanted it in my head. There's a world of difference between the two. The way to get it into my head was to read. The only way I could read enough would be to join the engineering branch. This is what I made up my mind to do, as soon as I got the chance, once the war was over.

There was another attraction down below, too. There, everything that was man-made had a rhythm, a perfection, it seemed to me, that aimed at the creation of something: of speed, of power, of fresh water, of electricity, of life for the ship. Topsides practically everything we handled was aimed at some form of destruction, at least wherever I was involved. Destruction by aggression or by consumption. So I came to learn of the paradox of modern society: the aggression to defend the dynamo—the dynamo to fuel the aggression.

In the long cold night watches, watching the black shadows of our merchant ships plodding on as we rushed back and forth ahead or astern or between them, with my duffle pulled up around my ears, trying to pierce the gloom with my watery eyes, I thought of these things. Also, I remembered the cool nights under sail on board *Second Apprentice*, and how, it seemed to me, that under sail there are no two opposing forces in the craft, only one single entity, all directed in the one aim: to consume least, to destroy least, and by the very act of shifting from one place to another to be creative; to take life from what is around the boat, and to impart life unto all about by her very presence. The knowledge of life *is* life.

We were at sea, escorting a convoy from Halifax to Iceland when the news of Pearl Harbor struck us. I don't recall any rejoicing or relief as far as we matelots were concerned, although I expect the officers had an extra glass or two of pink gin. The full import of what had occurred so far away did not strike home until a couple of days later, when an American tanker, which had until then been steaming alone somewhere, joined the convoy. There was short daylight in those days, in December. The American's flag, as she passed us on her way to take up station, was suddenly lit up by a thin beam of sunlight. There had been silence up to that moment—she was not a particularly handsome ship, dirty grey—but suddenly from the fo'c'sle break, outside the ship's galley, where the off-watch matelots gathered for fresh air, there was a loud cheer. In minutes this was taken up by all of us, and our Skipper ordered our ensign dipped to the Yankee tanker's salute with her siren, and we played 'Where have you been all the day, Billy Boy?' over the Tannoy, and the American crewmen waved back at us. So did their officers.

When we pulled out of Heflavik, about three weeks later, after the merchant ships had been sorted out for a convoy to Murmansk, about two days out, we met up with our first Soviet ship. She was a big sea-going tug, very dirty and shabby-looking. This was a great disappointment to Prof. We had been told that we would be meeting up with 'units of the Soviet Navy'. All the Lefties on board were in a state of high excitement, Prof among them, of course. When the Red Navy finally showed up their faces—all our faces—dropped a mile. The tug looked as if she had just sailed out of a coal-loading dock. She came very close to us to pass messages and take on food and medical supplies, and she was filthy. Her crew, too, were very unimpressive, and there was a sullen Soviet matelot standing guard on the tug's deck with a tommy gun the whole time she was close to us.

The Soviet matelots' uniforms all seemed to be of the same size, regardless of the size or shape of the wearer. Later we were to see them painting ship when they took over the battleship *Royal Sovereign* in Scapa Flow. They dipped their hands in the paintpots and smeared the paint on. It was incredible to us that they had no paint-brushes! It was incredible to us that in a navy from the workers' *Erewhon*, the matelots could be worse off than we were.

The Russian matelots looked so brow-beaten and scruffy that we couldn't help feeling sorry not only for them, but for the ship they were taking over, which had been one of the prides of the Andrew, a sister ship to *Revenge* and *Resolution*.

At the war's end she was supposed to be returned to us, but the buzz was that she was so incredibly neglected and in such a ruinous state that she was never taken back and ended up simply abandoned and scrapped.

There was an ensign dip from our Skipper in reply to the Soviet tug's dip, but we could see that there was little enthusiasm in our Skipper's gesture. Prof said he was married to a Russian emigré from the Revolution. It was one of those cases where I would have been surprised either way, if it had been true or not.

At first, as the Red Navy tug came close, the stokers on board, who were practically to a man all Labour supporters, and whose great hero was Uncle Joe Stalin, cheered and waved their fists at the tug; they got no response but sullen glares. It was difficult to see which glares were more sullen —those from the tug or those from our bridge. Then our cox'n slithered down the ladders from the bridge and ordered everyone down below. As they passed into the screen door and so into the fo'c'sle a little buff-stoker emerged from the engine room hatch, almost directly below my gun, and shouted out as loud as he could, 'Bing for king—Joe can't sing!'

That was the first time I ever heard that, although I was to hear it a hundred times, later, in the next three or four years. I have often wondered if that little stoker originated the slogan.

That first convoy to Murmansk was very bloody indeed. It passed, in the middle stretch—up what we later called 'Blood Alley'—around the North Cape of Norway. We had to pass quite close to Norway because of the Arctic pack ice to the north of us. This brought us well within range of the Luftwaffe bombers and fighters. At the same time the U-boats had only a narrow gap to watch—and watch they did, and their pickings were murderously high. Of the more than twenty-eight ships we had in convoy, I think only seventeen got through, although I may be wrong, because some ships took off alone and headed to Archangel, or at least so we were told.

The reception in Murmansk was not at all a 'hero's welcome'. It snowed practically the whole time we were there —thick, driving snow—so we could see little of what was going on ashore. Only officers were allowed ashore, and then only on duty. Now and again we saw the grey shapes of workers on the docksides, but they scarcely glanced at us. Among them were—we eventually recognized a slight difference in shape and gait—women. But they looked huge and tough in their bundled-up winter clothes. There was no sign from them that they were being looked at by men who had been deprived of female company for weeks. No slight signal, be it ever so hidden or delicate, that females gave off the world over in similar circumstances, and which is so very evident to any mariner who sees them, whether he knows it or not.

Ups and Downs

On the Murmansk runs there was nothing for us but ceaseless routine and the prospect of death. There never was, in the eight convoys there and back that I witnessed. Apart from a sense of incredulity at being still alive, wondering when our turn would come, there was only the noise and the cold, and the shells, the 'piiinnng!' the rough seas and sloshing water on the mess deck, and there was little but wild talk of women and booze and soccer. It was like being in a mobile madhouse traipsing slowly each time, each way, through a slurry of freezing death; an inferno of hellish smoke and flame. Grown men went steadily and fixedly insane before each other's eyes, and most of them managed to hide their madness as best they could—yet still it showed; it still shows—in their eyes. It showed in the way they turned all serious conversation—anything at all ponderous or heavy —neatly and adroitly aside, so that they could deal with the appalling problem of living from minute to minute with death at their shoulders. All the time—all the time.

On the second trip back—a 'QP' as we called it—*Eclectic*'s turn came.

One minute we were steaming along, all at action stations, as we had become accustomed to being, as we knew full well we would be for all eternity. There had been five Heinkel torpedo-bomber raids earlier that day and now it was approaching dusk. We all looked forward to relaxing a mite when the darkness hid us, at least a bit, from the planes. We had, the four destroyers and one corvette in the escort, brought down four Heinkels since we turned the Cape. It was just before suppertime when the torpedo struck and blew the ship almost in half right where Number Two boiler room had been.

Practically everyone on deck and on the bridge seems to have been killed instantly. The stokers in Number One boiler room and in the engine room stood no chance. The superheated steam probably hit them so fast and hard they knew nothing about it.

I was in the port passageway, going forward with the supper tray when the tinfish exploded. I was knocked right through the passageway—about five yards—and finished up on the upper seamen's mess deck. That I recall clearly. The rest, until I knew I was in a crowded Carley float under a pile of bodies, dead and alive, in cold blackness, is not too clear. I was told afterwards that I had been picked up bodily by one of the killick seamen and thrown back again along the port passageway, then dragged out of the screen door in the rush of men escaping from the fore part of the ship.

We were soon picked up, we matelots in the Carley floats. It must have been about twenty minutes after the ship went down in two halves. Some men on the after half of the ship, which hesitated to sink, were picked up directly from it by the destroyer *Opportune*, just before she turned to us. Doing that in the sea at the time, knowing that U-boats would be lurking about to catch rescuers, was gallantry indeed. Our view of officers distinctly improved.

When I gathered my wits on *Opportune*'s deck, and stared around as best I could, there was no sign of *Eclectic* anywhere. Only the sea, dark and heaving and the blackness all around. I was half-covered with black oil fuel, just like most of the other *Eclectic* people—what few of us there were—and this had to be cleaned off, as best the *Opportune* dabtoes and sick bay tiffies could do it, before we were shuffled down below to their already crowded mess decks. *Opportune* had already picked up about thirty survivors off two merchant ships which had been sunk the day before. Down below it was muggy, and yet still cheery. I was served a tot of rum in the confusion. It was my first tot from the Pusser. I was seventeen years and nine months of age, three months before my 'man's time', eighteen, when I should have drawn my first tot. All I remember thinking at the time was that I'd done the Pusser in for at least *one* tot—that was until I learned that Prof and Shiner and Nobby Clarke had not been among the rescued. I crept then into the hammock-netting, hid myself behind the stacked pits, and cried my eyes out, until I was spied by a big three-badger who reached in and tousled my still-oily hair and murmured, 'Cheer up, mate—you got an extra bloody tot out of it!'

The following day we were transferred, very early in the morning, along with the merchant ship survivors, to a cargo ship, *Yarborough Castle*. This was done in her boats, and no sooner had the last of the survivors clambered on her deck than Jerry Heinkels came over and one dropped a bomb directly down her after funnel. We didn't wait for any order. What with the noise of roaring steam escaping from the blown-up boiler and the scrambling and shouting of men now driven out of their wits by the fear of sudden death, I was one of the first back over the side and down the Jacob's ladder into the boats, which had not even started to be hauled up when the bomb hit the ship. Within a matter of minutes everyone from *Yarborough*—the survivors of *Eclectic* and the two merchant ships, and what remained of *Yarborough*'s crew, all told about 150 men—were all jammed into the six lifeboats, most of us standing up, so as to make enough room, and the ship was sliding slowly and surprisingly gracefully into the cold, oily ocean.

By the time the lifeboats had rowed about fifty yards away from the sinking ship, she was off down in her final plunge. Then we waited to be picked up again by *Opportune*, which did the job in no time at all. No sooner had the last survivor been pulled up over her sides than her engines were racing and she was heading west as fast as Christ would let her.

Down below in *Opportune* now there were the ship's

company, those not on watch, say eighty men, plus 150 survivors. There were no more transfers. *Opportune* raced all the way back to Iceland for four days and nights, and dropped us off, a mob of scruffy stragglers if there ever was one, at Seydisfiord.

I have tried to write the facts as objectively as I can. But still I see the ships burning in the blackness. Still I hear the mutter of the men in the raft praying that she will go down fast so that the Germans will not see us in our frail float, white faces—those not layered thick in black oil fuel—looking like so much refuse waving in the wind. Still I see the frozen fingers, like so many claws, clutching the sides of the raft, and the lifebelts thrown from *Opportune*, and wonder if Prof glimpsed us being saved and muttered to himself, as the cold Arctic sea closed over him, that the Skipper was probably on our float, before he seized up and went down to discuss social evolution in the halls of Valhalla. Still I see the eyes of the men being dragged on to deck, safe and alive and not yet realizing it, their mouths stiff and grinning slightly, like so many death's head skulls, and talking rapidly, some of us, and sounding stupid while we were polite and thanked our rescuers as if we had been handed a cup of tea and a sticky bun.

But then I see us, a few minutes later, borrowed blankets across our shoulders, smoking a Woodbine easy and warm, as men do who have already died once, and still I hear some of the merchant seamen nearby muttering that this was all against union rules and they were going on strike as soon as they hit the pool.

Still I hear them say that the next time they sign on they are going to check the small print. Still I hear the men who had learned the hard way that every given minute of our lives, each and every one of us, and each and every minute, is more precious than all the gold and silver and diamonds and dead stupid things that are all around us. Still I hear it, even yet.

Still I see the dead body which floated close by in the waves past our raft as we made our way to welcoming, beautiful, dirty grey steel plates—a body torn into bloody gobbets, with the head and one arm gone and only greyish-pink meat where they should have been.

Still I hear again matelots in *Opportune* talking of sane things, like women and sport and up-homers and grippo runs and the last job they had where everyone nicked the akkers out of the till when the guv'nor wasn't watching, and was having it away with his missus every time the guv'nor went off for a weekend at Brighton with *his* horse, talking of a world full of sin and dishonour, and delight in tiny things that don't matter to anyone else; a world away from that death, destruction, misery, cold and bloody violence, and the thought of a freezing death, seized in the steely grip of that appalling sea. And music. Good music—uplifting, echoing of dreams of a pattern, a rhythm, a logic; anything but the shifting chaos of noise and cold and death.

I suppose I could write that I thought, in that Carley float, of books by a fireside, and birds in a garden, and flowers and wild ducks flying south over trees bare against the winter sky; and theatres and museums, but I didn't. All I thought about was simply staying alive as that disgusting body slid by.

13. Midst Pleasures and Palaces

As I walk along the Bois Boulogne,
With an independent air,
You can hear the girls declare,
'He must be a millionaire!'
You can hear them sigh and wish to die,
You can see them wink the other eye
At the man who broke the Bank at Monte Carlo!

As he strolls along the Bois Boulogne,
And his prick is on the stand,
The ladies think it's grand,
To hold it in their hand,
He'll give 'em a bob to finish the job
And pull the skin right over the knob
Of the man who broke the Bank at Monte Carlo!

'The man who broke the bank at Monte Carlo' was the song
broadcast over the Tannoy each time HMS *Eclectic* left Iceland for
Murmansk or Archangel—the infamous 'death run' through
'Blood Alley'—to help guard the convoys. Compare the matelots'
version with the original and decide which is the more obscene.

Most of the group of survivors from the convoy were taken
south from Iceland by HMS *London*, a cruiser, and I suppose
that was the last that we saw of them. Our separate little band

was shuffled on board a Royal Fleet Auxiliary tanker—a merchant ship on charter to the Andrew with mostly merchant navy crew and only guns' crews of matelots (so neither fish nor fowl, but highly vulnerable to high explosives)—and sent 'home' to Gairloch in Western Scotland.

Later I was told by an ex-able seaman from *London* that when she took Lord Beaverbrook to Murmansk on a political mission, a British soldier was brought on board the ship. He had been captured at Dunkirk in 1940, and escaped into the USSR from Poland in 1941. But in Russia he had been treated even worse than by the Germans. By the time he went on board the British ship he was a silent, nervous, thin wreck. This was only one of the many vague tales of the time, each one of which would make a book in itself.

In Gairloch we were taken on board a destroyer depot ship and from her sent a while later on leave. I was in for bad shocks. On arrival in the depot ship I read a letter from the wife of the mate of *Second Apprentice*, telling me that she had been sunk and Knocker, her husband, had been killed. The Skipper, Tansy Lee, and the deck boy had been blown over the side and the lad had been gravely injured, but Tansy was all right. That had happened in the summer of 1941.

But what followed was even worse. Aunt Lowri wrote to say that Dad's ship had gone down somewhere in the South Atlantic. The ship had been steaming alone, not in convoy, en route to South Africa. She was known to have been torpedoed, and the ship's company had taken to the boats. A wide search had been made for survivors, but none had been found. The shock had been too much for Mam; after lingering for a month, she died. Angharad was all right and was welcome to stay with Aunt Lowri and Uncle John for as long as she needed to.

All I remember after I read that is pushing my way down to the survivors' mess deck and scrunching up in a corner and saying to myself over and over again: 'The bastards . . . the bloody bastards!' until someone shoved a full tot of neat rum under my nose. Then I passed out.

They were very good in the depot ship. I thanked my stars I was not in Chatham barracks. The regulating office, once they saw what was up, cleared the way for me to go on leave fast, issued me with new kit, and gave me, as a parting gesture, a draft chit to HMS *Obstinate*, a destroyer in the Fourth Flotilla.

After the usual wartime shambles of a train journey, I arrived in Manchester in the wee hours of the morning and had to walk the five miles or so to Harpurhey. There was no one about in the cold January rain, and it was cold. When I reached the corner where I had met my paramour of the air-raid shelter I looked around, but there was no one, only a civilian firewatcher standing in a doorway in his gleaming, streaming cape and tin hat.

I reached Aunt Lowri's about 1.00 a.m. She was crying and wailing. I asked her to cheer up. It was too late for such things as crying. She sprang to go upstairs to wake Angharad, but I was now man enough to stop her. One wailing woman was enough for me. I slept on a couch because Aunt Lowri had an aircraft factory draughtsman lodging with her, poor sod, and sleeping in the spare room. Apart from a short air-raid alarm in the very early morning, which fizzled out, I slept well for the first time in months, and though I was in one of a row of workers' cottages in the slums of the industrial heart of Britain, with factories all around and trams rattling over the cobbled streets, I felt as cosseted as I may do later should I ever stay ashore in the country houses or seaside estates of rich magnates in Britain or America.

Next morning Angharad came down to breakfast, bravely trying to look as pretty as a lass of almost sixteen should look at breakfast, but I could see that the ravages of the past year had made their mark. I tried to jolly her up. Now she had left her piano-playing in Lewis's department store and was working in a small factory where they made the linings for steel helmets. Her job, she told me, was to rivet the chin-straps on to the inner lining. Ever after that, whenever I went to action stations, I had quick flashes of Angharad in her factory, and felt steel enter my heart. That led to a distinct improvement of the aiming of my gun. That and other remembrances.

I went with Angharad on her half-day off, on a Tuesday, to my mother's grave at the local Baptist cemetery. She had no stone, and I promised myself to save for one. It took me ten years to finally get enough together for a simple, decent marker, but I did eventually, when the Andrew paid me off.

That leave was miserable all the time I was in Manchester. Everyone was tired and downcast, although the simple-minded were shouting a lot about a 'Second Front' and getting youngsters into the Communist Party. I had my first fight outside a pub. This was with some character who was old enough to have known better and who told me that I was serving in a navy which was a mere tool of the Capitalists and which existed only to keep the Empire in bondage and the poor downtrodden Indians in slavery. By the time I'd heard a good ten minutes of his diatribe, all the while remembering Dad and Mam and Prof and Nobby, I'd had enough.

'Right, outside, you fucker!' That was the way we challenged a duel in our circles. It was hardly elegant, but very effective.

My protagonist, some kind of war-worker and about twenty-four or five, was bigger than me. He eyed me up and down and then with a smirk half-bowed me towards the door. I think he was intending to clobber me from behind as soon as we were outside the pub, but I was far too quick and wily for him. As he let go the door I turned fast and got both fists into his face. While he staggered, I put the boot in, just as I had

learned at Shotley from the Scotsmen. I was going to give him
the Gorgie Biscuit when a gang of locals grabbed me and
calmed me down, took me inside the pub and bought me a
couple of pints. There they told me that my sparring partner
had taken off, streaming blood, in the direction of the ARP
First Aid Post. I congratulated myself, rather woozily by
now, for not having murdered him; that was the closest I ever
came to killing anyone hand-to-hand.

When the pub closed for the afternoon, I was met outside
by a big elderly bobby. He gravely nodded towards me and
his helmet bobbed on his head and made his chinstrap cut
white creases into his red jowls.

'How long are you on leave, lad?' he intoned.

'Ten days. I've . . . hicc . . . four to go.'

'You're going to spend it all here?'

In a flash I knew what he was telling me. I also knew that
with his friendly eyes he wasn't suggesting I should go
somewhere else to protect his wards, but to get away from my
own grief, if I could.

'Er, hicc . . . no. I'm off to the Pool tomorrow for the rest
of . . . hicc my leave, sir.'

'Good idea,' said the bobby. 'An excellent idea. Couldn't
have thought of a better one myself when I was in the
Andrew . . .'

The news that I was taking off for Liverpool didn't go down
very well at Aunt Lowri's, although Angharad took it joking-
ly and wanted to know, quietly and slyly, who she was, but I
passed it off, slid her five of my ten pounds, and headed for
the Pool, through the cold rain.

In Liverpool I went to the Flying Angel for a bed. They
were over-full, of course, but gave me an address where I
could get lodgings for three nights. This turned out to be with
a sweet elderly lady who flustered about me as though I was a

Pekingese lap dog. The only problem was that she was extremely stout and had a huge goitre hanging from her chin. When she served the first meal, which was Spam and salad, her goitre wobbled alarmingly and almost put me off the rabbit-food on the oilcloth covered table. But the lady was so enormous, with little, black piercing eyes, and that by-now fascinating goitre, that it took all of my charm and diplomacy, such as they were, to escape from her cottage. I headed for a pub, somewhere in Scotland Road down by the docks.

The place was crawling with matelots and merchant seamen. By the time I'd had four or five pints and the women started wandering in, I was feeling quite at home and ready for anything. I soon got into the company of a couple of matelots from ships based in Liverpool, and they introduced me to some lasses, and the evening wore on with us trying to beat the clock before the pub closed at ten-thirty or before the air-raid sirens blew.

That was the time when I encountered my first American serviceman. It was in the pub toilet. I turned to go back to the bar and saw a soldier, dressed, as usual, in khaki. I gave him the usual greeting, 'What ho, mate?' and he replied in what I took to be an Irish accent. I finished buttoning my trousers and started for the door. Then I turned and stared, because this soldier had a huge canvas bag slung around his waist on a strap over his shoulder. It looked a bit like a big pistol-holder.

'What you got there, chum? A bloody ack-ack gun?'

'Naw, it's a gas mask,' he replied. He turned to leave the toilet. I shoved off into the bar ahead of him.

'Where you from, mate?' I called over my shoulder.

'Tennessee.' The soldier turned to join a friend, similarly uniformed.

'Well, good luck to you!'

He gave me a broad grin. 'Hey, thanks,' was all he said, then he sat down with his mate, quietly in their corner. That was a big contrast to the general GI attitude later, when there were thousands of them around.

One thing led to another in the pub and eventually I crossed Marlene's bows. She was about nineteen, I guessed, blonde and slim, with a good Scouse sense of humour, quick and penetrating. That suited me because that's the way I wanted to be, too, at seventeen, though I was cracking on that I was nineteen. The way I looked I suppose it would have been difficult for anyone to doubt me.

After I had bought her a shandy or two, Marlene offered me an all night in for thirty bob—because her boy friend was an RAF pilot and had been shot down and she had to feed the little 'un. Otherwise I wouldn't do it . . . well, not for money, see, Jack?'

It was the first time I'd heard *that* story. I didn't know that it was so common in Britain during and directly after the war that if each time it had been told it had been true, the Royal Air Force must have started the war with about six million pilots. But I fell for it, hook, line and sinker, as the saying goes, and wound up with Marlene ('Leenee' to her friend Lil—a mousy creature who showed off Leenee's peroxide blonde tresses to perfection). She and I finished up in a little hotel on Scotland Road, which Leenee told me was used by 'ships' officers when their wives come to stay in the Pool, see, Jack'. I fell for that one, too.

To a matelot from the grey steel confines of destroyers and such, flowered wallpaper on thin plywood partitions (even though we could hear every grunt and squeak from all sides) and a little sink with a fresh-water tap (even though it gave out a mere dark brown trickle) and a china washbowl (even though it was cracked) were the acmes of luxury and well-being. I quickly undressed ship and hung my uniform and cap on the wall, by the outside window. I was excited and happy, even though the hotel had cost ten shillings and Leenee had let me know that 'it's the wrong time of the month, really, but I know a nice bloke like you won't mind, will you?'

Even as Leenee clambered into bed, the sirens in the city wailed a warning. She wanted to get out of bed again, get dressed and go down into the hotel cellar. 'There might be one of them Yanks down there, and they have bottles of whisky with them, Jack.' She spoke as if the Yanks were a convention of Santa Clauses.

The last thing I needed right then was whisky, whether from a Yank or not, so I reached for Leenee and we set to.

There we were, going at it like knives, and me just on the vinegar strokes when there was an almighty bang and clouds of smoke and dust and Leenee shouting out at the top of her voice, 'Stop, wakker, stop . . . I told you we should have gone down to the bloody cellar!'

In a half daze I turned my head and stared around. The whole fireplace had been blown across the room, missing our bed and us by an inch, and in its place was a gaping black hole half the extent of the wall.

'Jesus Christ!' was all I could say. I turned the other way, Leenee wiggled out from under me. The blast had blown the sheets and blankets off the bed, we were stark bollock naked, and the blast had also *blown out the entire outside wall of the room*! And not only the wall, but all my uniform, cap, and Leenee's clothes, too!

We lay there, with the cold night air blowing dust and the odour of a hundred and fifty years of patronizing by Jacks and Johns and their floozies over us, wafting it gently over our shivering bodies.

I suppose we lay speechless there for a good five or six minutes, staring out at the gently falling rain and the search-lights probing the sky, and the blaze of a ship on fire somewhere in the Mersey. It was such a blaze as to light up clearly the whole scene: the tattered rosy wallpaper, the fallen cracked—now shattered—china washbowl, the gaping hole where the fireplace had been, the rain-wet floor-joists hanging out in thin air over the dark street, and Leenee, thin and cold and scared out of her wits, crossing herself and swearing she'd never do it again, no, she'd go into a convent; 'Holy Mary, Mother of God! forgive us our trespasses!'

Of a sudden, there was the noise of an engine and voices below the gaping hole which had once been the hideaway of desire, and then a scraping noise. I stared at the windy space where the wall had been. The top of a ladder appeared. A minute later the top of a steel helmet. 'AFS' was proclaimed on it. 'Auxiliary Fire Service.'

Under the helmet was the small wizened face of a man of about sixty, wearing thick spectacles and a huge moustache. His blue overcoat was tightly buttoned around his scrawny neck. He looked like a government leprechaun. I stared; Leenee stared, silently. Leenee scrunched herself down behind me as best she could and peeped over my shoulder.

The fireman peered around for a few seconds, frowning at first. Then, through the still blowing rubble-dust he saw us. He grinned from ear to ear. 'Hello, Jack,' he shouted loudly. His eyes glinted behind his spectacles in wicked humour. 'Hello, Jack!' he repeated. 'Still at it, then?'

He turned and shouted down to his mates. There was a muffled reply from outside. The fireman turned again. 'We got your cap and jacket down there, Jack,' he shouted, 'but we can't find your trousers nowhere.' He thought for a moment, grinning. Then he added, 'Still, you won't mind, eh? You can manage better without 'em, eh?'

Then he threw a blanket into the room. 'Here, wrap your missus in this,' he said, kindly.

I bought a pair of trousers from a matelot in the same pub where I had met Leenee. I don't know the real name of the place, but we called it the 'Blood Bucket' because the outside walls of brick were painted bright scarlet, supposedly to hide bloodstains from the frequent fights. Early 1942 was no time to steal anyone's girlfriend in Liverpool. Having your teeth kicked out or a few ribs busted meant nothing when your next trip might be up Blood Alley, or across the U-boat infested Western Ocean.

I found out later that the blast was caused by one of the new cannon-rockets the Nazis were using.

When I returned to the depot ship and was waiting for the arrival of *Obstinate* so I could be sent on board, I had a chance to find out what was going on in the world and how the war was going. It looked bad. In the Far East the Japs had sunk our two main standbys, the battleships *Prince of Wales* and *Repulse*, and the day I joined *Obstinate* they incredibly took Singapore.

In Russia the Nazis were at the gates of Moscow, waiting for the spring to overrun the rest of that country. But for us the worst news was that the Nazi battleships *Scharnhorst* and *Gneisenau* had escaped from Brest, in North-West France, where they had been bottled up ever since the *Bismarck* sortie. They were now in German waters again, from where they could sneak up the long Norwegian coast, to wait there, ready to pounce on our northern convoys. That was bad. It meant that instead of having a small base, which could be watched easily, they now had almost a thousand miles of jagged coastline to hide themselves in until they were ready to come out and do their worst, and they would have the twenty-four-hour northern darkness in winter to aid them. Now, besides the Luftwaffe, the U-boats and the *Tirpitz* to worry about, there were two more murderous menaces for us to contend with. We were told that both *Scharnhorst* and *Gneisenau* had been damaged by tinfish from our Swordfish planes as the Nazis had pelted up the English Channel, but we had no way of knowing that they would be out of action for almost a year.

Obstinate was an 'O'-class destroyer, completed in 1940, and a big improvement on the older destroyers in every way. She had three 4.7-inch guns and eight torpedo tubes as her main armament, and six groups of four Bofors guns as ack-ack defence, as well as depth charges. But even more important to us matelots, her mess decks had been laid out with slightly more thought for the men who would live in them.

As soon as we newcomers—there were about a dozen of us—stepped on board, we knew that this was a happy ship. There was a free-and-easy air aboard, and a pleasant rapport between all ratings, Chiefs and POs and even with most of the officers. It was a new experience to me, to be addressed by a subby or even a lieutenant as if we were real human beings.

The subby who met us at the gangway was cheerful and smiling.

'Now, chaps,' he said, 'welcome on board. You have your mess numbers, so pick up your gear and off you go to your messes; lunch is up. Have a good meal and get settled in, eh?'

I almost fainted at being addressed so by an officer. I knew he meant 'dinner', not lunch, but it took me a good ten minutes to get over the surprise of having, for the first time since I joined the Andrew, had an officer talk as if he realized that we actually *ate*, and had bodily functions besides marching, drilling, firing guns and simply *being*.

My mess was the after seamen's mess, along with a hodge-podge of cooks and stewards and other odds and ends, but the majority were dabtoes. I didn't know it at the time, of course, although I might have guessed, that they were a crowd of the finest men I ever came across in my life, for all their personal peccadilloes; and not just my mess—the whole ship, with very few exceptions, from the Skipper down.

The Skipper was Scottish and when the ship left harbour he had an AB playing the bagpipes on the flag deck. This was to be our custom every time we left harbour and every time we came back in, and mostly when there was action. If the AB couldn't play the pipes, then a Scots wardroom steward was roped in, and sometimes even the Skipper himself had a go. The tune they played leaving harbour was the hymn 'Amazing Grace'. It is an old Scottish air, and every time I hear it now a lump comes to my throat. Perhaps my American friends think that I'm a religious man, and so I am in my own way, but it is not the religious aspect of the music that hits me, but the memories. How many dead men heard it . . . ?

I was still under age—too young to draw my tot. That might have been the cause of a slight coolness towards me when I joined the mess, but as soon as I was a 'man' of eighteen—about three months after I joined *Obstinate*—that was all forgotten. Now I had some leverage in the mess. Now I had something to barter besides mere friendship, or perhaps relieving early someone on watch.

I soon got to know all the fifteen men in my mess very well, and sorted out the ones to cultivate and the ones to—not avoid—there was no such possibility in a crowded ship —*slide by*.

They are all around me now as I write—Pony Moore, the senior killick, with his tales of runs ashore in Honkers and Singers, up the Gut and Gib, in the peacetime Andrew, which he made sound like a cruise on the Prince of Monaco's yacht. Pony's oppo, Flossie Herbert, also a killick, a handsome man of about thirty who'd once slept with the wife of a French cognac distiller. Every time Flossie went into a bar her name was on one of the bottles, so he said. Then, in descending order of seniority among the dabtoes there was Tinger Ling and Rasher Williams, both serving over their time for pension in the Andrew—they had both joined as boy seamen in World War I. Rasher had once been messmates with Jack Cornwall, the boy seaman who had won the Victoria Cross at the age of fifteen for standing by his gun position for hours, waiting for orders when all the rest of the gun crew were dead around his feet. When Rasher recounted the tale I recalled wryly what Knocker White had said when he was bollocking me for doffing my shoes on the mast: 'Even if you've got a shell up your ass.'

There was Rosy Lee the London barrow-boy, and Jock McAllister, the two-badge sheepshagger from the Hebrides, with his angel face, his soft, musical voice and pink cheeks. It was said of him that he would fuck anything moving, and I can believe it. Brigham Young and Pincher Martin were HOs in their early twenties. Pincher came from a well-off family in Southampton, and always had plenty of akkers. The older matelots said he drew a weekly allotment from Pompey Lil for making her come five times in one night, but I expect they were kidding me.

The most intellectual of the mess was Roger the Lodger the Sod, who had the *Daily Telegraph* smuggled out of the wardroom by one of his oppos, the bagpipe-playing wardroom steward. I quickly made pals with Roger and made sure of getting a look at the *Telegraph*. The *Mirror* was all right, but we thought it wise to get the other side's story, too.

Roger was well educated, and when he was not on his guard he spoke with a very concise Oxford drawl. But when he was in the mess or on watch he could put on an excellent Cockney dialect, too, and had a swearing vocabulary which would have made any three-striper envious. The reason that all his messmates most admired Roger, though, was that whenever there was a superior around, an officer or some rare officious Chief or PO, Roger would always address him first in Cockney, so screwed-vowelled that Authority's face would twist up to hear it, and end up in pure Oxford English. That always left the officer in a tizzwazz, not knowing with whom or what he was dealing.

There were others, too: Harry Tate, a quiet three-badger, and Spider Crabbe, his oppo, and Taff Williams and Organ Morgan, two inseparable Welsh HOs from the mining valleys of South Wales. It was the first mess I'd been in where I wasn't the only Welshman. Taff and Organ treated me like a younger brother—they were in their mid-twenties. Most of the time they were quiet in the mess and, I was proud to note, the only ones who didn't curse continually. The only times they were in real evidence were when they came off from a run ashore—for example, to the Fleet Canteen in Seydisfiord —full of beer. Then, regardless of shoes and trousers and underwear thrown at them from the matelots in their swinging pits, they belted forth their rendering of 'Cwm Rhondda' in perfect harmony, in Welsh; the strange Welsh of the valleys, and I joined in, low, in the softer vowels of West Wales: '*Strong deliv'rance, strong deliv'rance, be thou still my strength and shield . . .*'

The turbulent Taffs belted it out every time they came off sozzled. The English, the Scots and the Irishmen in the mess had to tolerate it. You can't tackle a trio of Welshmen in full voice, now can you? At least not until they've finished their song. You can't show that besides not being Welsh, God help you, you are also a bloody unmusical-eared barbarian, can you?

14. *Promises and Threats*

Now the first place we called at was Malta;
The girls wouldn't fuck—but they alter—
Ten dollars she said, so I hopped into bed,
To the tune of my Spanish guitar . . .

Chorus: Plonk, plonk, plonk, plonk, plonk, plonk . . .

The next place we called at was Aden,
The girls wouldn't fuck but we made 'em;
Ten dollars I'd pay for a blowthrough each way,
To the tune of my Spanish guitar . . .

From 'My Spanish Guitar'. This lower deck ditty has about a
hundred verses, mentioning common naval ports of call.

By my eighteenth birthday, May 8, 1942, things were
hotting up in the Home Fleet. We had a lot of new ships
—many of them old American 'V & W' destroyers, many
new US Navy and Canadian ships joining up, frigates and
corvettes and such, and quite a few of our own ships were
newly built. We also had a new admiral—Bruce Fraser. He
was a Scotsman. That pleased most of the Scots among the
matelots in *Obstinate*. The previous admiral had been extremely distant. He had always been referred to as the
'fucking admiral'. There was none of that with Bruce Fraser.
He was popular on board his own flagship, *Duke of York*, and

he seemed to take delight in our Skipper's bagpipe playing and always gave us a special wave when he passed our ship.

But our losses were heavy. In convoy after convoy across the Western Ocean, usually to and from the waters off Newfoundland, where the Canucks took and handed over the escort, we were lucky to get through with less than thirty per cent losses. In some cases it was much more. In the north, on the Murmansk run, the losses were generally over forty per cent, escorted and escort.

The main effort of the Home Fleet itself, the battleships, cruisers and destroyers, as opposed to the convoy escorts (and it was very often impossible to make any distinction between them) was to keep the Nazi battleships *Tirpitz*, *Scharnhorst* and *Gneisenau* bottled up on the German side of the North Sea; to prevent them breaking out into the Atlantic and slaughtering the convoys.

The Andrew had already spiked one of the Nazi navy's guns in February, when HMS *Campbeltown*, an old American World War I destroyer, manned by the Andrew and loaded with dynamite, had rammed full pelt into the dock-gate at St. Nazaire, in North-West France. She deprived *Tirpitz* of the only drydock big enough to take her outside of the North Sea. But *Scharnhorst* and *Gneisenau* were a different matter. There were a dozen places in France or Spain they could head for if they were damaged out in the ocean. Our main concerns were a sortie by *Tirpitz* and a breakout by *Scharnhorst* and *Gneisenau*. The menace of the three Nazi ships rarely left our thoughts the whole of 1942. It must never have left the thoughts of the My Lords of the Admiralty in London. The mere threat of a sortie by these three ships almost won the Western sea-war and the Soviet front for the Germans in July 1942, as we shall see.

I think we saw the first American Navy ships to join our North Atlantic and Arctic Fleet before May, but I'm not quite sure. It may have been as early as March. What I do recall clearly is that I had been on watch, the middle watch, and so got up the latest, at about eight o'clock in the morning. *Obstinate* was a very easy and humane ship—but she still got her work done and scored enemy kills—even more so than the bullshit pusser ships I'd been in before. I went up to the after bathroom, a tiny cubbyhole of a place with four little sinks and a shower in one corner. There I had a shave; I'd started about three months before, slyly, in the night watches so few would see me and take the mickey. I looked through the bathroom scuttle and noticed some strange ships, destroyers with two funnels and no scuttles, a couple of cruisers and the like, and it took me a moment or two to realize that the ensigns being hoisted on their stern-staffs were American. I don't recall feeling anything but curiosity. I thought all navies could only be judged by the standards of the Andrew. That's understandable enough, surely.

Rosy Lee and Roger the Lodger the Sod came into the bathroom. 'Yankee ships over there,' I said, half absently.

'Yeah, they got Errol Flynn wiv 'em,' replied Rosy, "e's goin' ter win the bleedin' war for us!'

'Sooner him than me,' said Roger. Then he doffed his pants and stepped into the cold, trickling shower. He had an anchor tattooed on his ass.

'I thought he was Australian—I mean Errol Flynn,' I half-asked Rosy. That's the way I was mostly in those days; I'd believe anything, and the English keep such straight faces when they kid.

Roger the Lodger threw his bar of pusser's hard at me.

For the date-watchers, it was the day that the news of the sinking of the cruiser HMS *Edinburgh* came through. She had been torpedoed by Nazi destroyers in the Barents Sea while escorting QPII—that was the eleventh convoy back from Murmansk. There had been three little minesweepers with her. While one of them stopped to take off *Edinburgh* survivors—including their Admiral, Bonham-Carter—the other two had steamed full pelt at the Jerry destroyers and chased them off. That caused quite a stir on board because we had done convoys with HMS *Edinburgh* and even rafted up alongside her a few times in Iceland and made oppos with many of her matelots. It was no wonder that this was the main topic of the day, and not the arrival of the Yanks.

All that spring and summer we plodded on, along with the merchant ships. Our destroyers—all our naval ships—were camouflaged in crazy, abstract designs of grey, black, green, yellow and blue paint. When we looked at the other escorts it was difficult to figure, at a distance, which was sea, sky and them. Their offset course and direction never seemed to be what they seemed to be. In the cold north everything was grey, eternally grey, as if the world would be grey for ever and ever; everything—ships, faces, snow, rain, sea.

All the time we were escorting there was rarely a break in our monotonous plod on the flanks of the convoy. Only at night, mainly, when a sudden order was given from the bridge, the engines below rose to a screaming crescendo, and we looked aft, to see the wake rise, cold and frothy, and the waves spill back from it, like smashed cellophane. Topsides on the guns—I was an AA1 now and drew my tot along with the rest; a real Jack me-tickler-tin—I watched the moon, the only familiar thing that was not of the escort, and sometimes wished I was on her, and not in this crazy game of dully dodging death morning, noon and night.

Between watches, down on the mess deck, the heat from the steam pipes warmed us, but not to the marrow. It warmed all the fittings—the table, the steel bulkheads, the hammocks—and yet it left a cold lining on and around them. In the very centre of that crowded, muggy space, there was always, at sea, a freezing void; death was never further away than through one-eighth of an inch of steel plate. The ship's side always cried tears of condensation, the cold, cold moving tears of a helpless friend.

All the time the merchantmen seemed to move sideways, and we in the escorts slid around them like eager eels slithering around crabs in the unseeing dark, feeling, sniffing, reaching for lurking predators below in the dark deeps. Sometimes, on the night watches, when an Asdic 'piiinnng!' had changed to 'poiiinnng!' we found ourselves talking to the Jerries down below, sometimes aloud; 'Come on, you bloody bastard, come to Mammie, do!' and everyone on watch spoke through gritted teeth. Brigham Young, the wonder from 'Zummerset' used to spit a mouthful of kye over the side and call out, 'Get a gobful of that, Herman!'

But most of the time it was quiet waiting, trying to find a little corner out of the wind, yet where we could still keep a lookout for the telltale wake of a tiny periscope in the blackness all around, above and beneath us.

On the Murmansk run our only sight of land, more often than not, until we reached that unhappy gateway to the proletarian Nirvana, was Jan Mayen Island, dull, grey and leaden, perhaps glimpsed through a snowstorm. Sometimes, with a cup of cha in a frozen mitt, Flossie Herbert, the three-badge killick, tauntingly entertained us with tales of his runs ashore in the peacetime navy; in Hands, Knees and Bumpsadaisy or up the Gut, and incredible stories of impossible romances with improbable émigré Russian princesses in Shanghai. We listened, none of us doubting. We knew that his were the only romances we would ever know, and we lived and re-lived all his escapades, each of us for ourselves. Later, quietly alone in our pits in the steaming mess deck, with the ventilator louvres shut off because the blast of air was too cold, and the coughs of incipient tuberculosis all around us, we hugged Flossie's accounts unto our hearts, to keep the thought of the one-eighth of an inch of steel and the cold black water outside, and the tinfish racing towards us out of the eyes inside our heads.

One day passed just like the one before, just like the one to come. The good days of avoiding death for yet twenty-four more hours passed like grey flags hoisted up and hauled down on some remote flagpole half shrouded in mist, fog, rain and snow.

And all the while the great seas sank and heaved, grey and eternal.

July 1942 started with promise of life for another two weeks, perhaps, instead of one, as had previously been the case. There were more American and Canadian navy ships about, although they seemed to be for the most part still getting themselves organized, and convoying from the States and Canada to Iceland. The main burden of the Russian convoys was still on the Andrew.

I write this in a tiny corner of a small port in the United States, on American Independence Day. Right now, outside me, as I lift my head and look through the window into the brilliant July sunshine outside, Americans—most of them born long after the events of which I am writing—are going about their holiday in a professional way, as all Americans seem to. They look as if they have been on holiday, and will be, for ever. All around are green trees, some blossoms, a church spire—fibreglass, but still aspiring—raises its admonishing finger. On the radio, on the television, commentators who read things of which they are seemingly only dimly aware, are busy telling their countrymen what July 4 means.

Let me tell you what July 4 means to me. Be patient. Let me try to set the scene if you will.

I've already told about the menace of the three Nazi battle-cruisers, *Tirpitz*, *Scharnhorst* and *Gneisenau*, which were thought to be all somewhere in the fiords of Northern Norway. That is the first salient fact about these events. The second fact is that the Gods of sea-warfare decreed that when up against a bigger ship, *any number of smaller ships are only slightly stronger than the strongest of their kind.* The third is 'know when to cut your losses'.

The facts are plain: thirty-six well-laden merchant ships left Hvalfiord, Iceland, for Murmansk in convoy PQ 17 in late June of 1942. Only eleven reached Murmansk. Two returned to Iceland early, because of machinery problems I think. Ten were sunk by the ever-watchful U-boats. Thirteen went down under a rain of Hermann Goering's bombs. The ships were led out from Hvalfiord by six destroyers, *Obstinate* among them. The destroyer escort-leader was HMS *Keppel*. There were two American destroyers with us; USS *Wainwright* was one of them.

On July 4, in the morning, the escort commander in *Keppel* received orders from London to abandon the convoy because the Admiralty had information (probably from a double agent) that *Tirpitz* had left her anchorage for sea. That was the surface crux of the affair.

Up to July 4th, we had had a very hot run indeed, with our ack-ack guns firing so much that the main concern was running out of ammo. Our total score up to July 4 was, I think, five Nazi torpedo-bombers shot down. That was us—I don't know the score for the rest of the escort and for the gunners on some of the merchant ships, but Jerry must have been smarting. Until July 4 all was going well, with no sinkings or damage to any ships beyond probably a few bullet and cannon holes here and there.

By the time we all grouped up east of Iceland, there was a quite formidable convoy and escort—thirty-three merchant ships, twelve of them American, two tankers, three rescue ships (one the scruffy Russian tug), two submarines, all guarded by six destroyers (two US), four corvettes, two ack-ack ships, three minesweepers and four trawlers. We had been practising manoeuvres with dummy torpedoes and smokescreens, so as to give a good account if the *Turpers* did come at us, and we thought we could give her a pretty nasty shock. In a day or two everything was sorted out—imagine trying to organize the fuel, stores, medical help, ammo, and so on, for ten thousand men in fifty-nine ships, mostly newly met!

The first few days out we escorts were busy as bees, attacking U-boat after suspected U-boat. None were sunk, so far as we knew, but that was our method, to deter them from later attacks. We shoved depth-charge after depth-charge over the stern, getting rid of most of the barrels of TNT which had been stowed the whole lengths of the side decks, from the poop to the fo'c'sle break. Jerry must have got the message, because after the first few days he made himself scarce.

On the afternoon of the second day east of Iceland we sighted a Blohm and Voss spotter plane and knew that Jerry also knew that we were out, and where we were headed. Slowly, round and round he buzzed. We were frustrated watching him, well out of range, down on the horizon, listening to the loud buzz of engines and not being able to do a thing about it; knowing all the time that his radio messages were being picked up in German Naval Headquarters, and being transmitted to the Big Bad Wolf—*Tirpitz*.

The first bomber raid was hard by Jan Mayen Island, which we could see clearly during the attack from *Obstinate*'s position to the north of the convoy. The Nazi planes hung back in the face of our heavy firing. The American destroyers really let rip; they didn't seem to care about wasting ammo, which was always our main concern! We were often being bollocked and charged for wasting ammo.

'Them Yanks got 'Enry Ford down below, churnin' bloody shells out,' commented Rosy Lee, the barrow-boy who was my gun loader (actually he watched the gun loading itself automatically, which suited Rosy down to the deck. He was happy anywhere he could just stand back and watch, and have a crafty smoke. Woodbines were his brand.)

A little while later the convoy and we steamed into a thick fog bank. Those were the only times I was ever at sea in fog and glad of it. It was the best protection we had from the Nazis. Brigham Young, also on my gun's crew, said that 'we ought to have a fucking machine for churning it out, all the way from Ikkey to Murmurs'. We all lit up fags; the fog was so thick the officers on the bridge couldn't see us.

The Jerry spotter plane must have been going spare. A couple of times he roared low overhead, trying to find us, but then he went away back to Norway for 'supper of Bratwurst und Lager, und die Fräuleins . . . ja!' as Rosy put it.

It was light just after 1.00 a.m. on July 4 in those latitudes. At about three, the first merchantman—a US freighter loaded to the gunnels with ammo for the Red Army, took a tinfish and suddenly disintegrated into flame and smoke. One of our rescue ships headed over to seek survivors. Everyone in the convoy and the escorts knew that it was merely a gesture. No one could have survived that blast, which physically shook us, even at five miles distance.

It was quiet then, until about mid-morning, when the escort received the signal to retire to join the big fleet units so they could defend other convoys from, or tackle *Tirpitz* and 'one other German unit', which were 'loose', according to what our tame sparker told us later.

But before that—and this was the only saving grace of the whole sorry tale, at least to us matelots—at eight o'clock, as the watches were changing, a sort of low moan went around our ship's deck, from man to man, from the Skipper on the bridge down to the youngest OD waiting for orders. It couldn't be heard over the ship's engines, of course. It was as if we *felt* it.

I was clambering down the ladder from my gun deck, and stared around. All the American ships were lowering their flags! One after the other, in quick succession, their ensigns were coming down, *even on the destroyers*. To us, this could only mean one thing, and one thing only. In the Andrew, once a ship has her anchor up and her steaming ensign hoisted, it never comes down until the voyage is over. To haul it down meant only one thing—the Americans were showing *surrender!*

'The bloody yellow-streaked, steak-yaffling, gum-chewing piss-pots!' shouted some killick stoker garbed in oil-streaked overalls.

'So much for bleeding Errol Flynn!' yelled another.

Then Pony Moore, our killick, who'd been to Brooklyn early in the war, and who had rushed to the flag deck shouted down, 'It's all right! Look, they're *hoisting clean flags*. It's the *Fourth of July!*'

We peered at the Yankee ships. It was true. One by one they were hoisting what looked like brand new ensigns, until all thirteen had them worn bravely from their sterns.

'Fourth of July?' said one young OD. 'What the fuck is *that?*'

Old Flossie Herbert turned to him scornfully. 'It's their bloody Independence Day, of course, you twit!'

'Why don't we have one?' asked the OD.

''Cos we've *always* been independent, idiot,' butted in a stoker PO quietly, as he headed down the Number Two boiler room hatch for another sweaty forenoon watch.

At about mid-morning we, the escort, fell out of the

convoy, formed up, and started to steam back towards Iceland. What followed was the nearest thing I ever saw to fullscale mutiny on board one of His Majesty's ships. It was the only time that I ever saw the ship's company, those not on watch, confined to their messes, and the Jimmy, with the cox'n alongside him, come into the messes to explain what we were doing and why we were abandoning the convoy. It was the only time I saw matelots threaten to refuse duty and not be put under close arrest to await courts martial. That couldn't be done. Everyone (I suspect even the officers, too) was against leaving the convoy. In the afternoon, as we steamed in line with the ack-ack ship *Pozarica* and the USS *Wainwright* ahead and astern, it was touch and go, on our mess decks, as to whether we should seize control of the ship from the officers and rejoin the convoy. I was for seizing the ship at first, along with most of the others. Cooler heads prevailed, mainly the older heads.

'You know what'll happen?' as Pony Moore put it. 'Before you know it we'll have the bloody *Duke of York* as well as the bleeding *Tirpitz* and the fucking *Scharnhorst* and the poxy *Gneisenau* up our asses. They'll forget they're at bloody war. Naval officers stick together, mates, just the same as matelots do, if they get the chance!' Then he said, mysteriously, 'They don't forget Kiel and Inverkeithing . . .'

That final argument decided it. We let Pony go to the cox'n and ask him to pass on to the officers (that meant the Skipper) that we all understood and were with him, as long as there were no recriminations after we reached the Fleet. The Skipper sent for Pony and the other senior killicks as soon as he knew they were with the cox'n in the Chief's mess, and told them that he would forget the whole thing. He told them it was one of the worst orders he'd ever received, to abandon the convoy, but that our overriding duty was to the Admiralty, who were thinking of all the other thousands of ships out in the Atlantic. It was a case of risking one convoy's loss against the risk of losing the whole sea-war. The Germans, if their big ships got control, might even risk an invasion of Britain.

That was what Pony told us when he came back down aft. We all jacked in our hands at mutiny and returned to duty, but there was a resentful sullenness on board for a good month and more, and in a few weeks many of the leading lights of the protest had been drafted to other ships—mostly, I learned afterwards, to the Far East. But I doubt if any of the officers slept at all soundly on board during the months that followed.

In the short spells between convoy escorts to Murmansk or Archangel, we had a chance to inspect at close quarters our opposite numbers in the US and Canadian navies. *Obstinate*'s particular 'chummy' ship in the US Navy was the destroyer *Wainwright*. Our Skippers had made friends, and so managed to either anchor close together, or even, on rarer occasions, raft up alongside. But this practice was stopped after a while, because it affected our matelots' morale a great deal.

It was the first time we had ever seen, or even dreamed of, such luxuries as real steaks and ice cream on board a ship, or a ship's laundry, or a choice of three or four different meals. But most telling, for us, were the easy-going, friendly relations between the American men and their officers—especially ashore. To us, they were unbelievable. Most of us, until we joined *Obstinate*, had never seen a matelot and an officer actually greeting each other in a canteen, and the officer calling the man by his first name, or by anything else but his rating, or addressing him as anything else but a mere moving object. The first time we witnessed this on board the American ship there was a stunned silence on board *Obstinate*. Most of us youngsters simply could not believe our eyes and ears. It is not easy to explain. It was as if each individual American gob had a share in his ship, the whole ship, and not just in one or two small corners of it.

We already knew that the Yankee ships were dry, so we made the best of it, when we were alongside, and swapped our rum rations for their nutty and cigarettes and food, and got them to take in our dhobying, which the older hands among them were only too willing to do in exchange for our bubbly. They loved Nelson's Blood just as much as did we. We had to be a bit careful with the younger Yankee sailors. They had not the stomachs for rum that we had. A couple of sips could get many of them flat out flakers in no time at all.

My Lords Commissioners of the Admiralty must have got wind of what was going on between our matelots and the gobs. Towards the late summer of 1942 we didn't find ourselves so often near a US ship. My Lords must have concerned themselves about how they would ever manage to get the HOs back into the stables once the war was over.

Besides a glimpse of humaneness in warships, though, there was another side to the coin.

In Iceland, we British were not very welcome. Our boot-necks had seized control of the island in 1940, to prevent the Nazis from making a most dangerous base for their navy. The country had been occupied by Canadian infantry ever since. Only now was part of the garrison handed over to Yankee leathernecks.

The Icelanders, on our rare runs ashore, treated us with a coldness which showed quite clearly the disdain or even contempt in which they held us. Our officers could avoid this, in many cases, by organizing hunting and shooting parties for themselves. The skipper of the cruiser *London* was a familiar sight, going ashore in plus-fours to collect wild flowers for pressing. But to us ordinary common or garden matelots, Iceland was exactly what its name conjures. We had no means of overcoming the coldness. Our pay was very low by American standards. The only thing the vast majority of us had to give was a smile and our lives.

As time went by it was wearing for us to see how the American newcomers were welcomed, and how dances were given for the Yanks, with the pretty Icelandic girls in droves attending, the females to whom we were so obviously worthy of nothing but a cold stare. It was dulling to the manhoods of men who continually, day and night at sea, for three years, had stared death right in the face, with the same cold stare that the majority of Icelanders cast towards them, whilst newcomers were welcomed royally.

After a while we hoped that the ship would anchor well away from the shore, so that we would not see the bright lights of the dancehalls packed with the lasses and the Americans, nor hear the music of Tommy Dorsey or Glenn Miller wafting out over the frosty foreshore. In time we became accustomed to being in our womanless, shore-comfortless limbo, but we never completely accepted it. Many matelots among us resented it, and often their resentment was transferred, after the first few weeks, towards the Americans, and especially towards the US Marines, who were, it seemed to us, and in comparison with our own risky, sparse lives, living ashore the life of Reilly, lording it in comfort with the local lasses fawning over them.

In time, no Americans, or very, very few, would come into our fleet canteens. There was no attraction for them there, and the chances were that within an hour they would be bleeding hulks on the deck with their noses and ribs stove in. When there's nothing to lose you can put it all in.

I personally never had a set-to with an American. This was not due to any particular virtue of mine above others. It was simply that I never had the money to afford to drink beer. Most of my pay was—it sounds maudlin, but it's true —going into a savings account to pay for a gravestone for my mother, and the rest for small luxuries like a bar of chocolate perhaps once a week.

But we had our consolations. We had films on board most times we went to anchor, if it wasn't raining or snowing, and now and again all the older hands would get together and give us a 'sod's opera'. That I wouldn't have missed for all the washing machines, cigarettes, nutty and females in Iceland.

The other consolation, for many of us, was that at least we had our rum and our officers had their gin. None of the Yanks could get a drop on board their ships. For that we blessed the American ladies from afar, in our cold, lonely anchorages and sea watches at the guns. We reckoned that the Yankee ladies, at least, were on the side of us Goddam Limey matelots, even if no one else was.

15. *The Cockpits of Hell*

With a bottle of Pepsi-Cola,
And a carton of ice-cream,
We're fucking good kids in harbour,
But oh, my Christ, at sea,
Oh, my Christ, when we leave the jetty,
Oh, my Christ when we get to sea,
We're a shower of no-good bastards,
The United States Marines!

'With a bottle of Pepsi-Cola', to the tune of the 'Policeman's Song'
from *The Mikado* by Gilbert and Sullivan. Probably better known
in the USA as 'From the Halls of Montezuma'.

Definitely World War II, this is a bitter comment on the
glamour and publicity bestowed on the US Marines. The Royal
Navy had been at war since September of 1939, a continual day to
day struggle against the Nazi submarines, airforce, surface raiders
and weather, when the US Fleet appeared in Iceland in March,
1942. Most often it was sung in jest, and I have heard US Marines
joining in, but rarely, and only the older hands.

I must reiterate to my many American friends (among them
many Marines past and present), that this song was sung more
jocularly than in any other way. To miss it out would be to hide a
truth. I know many—most of my friends (among them many
matelots)—will not agree with the sentiments in it, but that they
would fight to the death for its right to be published. The same
terms were often in the matelots' songs about themselves—('We're
a show'r of bastards', etc.)

235

My happiest wartime days at sea were in HMS *Obstinate*. She was a well-run, efficient vessel in a well-run, efficient flotilla, in, as far as we could tell, a well-run, efficient Force. It was quite a change—almost like not being in the Andrew, but in some other navy.

Looking back, it strikes me that wherever repressive discipline and martial bullshit prevails, so does inefficiency, and the more the bullshit, the higher up the ladder, probably, is the inefficiency. There ought to be a law about this somewhere, and if there is, then it should be called the Law of the Barents Sea. There was no bullshit there. Everyone knew, by that time the hard way, what they were doing, from the Rear Admiral of Force R in the Shiny *Sheff*, down to the lowest second-class stoker.

The Battle of the Barents Sea was, at least on the naval side, a purely British and German affair. It was classical, and for us it did much to settle a very sore old score:

On April 8, 1940—before many of us in Force R had even joined the Andrew—HMS *Glowworm*, a little destroyer of only 1,300 tons, patrolling in the Norwegian Sea, sighted, suddenly emerging from a fog-bank, the 10,000-ton Nazi cruiser *Hipper*. *Glowworm* turned towards *Hipper* and rammed her at full speed. *Glowworm* sank, of course, along with most of her men, but she put *Hipper* out of action for months.

Now *Hipper* was out again, and we all knew it. As Admiral Burnett signalled (or words to the effect), 'Now's the chance to get back for *Glowworm*.' He needed to say no more.

We left Iceland with convoy JW51B. We were a heavy escort compared to previous ones; the two cruisers *Sheffield* and *Jamaica* and eight destroyers of the more modern type. *Obstinate* was one of these destroyers. The big convoy's destination was Murmansk. It consisted of merchant ships of many nations, but there were more American Liberty ships than anything else, if my memory serves me right. It was an important convoy, loaded with ammo, guns, trucks, tanks, and planes for the Soviets. Leningrad was under siege, and, although we didn't know it at the time, the Russians were limbering up for the Battle of Kursk, which was the crucial turning point ashore, of World War II in Europe. These supplies we guarded probably assured Russia her great victory. We can surmise that had the Battle of the Barents Sea ended in defeat for the Royal Navy, the Soviets might have been defeated at the Battle of Kursk.

We started out from Iceland in mid-December, and headed for the Barents Sea, to pass around the North Cape of Norway. The icepack drifting south forced us much closer to the North Cape of Norway and the waiting Nazi planes and ships, through a narrow gap where the U-boats concentrated for their attack.

It was miserable watch-keeping in winter; our main occupation, day and night, was knocking ice from the gun breeches, the mast and the rigging. In a destroyer plunging around in high winds, that is not a passive duty. It snowed most of that trip, even more when the wind was down. The snowflakes fell like confetti at some hellish wedding. Doom cracked wide open in smoke and noise.

Hipper appeared suddenly out of one of the snow flurries and every destroyer in the escort opened up on her. We had been waiting for her this time, warned by our still-primitive radar; not like poor little *Glowworm*, which had had no warning at all.

Hipper looked like a ghost ship, almost white behind the white snow against a grey background of sky and sea. Little round flames sparked all over her where our shells were striking home. It was all over in about five minutes. The Nazi was there, then she was gone, firing her much bigger broadsides at our flotilla leader *Onslow* as she tore back into hiding at full scuttle.

We had a running commentary, in *Obstinate*, from a sparker who passed it on to a wardroom steward, who passed it on to . . . anyway, in action, a destroyer is a network of jungle telegraphs. *Hipper* hit *Onslow*, forward and in the engine room. *Onslow* was knocked temporarily out of action. She requested *Obdurate* to take over as flotilla leader as her captain had been wounded. We could plainly see *Onslow* now, plunging and rearing still, on her way back to the convoy, with thick black smoke pouring from her stern—a smoke screen—and greyish-white smoke from amidships —shell hits.

'*Onslow*'s flooded her forward magazine!' someone shouted from the after torpedo tubes. *Onslow*'s signal lamp stuttered in like the flicking tongue of some hellish lizard, quick stabs from the smoke pouring out of her lower bridge. Now she was heading south of the convoy, out of the battle, to lick her wounds in isolation, to fight against herself.

As we searched the sea and sky for *Hipper*, aircraft, U-boats and other, more incidental enemy, we saw in our minds' eyes the worst of all: *Onslow*—her A & B guns out of action, no ammo from the flooded magazine forward, her radar destroyed, her aerials ripped asunder, and a gaping hole in her hull forward, with sea smashing through her forward mess deck, fire and water all together and thick black smoke, and the ship listing ever more and more—going . . . going . . . but not quite, not yet, not bloody *Onslow*!

Then we saw—and we knew later we were right—the forward wireless office with everyone dead and drowning in the water and the blood of their oppos, and the whole of Number Five mess mashed to a gravy of pulped bone and blood, and ditty-boxes, the taxi-cases, kit-bags and hammocks and Number Five tropical suits all neatly tied with blue wool ready for the next kit muster, tumbling into the cold Arctic seas and trailing astern of *Onslow* like the dying wails of grieving mothers at a wake. We saw the ammo parties hurled up through the caisson, lying broken on deck, like drunks after a wild run ashore waiting for ever for the liberty boat to take them back on board. We saw a young OD running forward in panic, stepping into the guts of his leading hand and slipping on his blood, falling over and down a hatch to break his neck on the hammock-netting rail. We saw the old hands, still dripping with complaints, steadily and sturdily passing fire buckets from hand to hand along the deck and all the 'X' and 'Y' doors clanging shut to make a fiery citadel of hell, smoke and flame, screams and moans, pain and death. As the OD slipped away quietly, what was left of him, through the doors of the kind hereafter, we were with him, watching on at our guns, silent.

'She's going to make it!' called the torpedo officer, a decent sort. '*Onslow!* By heavens! Good old *Onslow!*' We knew her sightless Skipper was still in command in his cabin.

Then we knew that in *Onslow*, with the fire under control, a double tot was being dished out, '*Splice the mainbrace!*' and a cold meal of frozen spuds and corned beef, and *Onslow*'s Jimmy, as cool as if he were at Henley Regatta, giving orders right and left and centre, Skipper for the time being—and *Onslow* was saved. In the falling Arctic night we saw her rejoin us, her flotilla, and cheered like madmen, even though by then we knew the German battleship *Lützow* was out and on the prowl, and that *Hipper* had been merely her screen.

Then another destroyer, HMS *Achates*, busy laying down a smoke screen between the convoy and *Lützow*, was straddled by German shells, and went down in death, gently, while a merchantman, *Northern Light*, took off what was left of her men. All night long we and the other destroyers darted out from the lines of the convoy, as if on messages of our own, and fired everything we had at *Hipper*, until in the early hours our cruisers *Sheffield* and *Jamaica* steamed right at the Nazi's guts, pounding away with their six-inchers, and set her well on fire, to slink away at full speed south, back to her bastard masters. In the process *Sheffield* happened upon a Jerry destroyer. *Sheffield*'s signal, passed on to us gun crews, was laconic: 'Enemy destroyer sighted,' then, three minutes later, 'Sank same.'

Our Skipper got on to the ship's Tannoy: 'Three cheers for the Shiny *Sheff*!' he shouted, and cheer we did.

One of the cooks brought us up a cold turkey sandwich each, and we ate it standing and sitting at the guns in the snowstorm. That was our New Year's dinner. But we somehow knew that we had more than just cold turkey. We knew somehow that little old *Achates* and brave *Onslow* had somehow won a great battle—which indeed they had. If it hadn't been for *Onslow* and the other 'O'-class destroyers getting stuck into *Hipper* right away, and bashing away at her like mad with all we had, *Hipper*, with *Lützow* backing her up, would have made smoke, dust and fish-food out of Uncle Joe's tanks, planes, trucks and ammo, and murdered another four or five thousand Allied merchant sailors.

During the spring and summer of 1943 the Andrew and our allies were getting into our real stride. The trans-Atlantic convoys, as well as the Murmansk runs, were turning into U-boat slaughters as we improved on our group-attack tactics against their wolf-pack techniques. During April we destroyed fifteen U-boats, and in May, forty-one. We didn't know the numbers, on the lower deck, but we knew that in six cases out of ten a U-boat setting out on her bloody business would not be allowed to return to Jerryland or wherever she was based. We guessed that if this could go on we would overtake the Nazis' production, and that would mean the end of them, and victory might be in sight.

On one convoy, ON5, en route to Newfie, we passed

another, SC128, bound from Newfie. A wolf-pack of thirty U-boats massed to attack the eastbound convoy first, of course. They missed them, and decided to make up for their error by attacking us. By May 6 we lost eleven merchant ships, with no U-boats sunk. Most of the other ships of the convoy support group, the destroyers, and most of the close escort group, frigates and corvettes, were short on fuel and had to take off ahead to reach Newfie to fuel up. There were only two destroyers left for the support of the convoy. By then we, too, were low on fuel and depth-charges. We were sitting ducks for the great pack of U-boats. We didn't know at the time that Doenitz, the Nazi admiral in charge of their U-boat campaign, had guessed at his chance to wipe out the whole convoy and escort and ordered his U-boats to surface if they ran out of torpedoes and attack with gunfire.

By God's grace a fog came down that night, and so made the Nazi effort much more difficult, but there were still twenty-four attacks; all without hitting one of our charges. *Obstinate* charged up and down the lines, all round, this way and that, with too few depth-charges to waste any, making pretence of being six destroyers with full loads of weapons. We were reckless with our fuel to the point of desperation. We scored two U-boats for sure, and two probables, but there were so many of them about, our Skipper couldn't hang around to sight oil or wreckage. Two of the frigates sighted Jerry U-boats on the surface, through the fog, turned, and rammed the submarines, sending them straight down to the bottom. There were no Jerry survivors because no one, not even our officers, could stop to be kind, with dozens more U-boats lurking everywhere.

Next morning the escort ships which had gone to refuel were back with us. They soon got stuck in and sank two more U-boats, while a Canuck flying boat sank another. By my nineteenth birthday, on May 8, the U-boats had made themselves scarce and I don't think we got another attack or sighting after that all the way to Cornerbrook, Newfie. Our passage from what we called 'Oversea' to 'Westomp', both of them merely otherwise empty areas of grey sea, on opposite sides of the ocean, took sixteen days, and for ten of them we were at action stations.

Pink, Loosestrife, Oribi, Pelican, Vidette; what innocent names they had, those little ships of the Andrew that turned the battle of the Atlantic! How the Nazis must have frowned when they turned to their dictionaries for translations, into German, of the ships' names! How different from the high and mighty sounding names of their ships! How indignant they must have felt to have their arrogant marauders destroyed by ships with the names of flowers and birds! How very, very and *bloodily British*.

In September came the cheering news of the midget-sub attack on *Tirpitz*. The buzz was that she was out of action, but of course no one knew for sure. As it turned out, she was indeed, until she was finally laid to rest by the RAF in late 1944. But in late 1943 this still left the *Scharnhorst* and *Gneisenau*. All the lower-deck strategists guessed to a man that Fraser would be after those two during the coming winter, and they were right, as usual.

'Outside', things now seemed to be going well on all fronts, although we were still at it, day and night, night and day, on the convoys.

The air on board the destroyers was now very relaxed, except when at action stations, and I think it was the only time in most of my naval service when someone or other was not under punishment, although even then, at odd times, we would have a matelot clomping around the upper deck with a Lee-Enfield held at arm's length over his head: 'Get those bloody knees UP!' to a background of heavily-loaded merchant ships plodding on and on. In those days the Andrew's punishment verse and chapter, all still on the big varnished noticeboard in the port passageway, seemed the most ridiculous, the most insane. How can a man already probably under sentence of death, already suffering cold and malnutrition from unheated meals, already worried to death over lack of mail from his missus in Yankee-crowded Britain, be further punished? But punished we were, and sometimes for the most trite offences—being late on muster, being out of the rig of the day at anchorages, fighting (although that was most rare), or being found wanking in the heads and accused of skulking.

We had two visits to the West Coast of Scotland that year, and I was ashore for three days there. On the second visit I got into a barney with a Canuck airman and was picked up by the MPs. My reward was seven days Number Elevens and dipped my chance for killick. I'd passed the exam only a week or two before. Such were the slippery lower rungs of the ladder of advancement in the Andrew. My leave was stopped, and I spent two days trotting up and down the jetty with my .303 wobbling aloft under the amused, sometimes pitying, stares of the dockyard mateys. I'd had a bloody good go at the Canuck airman, though. He'd made some remark, outside a pub, to impress his girl-friend, about 'dry-land sailors'. I'll bet he thought twice before he made that remark again. I suppose, looking back, that it wasn't his fault. It must be very difficult for a Canuck to recognize the difference between an Englishman, so slow to anger, and a Welshman, who at nineteen is often a case of grievous bodily harm waiting to be provoked.

My own main moments of relief, on those calls to Britain, were a couple of letters from Angharad. She was all I had now, all that was left of Wales and Llangareth. To me the sea and the hills of Wales were in her letters, but the dreams of Wales were always in me. When I stared through the snow or rain, or in sunshine, at the black, frowning mountains of the Vatnajökull, in Iceland, or the gentler—much gentler—hills of Scotland, I always remembered Wales.

As we left Scotland, I stood at the fo'c'sle break and watched the gaunt, sea-girt bastion of Ailsa Craig darkly demanding the sun, and above the haze, the lovely Scottish haze like bridal gossamer, the twilight of Kintyre, and thought of all the people living quiet, sane lives, of milkcarts and plane trees, bobbies and baskets and how the Scots, Celts to a man, sing when they talk; not only like the Welsh, with their cadence, but with the consonants of their words, too. And sweet the lasses! Scotland! The hardest land in the world to arrive at—and the hardest to leave!

Bonnie Scotland! And the Mull of Kintyre, where even the seabirds aloft sound like harps twanging and rolling in the gloaming and shouting, 'Where're you bound, you *fool*!'

Will ye no come back again?
Bounding o'er the foaming main?
Many's the heart'll break in twa,
Will ye no come back again?

Then Brigham Young and Roger the Lodger the Sod were at my side.

'Did all right in Haggisland, eh, Taff?' said Brigham.

'Robbie Burns would have been proud of you,' muttered Roger. I had to turn away at the pipe, 'Men under punishment fall in on "B" gun deck!' It was time for me to pay my own private homage to Sauchiehall Street and the bonny lasses thereon. As I climbed the ladder I thought, 'Nothing like a bit of rifle-toting at the double to keep you warm in the Mull of Kintyre on a wet, misty autumn evening.' That's the way a matelot AAI, nineteen years old, under punishment by edict of My Lords Commissioners of the Admiralty and everyone else in the Andrew down to the Chief Gunner's mate, thinks.

Scharnhorst was sunk on Boxing Day, December 26, 1943. It was a beautiful Christmas present for the British people, and God knows, after three and a half years of calamities, defeats, frustrations and shortages, they needed it. It was again a purely British and German affair, except I think for the Norwegian destroyer *Stork* and certainly the last remaining warship of the old Polish navy, *Blwstkwa*.

We were all pleased that the latter was at the kill. We matelots got on pretty well with most of the continental matelots, Norwegians and Dutch especially, though not so much the French, what few there were in the northern waters, but we *loved* the Poles. They were funny, and they wanted little but booze, music, women and to kill Nazis. I believe that after the war most of the Polish matelots settled down with their British wives in Scotland. If that's true, then Scotland could not have done better than to have those men add their genes to her own.

Fraser set his trap well. It was a juicy bait: a great many ships loaded with war supplies for Russia. But this time the bait was surrounded by dynamite in the shapes of fourteen destroyers as close escort. Astern of them, over the horizon, steamed three cruisers: *Sheffield*, *Belfast* and *Norfolk*—three hard nuts if there ever were—and, hovering away to the west, a distant cover for the battleship *Duke of York*, the cruiser *Jamaica* and four more destroyers. For one of the few occasions in the northern sea war, the Allied Naval Commander was in a position to have practically all of his 'heavy mob' pounce on any Nazi surface ship.

Raeder, the Jerry admiral-in-chief, fell for the trap hook, line and sinker. We didn't know, of course, that Hitler was demanding a major naval action by a Nazi surface ship, and otherwise threatening to scrap the Nazi surface navy and send all the officers and matelots to the Russian Front, or into U-boats.

Our mess deck strategist, Roger the Lodger, nevertheless told us that might happen, quite clearly, but he was poo-pooed by Rosy Lee, the London barrow-boy. 'Bleedin' Adolf?' commented Rosy, ' 'e don't know the fuckin' sharp end of a ship from the blunt!' History seems to show that Rosy was right, too.

Scharnhorst weighed anchor in Altenfiord on Christmas Day. We all knew that she had weighed. We were having our Christmas dinner (lunch to officers and others) when our tame sparker, who had a crush on Pony Moore, came flying down the ladder: '*Scharners* is out,' he bellowed, 'and steaming north!'

Rosy jabbed another forkful of Christmas pudding. 'Good,' he said. 'Spoil their fuckin' Christmas pud, too!' Our ship gave a lurch right then, and sent his pudding flying over the mess deck.

We were at action stations most of Christmas Day and night. The taunting and jabbing of *Scharnhorst* by twelve destroyers started in the late afternoon of the next day. In we hared, at full pelt over the southerly horizon, widely apart, until just out of range of *Scharnhorst*'s guns, which were blazing at us, but the small splashes fell short by a mile or so. Smartly about turn and, quick as gnats, back a couple of miles, about turn, repeat the performance, over a heaving grey sea in bitter cold. The light was not clear, more like twilight than daytime. Now and again we caught glimpses of one or the other of our cruisers quietly shadowing *Scharnhorst* with their radar. At the ack-ack guns we stayed closed up, but sighted no planes. This was a big surprise, and for some time afterwards we wondered if the Luftwaffe had ordered, incredibly, to let two battleships have it out between them, just once more, for old times' sake.

On about our tenth or twelfth dash, in and out again towards the Nazi, suddenly there was a roar overhead, exactly like an express train coming out of a long railway tunnel. We all knew what it was, all right. *Duke of York*, with our bonny little Scots admiral on her bridge, had got close enough to *Scharnhorst* and had opened up. Automatically, we all followed the shell-roar north with our streaming eyes, and, in the gloaming to the south-east, saw star shells burst in beauteous splendour, like chrysanthemums on grey velvet —and under the glare, tiny and innocent-looking, like an ant on a clothesline, a mere dark blip on the line twixt sea and sky . . . something.

It must have been about five o'clock in the evening. Another star shell, and then another, and now we could plainly see the Nazi's fighting top over the horizon, pale gold in the light of the phosphor glares. Otherwise there was nothing but night and our awareness of fatal events.

Our ship and the other destroyers we could see slowed down. Apart from the rushing shells, now from both *Duke of York* and *Scharnhorst*, there was only the low moan of our engines, the slock, slock of our screws, and the eternal sound of the moving sea. The men at the guns spoke in quiet voices, as if to themselves, their breath condensation resented for misting the view. The silence was as if we knew—we didn't —that we were witnessing the last great slogging match between two great naval dinosaurs, without any interference from the air.

'Bloody Marquess of Queensberry Rules, that's what it is!' Rosy Lee exclaimed softly.

As soon as *Scharnhorst*'s top turned to silver, there was an almighty crack! from her direction. Then another from *Duke of York*, and a line of flame on the horizon to our north.

'That's a broadside from *Duke*'s six-inchers,' explained Pony. Seconds later there was a deafening whizzing noise from the whole sky as the *Duke*'s shells roared over our heads. Automatically I pulled my tin hat over my neck to protect it more and peered from under my brows. I'd forgotten we'd been recently issued with a new type of steel helmet, with a longer brim at the back. I wondered if Angharad had sewn the chinstrap into this new helmet and prayed that the *Duke*'s shells would burst right inside the *Scharnhorst*'s wardroom. Now the *Duke*'s tracer shells were whizzing like mad. It was like a fireworks display gone wild. The lines of shells converged on each other as they zinged across the sky. They all met right over *Scharnhorst*.

'*Duke* ain't even opened up yet, that's only her secondary guns,' said Pony, and just then there was a roar to the north of us which almost knocked me off my seat. I turned around and saw the *Duke of York* steaming at full pelt at an angle, towards the place where the *Scharnhorst* would be heading if she maintained her course. The *Duke* looked frighteningly magnificent. She was almost entirely wreathed in gunsmoke and shooting flames. At first I thought she was on fire, but then the stabs of flame, quick and bright, a dozen at a time, but not all together, told the tale. I tried to imagine what it was like in her huge gun turrets, for the matelots and the marines—and their officers, too. I tried to imagine handling shells eighteen inches across in that noise and cordite smoke. The sight, the contestants, the noise, the event, were all colossal. It must have been after two or three of the *Duke*'s broadsides that the first Nazi reply came. First it was star shells—she was trying to light up the *Duke*. Hers were more silver than our own gold. They lit up the *Duke* like a Coronation coach, all silver and grey, only a couple of miles away. They lit us up, too, and I felt as if I had been stripped naked violently in a crowded boxing match.

Two star shells burst over *Obstinate* low and very, very bright. Red hot splinters showered the ship. Everyone on 'X' gun deck caught a few pieces which pierced lifejackets, duffel coats, jackets, and entered muscles already tense with pain and strain. I caught some in my right shoulder and left foot.

Then *Scharners* opened up with her eleven-inch broadside. We, on *Obstinate*'s 'Y' gun deck, were swivelling around like spectators at Wimbledon, at first scared stiff that *Scharners*, like *Bismarck* with *Hood*, had got in by a lucky first straddle on the *Duke*, as she was surrounded by smoke, flame and waterspouts for a few seconds, but *Duke* rammed out of that mess with all her guns still blazing. We cheered.

Another blast from *Scharners*, another swivel, another breathless hesitation, another cheer from us, and so it went on, with both the *Duke* and her enemy racing towards the east; the destroyers and cruisers piling on speed to keep up with the two locked giants, both of them heading for the same spot.

The fight roared on for another few minutes, then there was a lull. Over the scream of our engines, the whole ship was quiet for a long moment. Suddenly there was a loud shout over the Tannoy. I'm not sure, but I think it was Jimmy, whose voice used to crack when he got excited (didn't all our voices crack?). '*Scharnhorst* is retiring! *Scharnhorst* is retiring! Tally Ho! Tally Ho! This one's for Christmas, men!'

It was the first time I can ever remember a Royal Navy officer addressing his men as 'men'.

There was a pause of several minutes in the firing as all the ships—those we could glimpse in the dark night, those we could not—charged. East . . . east . . . bugger the sea . . . bugger everything . . . get the *Scharnhorst*! I could have sworn there were blood flecks on the lips of the gunnery officer when he came to check on us. His eyes were wild, like a hunting dog's on the scent, bloodshot and murderous.

'We'll never catch her,' he moaned. 'But there's a fiver for anyone who can get any kind of shot at her and hit her—if we ever come close enough!' The cry was on, all right, when an officer offered reward. 'Bugger the King's Regulations and Admiralty Instructions, too!' as Rosy muttered when Guns was out of sight.

We stared more in the *Duke*'s direction, I think, than in the *Scharners.*'

We were all praying for the *Duke*. If *she* went we *all* went. We knew that. Suddenly there were three bright orange stabs right on her, and a low moan came from everyone. But she passed the spot, again lit up by Jerry star shells, again untouched, blazing away with everything that she had.

'Old Fraser'd throw his bloody hat at *Scharners* if he could get close enough,' said Pony. 'He'll have that fucking Jerry skipper's guts for breakfast.' I laughed, but I think it was more hysteria than anything else.

Now we crossed over the *Duke*'s wake, to leeward of her, and the wind smothered us in the stink of her cordite. For a few seconds it was almost impossible to breathe. What it was like on the battlewagon's open bridge I can only guess. If cordite smoke causes cancer, then most of the *Duke*'s crew must be dead by now. A mile and more astern of her it seemed like our ship was charging through a solid wall of cordite smoke.

There was another lull when we got clear of the cordite smoke. Then it was our turn, the destroyers, the killers. *Scharnhorst* must have been severely damaged. Now we reverted to the role for which we had originally been intended. Not for husbanding slow fat merchant ships from the unwanted attentions of sly predators hidden below; now we were *destroyers*, the hit-men of the Fleet, the private murderers on embassy from the King of England. Now watch out! Watch out, you bastard Nazis!

Our stern went down, the bow shot forward, there we went—*Onslow, Obdurate, Opportune, Orwell*—there we went like staghounds at last, at long, long bloody last, off the leash. *Cavendish, Chieftain, Cheviot, Caprice.* Faster and faster, plunging and swaying, pulsing with strain until her whole hull screamed in protest, *Obstinate* headed for the flame and smoke to the south-east now, closer and closer in the pitch darkness, in the freezing wind, closer and closer. All we could see of the other nine destroyers were their pale wakes, until Captain (D) in *Onslow* opened up with his four-inchers. We followed. Crash after crash shook our hull, already battered by the flashing seas crashing alongside. *Obstinate* reared and pitched and rolled and wallowed, and how the Torps got the tinfish away in any semblance of an aim I'll never know. Out slid the tinfish, long and sinister, and splashed into the darkness. Then they tore off with an innocent-looking little stream of silver bubbles astern of them. Another torpedo salvo then, from the forward tubes, and over we went, heeling to starboard at fifty degrees, to turn and scuttle away from the range of *Scharner*'s armament. *Obstinate* was still firing madly, then off hell for leather; then back again, firing all our six four-inchers, and us at the Bofors guns, firing for all we were worth at the red flames a mile and a half away; then closer and closer, a mile, half a mile, turn at full speed and out again—and so on, and on, and on, for an hour and a half of eternity in the Arctic night at the northern edge of a suffering world. We heaved everything we had at the *Scharnhorst*, for everyone who had died and suffered because those bastards wanted to rule the roost. Rule a roost? We gave them a roost all right.

Before our Bofors, the red streaks across the night of our eyes changed to scarlet just before they disappeared into the orange-red glow that told us *Scharnhorst* had been hit well and truly and was blazing, and then the red-orange slowed down in its steady traverse across the unseeable horizon, and almost came to a halt. Even above the noise of the main guns, the banging of the Bofors and the screaming of the engines, our cheers must have been heard, my own included, but to me it was as if they came from somewhere else, from some other ship, from *Cameroon* and *Eclectic*, *Yarborough Castle* and a thousand other ships on the bottom of the cold ocean, and all the wide open mouth-sockets still nodding in them far down in the black depths. There was a scream from *Ganges*, too—the most blood-curdling of all. '*Get that—and that —and that!*'

'We got the bastard!' shouted Rosy Lee. 'That's one for my old man!' Rosy's dad had died in the Somme in 1917, before he'd been born.

I had my hands locked on the firing trigger of my Bofors. The barrel was steaming vapour. *Bang! Bang! Bang!* 'That's one for mine, and for Mam, and for Angharad, and Bert and the nipper, and Tansy . . .' and I was crying and shouting until Pony Moore swiped me with a knife lanyard. 'Shit in it, Taff,' he ordered over the bedlam. 'Maintain your aim, fuck-dust!'

There was a lull a few minutes later, and no firing from *Scharners*, until one of her smaller guns opened up firing single shots at several seconds' intervals. 'They must have a *Ganges* bloke on board,' observed Pony. He was flanelling me, but it made me feel better, even though I felt the pain and panic of the Jerry matelots dying a mile away.

Suddenly a voice blared over our Tannoy: '*Jamaica*'s going in to finish her off! Stand by all action stations! Prepare to pick up survivors!'

We were about a mile from the burning battleship. We could see her clearly delineated in the fire spurting and rolling from her decks, solid lumps of bright scarlet flame. Then *Jamaica* opened up and smashed six-inch shells, eight at a time, time after time, into the Nazi wreck, for a few minutes. Then *Jamaica* stopped firing. There was another lull as we watched, fascinated and horrified. Then two unmistakable explosions, deep and muffled, as if the ocean floor itself were erupting, shook the enemy ship, and we knew that *Jamaica* had got two of her tinfish into the guts of *Scharners*. When the smoke cleared, as we waited about ten minutes, we could see nothing on *Scharnhorst* but one solitary searchlight swinging about as if let loose, turned down on the sea. Then it was gone.

We went to pick up survivors. There were very few in that cold, heaving, uncaring ocean. The North Cape seas are unkind to all matelots, from all nations. The Arctic waters know no difference between Aryan bodies and any others. Three minutes is about as long as the strongest could hope to last after the water closed around them.

We could see bodies, black, sludge in the crests. Sometimes we caught, in the glare of our searchlights, a wave of a hand. We picked up eight men. Two died very soon after being hauled on board. They were returned, eyes and mouths open, respectfully to the sea.

The other destroyers picked up between them another twenty-eight of *Scharnhorst*'s company of almost 2,000 men.

Otherwise there was nothing. Nothing but the black, gleaming sea and the floating dead, bits of wreckage and oil, to mark the deaths of nineteen hundred good German sailors; all victims of the dreams of an evil-minded megalomaniac.

So much for glory. So much for uniforms and medals, bands and trumpets, bayonets flashing in the sun and all the other military bullshit which entices the young into the cockpits of hell.

16. *Take Me Somewhere East of Suez*

Underneath the lantern
By the barrack gate,
Darling I remember
The way you used to wait;
'Twas there that you whispered tenderly
That you loved me.
You'd always be
My Lili of the lamplight,
My own Lili Marlene.

Orders came for sailing
Somewhere over there,
All confined to barracks
Was more than I could bear;
I knew you were waiting in the street.
I heard your feet,
But could not meet:
My Lili of the lamplight,
My own Lili Marlene.

From 'Lili Marlene', music by Norbert Schultze, German words
by Hans Leip, English words by Tommie Connor.

(In memoriam, the matelots of *Scharnhorst*.)

Two of the German matelots were brought down to the after seamen's mess after they'd been checked out by the radio officer, who knew German, and warmed through and prodded in the sick bay.

When we finally dispersed from action stations they were already sitting in the mess, looking very sorry for themselves. Their working uniforms had been dried in the boiler room, and they were now fully dressed in their own rigs again. One was about twenty-two and the other about my age—nineteen and a half. The older one, Karl, was a stocky bloke with surprisingly dark complexion and hair. He came, he told us, in hand gestures and words which somehow we understood, from Düsseldorf, where he had been a mechanic in a garage until 1939. '*Meine Muter, mein Vater . . . tot . . .* RAF boom . . . boom!' He let us know his situation in short order.

The other one, the younger, Heinz, was thin and blond, with regular, handsome features, but very arrogant. He stared everyone in the eye with a despising glower for the first half-hour or so. Then he sulked for a couple of hours in a corner. By the time our rum was up he was crying softly to himself. None of our lads disturbed him. We were too accustomed to seeing men cry softly to themselves. We had met the enemy; he was just like us.

Pony Moore brought the rum fanny down, full of dark liquid smelling like molasses. (Ah, the bitter-sweet aroma of Nelson's Blood!) He set it on the table in the silence which always paid tribute to the brew, peered around and said, 'Sippers from all for our new chums, eh?'

There was a silent chorus of nods and grunts, and a little rum was slopped, out of the old brass measure into two stolen beer mugs, for the *Kriegsmarine*.

The bubbly cheered up the older one, Karl, and soon he was having a lively discussion with Roger the Lodger, in some kind of bastard English–German–French language, about pay and conditions in our respective services. It seemed that Karl thought about as much of German naval officers in general as we did of our own, but he excepted his own ship's officers, except one or two, just as did we. By that time we were calling Karl 'Curly' and Heinz 'Heenzies Beenzies' after the tombola call for '57'. Curly was very shortly one of the lads—in fact, by the time we landed our prisoners at Scapa Flow, Curly was reluctant to leave the mess. He'd loved the rum and food, which he said was better than theirs had been in *Scharnhorst*. We found that impossible to believe and Roger the Lodger said, 'The grass is always greener in your neighbour's field.' By the time he left the ship, taking little presents—nutty and fags and such—down the gangway, Curly was almost as British as we were. He had learned many of our songs, 'Three Crows' and 'Maggie May'. By the time he left we were for keeping him in the mess.

Heenzie was different. Curly gave Roger to understand that Heenzie was a typical Nazi via the Hitler Youth. When Heenzie became more accustomed to being a prisoner, about three days after they joined the mess, he suddenly pointed at Jock McAllister and me and shouted (he always seemed to shout when he spoke—it was one of those voices), '*Juden?*'

Roger broke out laughing, as Jock and I looked on perplexed. Then Roger spluttered, '*Nein, nein. Schottland! und . . .*'

'What's he saying, Roger?' asked Jock.

'He's asking if you and Taff [Roger meant me] are Jews.'

That caused an uproar of laughter in the mess, which made Heenzie, who had been nervously and closely watching our faces, start back in angry surprise. Both I and Jock McAllister, the two-badge AB from Campbeltown (a real hard case ashore if there ever was one—how he ever kept his good conduct badges amazed us all) were dark Celts of the Cym-

raig, of course, with the bigger-than-average noses and temper that come with that wonderful heritage—well, everything has to be paid for.

Jock stabbed his spoon into his nuts and bolts and almost
choked before he shouted to Roger, 'What's fuckin' German
for "shut your cake-hole, you Nazi cunt!" '

The rest of the mess were in fits of laughter by then. Roger
slapped me on the shoulder; my dinner plate went sliding
over the table—accidentally, of course—right into Heenzie's
lap. He jumped up and started shouting. Jock picked up
Roger's steaming dinner plate and shoved that right into
Heenzie's face. Then Pony got pissed off and slammed Jock
down on to the deck.

The upshot was that Jock got seven days' Number Eleven
punishment for 'striking a prisoner in contravention of the
rules of war and King's Regulations and Admiralty Instructions.' Jock also lost both his good conduct badges. That
meant a loss of a shilling a day to him. He, like me, had only
his sister, so it wasn't too bad for him, and Jock said that it
had been worth a bob a day to 'gi'e that li'l Nazi fucker a
dinner, a'richt!' Looking back, I'm not sure who was more
anti-semitic, in an unthinking way, Heenzie or Jock. I think
they were both so because of what they'd been *told* about
Jews, more than what either of them *knew* about them. There
were, so far as I know, none on board the ships in which we
served, and I can't imagine any Jews having been on board
Scharnhorst.

The cox'n moved Heenzie away from our mess to the
stokers' after the kerfuffle. We all bet he wouldn't ask *them* if
they were Jews. When Heenzie finally left the ship in Scapa
Flow, besides the plaster on his scalded nose, he had a fairly
new bruised eye, so we supposed that we had lost our bet, but
Stokes was too crafty—his world was too closed and self-
contained to let the King's Regulations and Admiralty In-

structions tell him what could be said in his mess and what could not.

We were given a late ten-days Christmas leave from Rosyth while the ship underwent a minor refit. I was treated for my shrapnel wounds; they seemed very slight. I went down to London after I called in on Angharad in Manchester. She was now courting a paratrooper in the First Airborne Division. I met him and liked him, and knew that Angharad was in love. It was no place for her big brother to be hanging around. Aunt Lowri was upset that I only stayed two days, but that was about all I could stand of her and Uncle John's continual complaints about rationing.

I gave Angharad a few of my saved quids and my ration card and left to join Brigham Young, another 'homeless' lad, at the Union Jack Club in London. It was cheap, the food was a distinct improvement on what we had on board, there were no restrictions on going out into the city and coming back in again. Apart from that we might just as well have been in Royal Navy Barracks, Chatham, except that from the staff we got mostly cold stares but no bullying.

I suppose that neither Brigham nor I had more than five pounds each when we started our week in London. We went up to the West End, around Piccadilly, the first evening, but the place was so crowded with Yankee GIs on Rainbow Corner, most seeming to have money to burn, many smoking cigars, a great number with girls on their arms, that we gave up on the West End and headed for Earl's Court. There were not so many Yanks there. The Aussies had the place tied up instead.

It was very hard on us visiting matelots who knew no one in London. In general, the average Londoners we met could not have cared less who we were, what we were, where we had been, or what we had done. Brigham and I were two more moving uniforms in a sea of them. Only we were not in a uniform which spelled money. We learned our lesson about London the hard way. Later we would find that the further north from London we found ourselves, the better the welcome, the more friendly the civvies, the more loving the girls. Birmingham and Manchester, Leeds and Liverpool were all good to us. Newcastle, Edinburgh and Glasgow were marvellous; Belfast and Derry's welcomes were ecstatic. We would never forget. We knew why it was so in those cities and seaports. They knew where we'd been, all right. London, as far as the ordinary matelots who were not Londoners was concerned, was to be avoided if at all possible, or to be arrived at, crossed and left as soon as they could manage it.

Many a time in London, after we ran out of our DF cigarettes, Brigham and I entered tobacconists only to be told that what fags they had were for 'regular customers only'. Many a time we were refused service in London pubs because there was 'no beer left' and had to push our way out through ranks of Yanks quaffing ale and being charged double the legal price.

The young women in London who, two years before had smiled and waved at us, now scarcely looked our way. Many of them showed their disdain, even. They knew that Jack had a pay scale about one-eighth of his American or Dominion counterpart. Brigham and I wound up, like many homeless matelots in those days, in the pubs around Victoria which were frequented by homosexuals. There at least we could get our fill of beer paid for by the regulars, before we avoided the rush at closing time and headed back to walk to the Union Jack Club. Otherwise I doubt if our money would have lasted more than three days at the most, not at the same rate of beer drinking, anyway.

Brigham was a good-looking lad of about twenty, with big shoulders and a stevedore's swagger—that's what he said he'd been before he was called up. His technique in the 'Queen's Head' in Chelsea or the 'Windsor Dive' in Victoria, or the pub in Portland Place where all the BBC queens hung out, was to swagger into the bar, with me traipsing alongside of him to counterpoint his masculine glory, and then stand at the bar, at one end, and order a half-pint each for us. There we stood, chatting about the bargirl, if there was one, and after marking out the rozzers from the Yard vice squad we waited, slowly sipping the beer and wishing we could slosh it down, to forget the Andrew and the pain and death. We never talked about that, of course; we talked about how we could find a woman in the Dilly, and if the Yanks had taken them all, how we could always resort to the peroxided older slags who hung out around the side doors to Waterloo station and did knee tremblers for the Yanks. Sometimes, when they'd had a good night, they would let a matelot have one free. (God bless them!) It was awkward, trying to fuck behind the opened gates, and cold, too, and the crowds all passing in and out of the station only inches away, but it was all we had. Once had been enough for me, but I didn't tell that to Brigham, of course, as we waited for some BBC announcer (his voice famous all over the world), to come in and buy us his usual pint. We liked him—he never pressed us for anything but our company for a few minutes. I can hear his voice now: 'Here is the news and this is . . . reading it.'

We preferred to start in Portland Place early. Then we made our way by bus to Earl's Court, and drank beer in 'The Boltons' pub, which was always crowded with men—some obviously with a lot of money—who would buy us beer. Some of them were decent types, who held good conversation and seemed to know what interested us besides women and beer—sport for Brigham, books, plays and films for me. Some of them were not nearly as pleasant though, and these Brigham was expert at getting rid of. His technique was not all that diplomatic by Whitehall standards, but for one of Bruce Fraser's bouncing lads in navy blue it was not too bad. He would lean over me, when some persistent bore or obvious sex-queen was hovering, and say, very quietly, 'Look, mate, we don't like you, so why don't you fuck off?'

It always worked, quietly, and we never got into a barney, or were asked to leave the pub, and after the initial shock the bloke would evidently shrug it off.

All the homosexual-frequented pubs in London had their share of matelots and squaddies and erks on the trot. Most of them had girl-friends with them, at least until it was time to be 'picked up'. They had to, of course, to keep their masculine pride. Those were the women that Brigham told me to watch out for. They were so jealous of their blokes that they would cause a fight at the drop of a hat. The only places where Brigham and I made any passes at other men's girls were in civvy pubs, and then mostly with Yanks' girl-friends. We were on solid ground in the 'straight' pubs, except where the Yanks had taken over, and those we avoided.

We finally found a happier hunting ground when we visited Roger the Lodger at his home in Hampstead. He introduced us to the arty lasses in 'The Flask'. But as usual on leaves from ships, that was on the day before we were due back. We were flat broke, of course, but the intellectuals looked after us. They thought we were a relief from farm boys from Georgia and South Carolina, I suppose. Being hosts to warriors can be a trying business, was the main impression I gathered in Hampstead. Brigham scored at 'The Flask'. That was why he came back to the ship three days adrift, just before *Obstinate* sailed. He'd caught a nap-hand from the mousy little woman who told us she was a school teacher, but Brigham didn't care too much. She'd fed him and bought him beer for two whole days, and in between the convoys and the patrols, what more could he ask?

I did a few more patrols in *Obstinate* in early 1944. I was content in her. I was twenty now and an old hand. I knew mine and everyone else's exact niche in the ship. I could rub along with no trouble at all, and have a fair time doing it. In between watches and action stations I was left alone, when I wanted to be, to read or to write, as I chose. I'd become familiar with D. H. Lawrence and Henry James, Proust and (above all) Joyce. The consensus in the mess was that I might be a bit tapped, but I was all right and good for sippers or a sub whenever anyone needed it and I could look after myself in a scrap. I was clean and I knew my job, and I knew how to avoid an argument with the wrong people, but could still hold a conversation of sorts with anyone.

The most important development that I underwent in *Obstinate*, though, was that I learned to be interested in everybody. Not just my messmates. I learned to be silently curious. I also learned how to concentrate on reading or writing in a crowded messdeck, with eight or nine different conversations and the noise of machinery humming all around me. Looking back, I can think of no finer training for anyone who wishes to write. I could have done with a few more mentors, though. Roger the Lodger the Sod was educated, but he was very cynical. Not in the way that Prof had been; Roger was no Socialist. Roger hated the idea of a working class. That might have been because he had been groped at the age of six by the milkman. At least that's what he told me. Roger's main idea of social improvement when the war was over was for all females over the age of sixteen to be fitted with Dutch caps, and to be allowed to be fucked whenever and wherever they felt like it. 'Mother-love— that's what spoils everything,' he maintained against all arguments from right and left. 'Damned mother-love.' Roger was the only matelot I can ever remember who used the word 'damned'. 'It's the most insidious emotion, the worst pressure anyone can endure.' Having met his mother in Hampstead for a brief moment, and having felt a bit like I did when the *Bismarck* was loose, I sympathized with him in the particular, but not in the general.

Things were much quieter in the North Atlantic and the Barents Sea by the summer of 1944. D-day meant that many of the escort ships had been transferred to support the armies in Europe. It also meant that many matelots got draft-chits out to the Far East. Mine came as *Obstinate* was on the way to support the American beaches in Normandy. The ship called at Pembroke Dock on the way south, to join the destroyer escort for the fast minelayer *Apollo*, which was to be Eisenhower's headquarters ship. She lay overnight in Pembroke Dock, but there was no leave. I stood on the deck for hours looking at the hills of Wales all around under the moon. It was the last time I saw Wales for thirty-five years.

We had a week's leave, and I went to see Angharad. She was getting married, but there were two weeks to go before the event, so I missed it. I was content enough for her. The bloke she married turned out to be AI at Lloyds. In 1946 they emigrated to Australia and he is very successful out there, with a fine family.

After a couple of days in Manchester I went to Hawick in the Scottish Borders. The buzz was that it was the only place in Britain then where the lasses outnumbered the lads by at least three to one, and most important of all, there were no Yankee GIs there. The rest of Britain, so far as I could tell, was crowded with them, even though the Normandy invasion was in full swing.

Hawick kept its promise. Wool mills there were turning out service uniforms, and they were packed with females. It was impossible to buy a beer in a pub; the locals always insisted on buying. They were doing well, and they knew that

Jack had little. They treated me royally, but I wished that Brigham was with me, so I could have shunted him off his particular road to hell, and brought him to the gates of Nirvana for a week. It is a great pity I didn't. He was involved after the war with a young woman who became a very famous singer. She was raped by a businessman in a Lancashire hotel. Brigham stabbed the man to death when he got ashore, and was later hanged for the murder.

My draft was shipped out to Trincomalee in Ceylon in a trooper. She was an old Union Castle Line ship and crowded to the scuppers with pongos and their officers, and a lot of RAF, too. I hated every minute in that ship. Most of the time we were kept below on the mess decks, only allowed on deck for about an hour a day. Our hour was at noon, when the sun was vertically above us and fit to scorch our ears off. After the Arctic and Britain it was quite a change.

Gibraltar, our first call, was no surprise to us. It looked exactly as it did in all the pictures the older matelots had shown me. We were not allowed ashore, but stayed sweltering at anchor for about a week, until a convoy to pass through the Med was formed up. It was strange to be in an escorted ship for once.

The Gully Gully men came on at Suez, of course, to show us how to take a live hen out of their mouths, and how to make our money disappear. For the rest of the 'passengers' it was mainly loafing about and tombola, but for us matelots it was cleaning ship—especially brass tallies on valve wheels. The army non-coms seemed to fall into two groups, either beer-swilling bullies, as crafty, each of them, as a cartload of monkeys, or pleasant, quiet, civilized humans. Most of the latter were in the technical corps, like the Royal Engineers. They reinforced my determination to volunteer for the Engineering Branch of the Andrew as soon as I could. One sergeant in the Engineers, Ernie Bramall, a man in his late forties who had been in the trenches in the First World War, and who loved classical music—who introduced me to it by taking me along to the gramophone recitals that a few of the non-coms attended—also had a great influence on my later life. 'Find something useful to do which is useful to others,' he told me, over and over. He also told me to emigrate to New Zealand after my time was up and go sheep-farming. I might do that one day—I've tried to do everything else he suggested.

We matelots destined for landing craft waited in Trinco —and waited, and waited. We had little to do in the hot days, and not much more at night. We were told we were waiting for craft to be released from the war in Europe. I made the most of it, and, although I felt a bit daft in my tropical shorts, far too long by any standards, and long blue stockings, I explored the area around the barracks, and sometimes sat under a waving palm tree at last, with my *Oxford Book of English Verse* and a bottle of cheap arak smuggled in by the head dhoby wallah who had the booze market in the barracks sewed up in Trincomalee just as tight as Al Capone had done in Chicago. I even got to Colombo once on a banyan party, and traipsed around for two days with a small gang of more intellectual matelots, Chiefs and POs, inspecting temples and churches. We were supposed to do that for three days, but I got fed up and scarpered on the third morning with an Irish lad. We got stuck into the arak, then the beer, and clewed up under arrest after a barney with some pongos in a cheap hell-hole.

I'd loved the ride in a bus to Colombo, through the mountains and valleys, watching the scenery, like North Wales, only there were trees even right up to the peaks. And the villages and people. But the ride back, jolting in an army truck, with its tarpaulin tied down all round, was a different matter . . .

The war was going well by late 1944. The Yanks had taken Guam and invaded the Philippines, and our pongos were steadily gaining ground in Burma, but it was going to be a long slog before we reached Singapore, it seemed to us then. Our job was to man the beach-attack and landing craft transferred from France and the Med as they were brought through Trinco on their carrier ships. Some of them already had some of their crews with them on the ships, others not. It was a case of waiting for a craft that needed you, whereas in Europe the vessels waited for crews that usually didn't need *them*, or let's say were not too eager to join them.

I missed two local drafts to landing craft; once through malaria and once through dysentery, so I was lucky for about six months, and lived a good soft life in Trinco. We had our 'action stations' at the ack-ack defences, but the raids were very, very few. I can only recall one, and that was a Jap spotter plane which was shot down way out over the sea before we could get one shot in.

The rest of the time it was the usual Andrew routine ashore: kit musters and drills, divisions and making work. At night it was sometimes leave in the town, but it was so crowded with servicemen that the delights of drinking beer in fly-blown hovels soon wore off. Then it was back steadily to the Fleet Canteen, for IPA beer and sod's opera, or sitting in the mess-barrack room, under a slow fan, reading, or writing letters to the BBC announcer and to a woman I'd met in Hampstead. She'd been terribly dowdy, but her letters were a Godsend to me, and I wish now I'd kept them. She became a well-known writer years later.

Finally, about February of 1945, I could swing the lead no longer. I'd made the mistake of allowing myself to be coaxed into the barracks boxing and rugby teams. It would have been difficult for a Welsh lad of almost twenty-one to have resisted. Besides, I thought in my ignorance that if I got into the sports teams, and shone at all, I would be kept back from sea, to play for the barracks. No such luck. All I did was get my name and number better known to the drafting office. I still hadn't learned to play the Andrew game as well as I ought to have done.

In May the European war finished on my birthday, but I didn't know it. I'd had sippers all round and was dead drunk.

When the drafting chief finally caught up with me, I was sent to an LCI—a landing craft for infantry. She was American-built and fitted with a Bofors gun, four Oerlikons and six rocket-launchers which hurled five-inch rockets in the general direction in which they were aimed. She was only about a hundred and fifty feet long, but the conditions in the mess deck were much better than they had been in *Obstinate*, even though she was small in comparison. For one thing we had a mess refrigerator. I think it was the first one I ever laid hands on. It conked out after the first few weeks, but we still treasured it, and kept the rum fanny and measures in its musty interior.

We named the ship *Lucky* and she lived up to her name, all right. Our Skipper was a young RNVR subby, not much older than me. He was very polite, considerate and easy-going. We also had a commissioned engineer who was at least sixty, who usually smoked a foul pipe so the smoke would keep everyone away, and who read Byron and Shakespeare. I got to know both those poets and his pipesmoke very well during the months that followed. He was one of only three officers I was ever on any terms but 'sir' with while I was in the Andrew.

We had fun and games testing out the rocket-launchers, until we got used to them. The first shots were so wild that the Commander in Chief, Trinco, ordered all LCIs to move out to sea at double the range of the rockets, before they practised firing them.

We left Trinco in convoy with some other landing craft, LCIs, LCMs, and LCTs about March or April, and we headed north for Madras, where we anchored for several weeks, rolling away uncomfortably in the heat and swell. I went ashore a few times, but recall little, except the vast contrast between the life of the white residents and the great majority of the Indians. I was also astounded by the distinct coldness of the whites towards ordinary matelots like me. Apart from Bermuda, a couple of years later, I don't think I've been anywhere where the local toffs treated the matelots with such open disdain. But we had the consolation of knowing that their days of lording it over India were numbered. Wherever I heard politics discussed in the British services among the lads, to all of them, after 1943, it was clear that the Empire was finished and over and done with and good riddance.

In Madras, dockyard mateys, who had been living in terraced cottages in Britain, here lorded it like squires of the manor. They were, these 'foreman' types, the most class-conscious, colour-conscious, biased, bigoted snobs I ever met. They had their living-abroad allowance, their raise in pay, their free housing in the European compounds, and their clubs where they were waited on hand and foot by Sikh ex-soldiers whose—for the most part—shoes they were not fit to polish, and they tried the same capers with us. No wonder we were barred from all their bars and clubs. No wonder we had to be back on board at sundown. It was nothing at all to do, as rumours and false history have it, with the Indians. We got along fine with them and made many friends among them. I had a special friend who was studying to be a doctor. We used to sit on the sea wall and discuss English and Indian history and literature for hours in the hot afternoons. But the British civilians I saw in India—it was impossible for me to accept that I was of the same race. Their women were, the vast majority, the most stuck-up, jumped-up, pretentious, supercilious herd of cows I ever clapped eyes or ears on. They knew what we thought of them and they got back at us through their female 'superiors' who, through their henpecked husbands, made damned sure that we had as unpleasant a time as possible all the while we were in Madras.

I remember later, when Gandhi took over India, that a cheer came from every British matelot who had ever gone ashore there when it was part of the British Empire. I recall thinking at the time I was in Madras that if the British in Singapore, the 'colonials' had been anything at all like these British buggers and bitches in India, then the Japs had done a fine job and good luck to them. It is shaming to recall, but it is true.

We moved up to the Ganges delta—off a Godforsaken place called Galachipa—for a couple of weeks. Then, as we were moving up the River Ganges to load troops and tanks, the news came that Japan had surrendered.

I don't recall any sharp relief or rejoicing. It was more a weary sharp breather between hot, sweaty tasks.

We still loaded the tanks, trucks and troops and steamed them down to Singapore. There we offloaded them just as if the war was still raging, except that we had no air raids to expect. Singers was hot, humid and unpleasant. There was a lot of misery ashore. I was detailed off for a working party at Changhi jail for a week or so. What I saw and heard there has left me with an abiding disgust for the older Japanese and all their works. It is unreasonable, I know. Most of the Japanese had nothing to do with it; but every time I see one of their elders, I see again the blood-soaked cell walls of Changhi prison, and the block where men and women were tied down for parts of their bodies to be cut off as punishment for trivial infractions of the code of Shinto. For years, every time I saw an older Jap I avoided him or her. I couldn't help it. I tried to reason myself out of that stupid attitude. But I thought of the ship- and planeloads of our blokes and the Aussies brought down to Singers for shipment home straight from the Burma railway, and heard again their horrifying tales, and I felt sick to my stomach that anything that pretended to be human could treat its fellows so. I knew there were decent older Japanese, kindly and civilized and cultured in their own and even in Western ways. But I didn't *want* to know them. I couldn't forgive their generation of that race of people for showing me how to hate my fellow man; really and truly hate to the death. I could not forgive them for making me despise them. I could not forgive them for the tiny corner in my heart which had nothing but hatred for them, God forgive me! I knew that many Germans were bastards too; that they slaughtered millions of innocent people of all races, religions and ages, but I hadn't seen Buchenwald, I didn't see Belsen. I *saw* Changhi; and it is far easier to hate what you have seen than what you have been told.

When we walked through the gates of Changhi after a day of clearing up their foul mess, and passed Japanese soldiers still guarding the gate, they were supposed to bow to us. I turned my head away from them. I didn't want the little sods' bows. I wanted them dead. Right there on the spot.

It took me a week to beg, plead and work my way out of the Changhi detail. I still couldn't sleep properly for months after.

I went ashore one evening some weeks after the Changhi work, got stinking drunk and clobbered a Sikh policeman (they'd helped police the city for the Japs). The upcome of that was that I lost my hook and was an AB again. I was soon drafted back to Yewkay in another trooper taking a lot of prisoners of war back from Calcutta, where they'd been in hospital. It was like being in a cross between a morgue, a hospital for the dying and a madhouse. Some of the tales I was told about the Japanese treatment of prisoners made my hair stand on end. After a few days of that I avoided the ex-prisoners as much as I could and haunted the ship's crew's living quarters. It was against the rules, but I had made chums with several of the ship's seamen, and they let me stay.

The yarn got around that as the ship left Gibraltar one of the officers was strolling on deck and came across a matelot gazing over the ship's side, lean and ill-looking. Later, as the ship steamed up the English Channel he saw the matelot again. To cheer up this, to him, obvious ex-prisoner of war, the officer said to him, 'Cheer up, old chap. I know you've had a rough time, but it'll soon be all over, eh, what? Three square meals a day and good British beer!'

'I bloody well hope so,' said the matelot. 'I've been in this sodding ship for five years now!'

Peace. But that's another story . . .

EPILOGUE

They shall grow not old, as we that are left grow old:
Age shall not weary them, nor the years condemn.
At the going down of the sun and in the morning
We will remember them.

From *For the Fallen* (September, 1914)
by Laurence Binyon (1869–1943)

(Reproduced by permission of Mrs Nicolette Gray and the Society
of Authors on behalf of the Laurence Binyon Estate)

GLOSSARY

AB: Able Seaman
action stations: station when the ship was ready for action
adrift: 1. absent without leave
    2. to return late from leave to the ship
Aggie Westons: sailors' homes set up by Dame Agnes Weston, providing cheap overnight accommodation in the main naval towns
akkers: cash
Andrew: the Royal Navy. On the lower decks the words 'Royal Navy' were hardly ever used
Arkkers: Archangel, USSR. Destination of Arctic convoys
Asdic: submarine detection gear
ass bandit: active homosexual

badger: *see* stripey
banyan party: an outing ashore
barrack stanchion: a rating who somehow managed to wangle a berth in Royal Naval barracks and who seemed immovable
baron: generally a civilian man (hetero- or homo-) who was well enough off to be hospitable
baron strangle: to accept a baron's hospitality
beat up to: to curry favour with or start a courtship (from the sailing term 'beating up to windward' on this tack and then the other)
beetle-crushers: 1. drill boots
    2. regulating Petty Officers
belay!: stop!
Bells-and-Smells: Malta
belt and braces: ready; expecting the worst. A ship could be so when she was incessantly at action stations
belt and gaiters, all: pusser-faced
Bible bosun: naval padre
blood bucket: ship's lifeboat

bobstay: foreskin membrane
bootneck: a Royal Marine (derogatory)
brass monkeys: cold weather (the term 'cold enough to freeze the balls off a brass monkey' from the days of fighting sail, when cannon balls, being iron, contracted with the cold so much that they became loose in their brass tracks, 'the monkeys', and so fell off and rolled around the deck)
brightwork: anything brass or bronze, such as porthole frames
bubbly: rum
buffer: Chief Bosun's Mate, the Chief Petty Officer in charge, under the First Lieutenant, of the day-to-day running of the Seamen Branch of the ship
buff stoker: Second Class Stoker, the lowest rating in the Engineering Branch
bulkheads: the 'walls' in a ship
bumfluff: an incipient beard
bunting-tosser: signalman
Burton, gone for a: to be killed (interservice slang, in reference to the famous tailors, who made suits)

cackleberries: eggs
camel-basher: Arab
can-spanner: tin-opener
canteen cowboy: someone who fancied himself ashore
Canuck: Canada and anything or anyone from there
Capers: Cape Town or any South African
Carley floats: a type of liferaft
cha: tea (interservice slang)
Chats: Chatham
chew: fellatio
chew bosun: homosexual who indulged in fellatio
chinky: dirty
chinky toe rot: athlete's foot
chokka: fed up, exasperated (from chock-a-block, when a rope is hard up against its block)
cottage: old hands' slang for mess
cox'n: the senior Seaman Chief Petty Officer onboard
crusher: Regulating Petty Officer
dabtoe (dabs): seaman rating below Petty Officer
Daddy's Yacht: where a hand who made a blunder was said to think he was

damager: the Naafi canteen manager, a civilian even onboard ship
Danskers: Denmark, Danes or Danish
DFs: duty-free cigarettes
dhobying: washing, laundry
dickey: a 'false' white front, laced up at the sides, worn in summer
  and in tropical waters
Dilly: Picadilly in London
ditty-box: A sailor's receptacle for odds and ends
divisions: muster of the crew
dockyard fusiliers: matelots under the command of the Captain of
  the Dockyard
dockyard matey: dockyard worker
doggo: ugly
dose: venereal disease
duff: pudding

easy shoes: gym shoes
Elephant and Castle: famous matelots' pub in South London
erk: RAF ranker (originally an RAF term)
Errol Flynn: a show off, who fancied himself with women

fanny: 1. an oblong shaped mess-can made of steel and polished
  with 'Brasso'
  2. vagina
fanny rat: promiscuous lady lover
fo'c'sle: the forward part of a ship, below decks, generally where
  the matelots lived. Incorrectly the fore deck.

gaff: house or flat
gas and gaiters, all: pusser-faced and loud mouthed
gash: rubbish
get: bastard (shoreside slang)
Gibbo: Gibraltar
gigolo: anyone who chased after women, not necessarily for money
Gully-Gully men: quay-side conjurers
glasshouse: detention barracks; naval prison (originally an army
  term)
God-walloper: naval padre
Gold Coast: California
Golden Rivet: a legendary rivet in the ship's hull, far below decks,

which older hands were supposed to entice younger hands to see, so that they could be seduced

gondola: hammock

goolies: testicles

Gorgie Biscuit: crashing your head very hard and fast into someone's face in a fight, then, when your opponent is down, kicking him

grippo run: an invitation to a party or an outing, usually by a civilian ashore

Gut, the: Straight Street, Malta, the Valetta 'Tenderloin' district

Hands, Knees and Bumpsa-daisy: Cannes, Nice and Monaco, the favourite peacetime runs ashore in the Mediterranean

hatter: passive homosexual

have a bastard on: be in a temper

hawsepipe, through the: an officer who had risen from the lower deck

heads: lavatories

Heffelent: *see* Elephant and Castle

Honkers: Hong Kong

hook, on the: at anchor

hooky: *see* killick

hope-and-glory: excessive patriotism

horse: girl-friend

HOs: Hostilities Only men

ikkey: ice in the Arctic

Jack: generic name for any rating—usually under Leading Hand —but by no means always

Jacob's ladder: a ladder suspended over the ship's side for climbing into and out of boats

jankers: punishment

jar: a pint of beer or ale

Jaunty: the ship's Master at Arms; the chief policeman (from 'gendarme', 'Gentleman at Arms')

Jimmy: First Lieutenant, the executive officer

John: a merchant seaman, a very old term used as a form of address

Glossary

Kay Gee Five: HMS *King George V*
killick: (hooky) Leading Hand; the equivalent, roughly, of a corporal in the army. The name comes from the anchor badge worn on the left arm
kippers and custard: any food of unknown origin
knackers: testicles
knee-trembler: stand-up sex
knockshop: brothel
kye (ki): cocoa

leatherneck: a sailor's name for a soldier
Liberty ships: merchant ships mass-produced in the USA and Canada in World War II
lid: cap; to doff your lid: to stand accused before an officer of some offence or default
Lily Langtry's Yacht: the dream ship, to which all hands aspired as crew

matelot: a Royal Navy rating's name for himself and his like. It is adopted from the French and pronounced 'mat-loe'. It is an honourable term
matey: a general form of address to strangers. *See also* dockyard matey
Murmurs: Murmansk, USSR. Destination of Arctic convoys
mystery: unattached young lady, usually pronounced 'Miss Terry'

nap hand: to contract gonorrhoea and syphilis at the same time
Nelson's Blood: rum. After he died, Admiral Nelson's body was placed in a barrel of rum to preserve it. It was sent back from Trafalgar to Plymouth in the fast frigate HMS *Pickle*. On the way home the matelots in *Pickle* tapped the barrel and drank the rum.
Newfie: Newfoundland
nozzer: a boy seaman recruit at HMS *Ganges*
Number . . . : 1. Uniforms in descending order of quality
2. Punishments in descending order of severity
3. Formulated medicines. Number Nine was an all-round laxative, doled out for any complaint less severe than cholera
nutty: sweets of any kind, including chocolate

OD: Ordinary Seaman, the lowest seaman rating
oggie: a West Country pie or form of address to a West Country man
oggin: the sea (probably from 'ocean')
OOD: Officer of the Day
OOW: Officer of the Watch
oppo: special friend (from 'opposite number')
ossifer: jocular name for officer

party: steady girl- or woman-friend, or sweetheart
pavement pounder: fried liver
Pee Oh Doublyew: HMS *Prince of Wales*
phantom flipper: a closeted homosexual matelot
pier-head jumps: last-minute draft on to a ship as she sailed
piggery: the wardroom; officers' mess
pigs: officers
pig's orphan: Petty Officer
pipe: an order made over the ship's loudspeaker system
'Pipe Down': the order to turn in to sleep (from the days of fighting sail, when the seamen put their smoking pipes away for the night)
'Pipes Out': the order to return to work
pit: hammock or sleeping berth
plates: feet (from Cockney rhyming slang 'plates of meat')
Pompey: Portsmouth
Pompey Lil: a legendary whore in Portsmouth
pongo: soldier
Pontius Pilate: naval padre
poodle-faker: someone who continually chased women ashore
Pool, the: Liverpool
pouf: homosexual
pox-doctor: 1. Venereal disease specialist
2. Someone who did not know much about what he was doing
Praed Street prowler or ponce: a legendary villain who waylaid matelots and made them adrift from shore leave in London
prat: an inconsequential fool
prick tobacco: loose tobacco leaves, issued duty free, which stripeys rolled up tightly into a cigar-shaped bundle and soaked in rum
pudding club: to be pregnant

Glossary

Pusser: anything supplied by the Admiralty
pusser's hard: navy issue soap
pyso: mean, stingy

quarter deck: the after end of the upper deck of a ship

rattle, in the: under punishment
red cap: a military policeman
ringer: officers wear rings on their sleeve cuffs. A lieutenant is a two-ringer; a lieutenant commander a two-and-a-half ringer; a captain a four-ringer
Rock-ape: a native of Gibraltar (not derogatory)
Rose Cottage: the venereal disease clinics at Royal Naval barracks. The origin is in the rose-like sores which are a symptom of syphilis
round turn and two half hitches, to take: to take a hold of yourself; to come to your senses or straighten up

Sally Army: Salvation Army
sand-scratcher: seaman rating below Petty Officer
scran: food
scranbag: an untidy person
scuttle: porthole
sheep-shagger: Scotsman (derogatory)
Shiny *Sheff*: HMS *Sheffield*
shitehawks: German reconnaissance planes; seagulls; greedy people
shit in it!: shut up!
shit-kickers: underpants or uniform shorts
short timer, a: casual sex with a prostitute; a 'quicky'
sick berth tiffies: sick berth attendants; also sick bay tiffy
siff: syphilis
sippers: a share of one's rum ration given to someone in return for a favour or as payment
skate: someone continually in trouble and usually under punishment
skin: a good-looking young male
skulking: hiding or idling
skurs: form of address to a hand wearing a beard, probably short for 'whiskers'
sky pilot: naval padre

Glossary

Skywegian: anyone or anything from Scandinavia
slash: urinate
snotty: midshipman
sod's opera: a matelots' social get-together and concert
soldier, like a: clumsy, lazy, inefficient, dishonest
sons of guns: in the days of fighting sail matelots were not allowed ashore. Their womenfolk were brought on board, and lived with their men in their berths between the cannons. Some women gave birth to babies on board and the male babies were brought up on board and spent their whole lives in the Andrew. These were 'sons of guns'
sparky, sparks: a rating in the Wireless Branch
Spithead pheasant: fish
splice the mainbrace: to be issued with a double allowance of rum, done on special occasions, such as the King's birthday, after sinking an enemy vessel or before collecting dead bodies from the sea
split ass mechanic: a member of the Women's Royal Naval Service
sprog: a baby or young child
squaddy: any kind of soldier
Stand Easy: a ten-minute break off work in the forenoon and in the afternoon
station card: on board identity document
stokes: stoker
strangle a baron: to accept a baron's (q.v.) hospitality
stripey: a matelot who wore two or three good-conduct chevrons on his left arm, usually with no other badge of rating. A two-badger had to be at least twenty-six and a three-badger was an old man of thirty or over
subby: sub-lieutenant
swinging the hook: to hide and idle

tally: name
tapes: ribbons on uniform jackets or the laces on dickey fronts
Telfords: meat pies (after the brand)
ticklers: duty-free cigarettes
tiddley: ship-shape, good looking
tiddley suit: best uniform
tiffy: engine room artificer
tinfish: torpedo

Glossary

townie: someone who hailed from the same town or area
train smash: sausage and tomato
Trinco: Trincomalee, Ceylon. Major British naval base during World War II
trot, go on the: to remain absent without leave
twinkle-toes: general soubriquet for a youngish homosexual with effeminate manners

ukkers: a game played on a Ludo board
underground pheasant: rabbit, regular fare in the Andrew. It is bad luck to mention this word in the animal sense on board any ship
up-homer: a place ashore to which one was invited by relatives or friends. A 'home from home'
up the line: 1. One's home
  2. Anywhere away from the Andrew in Britain or Eire

vinegar strokes: orgasm

wanker: a weakling, not to be depended upon
watch, on or off: duty; four hours on, four hours off
winger: a special friend, usually the younger partner in a friendship
wings: form of address to someone usually younger
work your ticket: to wangle your way out of the Andrew. The most common way was to pretend insanity

yaffle: eat
Yewkay: UK